Praying for the Harvest

D1707724

Praying for the Harvest

G U Y D U I N I N C K

Master's Touch Publishing Company
Tulsa, OK 74155

Praying for the Harvest
ISBN 0-929400-04-6
Copyright © 1997 by Guy Duininck
P.O. Box 54026
Tulsa, OK 74155

Published by:
Master's Touch Publishing Company, Inc.
P.O. Box 54026
Tulsa, OK 74155

CONTENTS

PREFACE

Praying for the Harvest is the outgrowth of a specific message the Lord put upon my heart to speak to local churches as I travel throughout the world. Because we are in the season for reaping souls, it is important that we know how to cooperate with God and do our part in causing the harvest to be great!

What I teach in *Praying for the Harvest* can be used by individuals and by local churches as a format for praying prayers that will make a difference in the harvest. *Praying for the Harvest* is a prayer assignment to believers and local churches. I hope and pray that you will be a part of fulfilling Jesus' instructions to, "Pray Ye Therefore."

May you be encouraged and blessed as you read. And may you help fulfill the will of God concerning the harvest by becoming involved through prayer.

In Christ, Who is my Life,

Guy Duininck

INTRODUCTION

"But when he saw the multitudes, he was moved with com-
passion on them, because they fainted, and were scattered
abroad, as sheep having no shepherd. Then saith he unto
his disciples, The harvest truly is plenteous, but the labour-
ers are few; Pray ye therefore the Lord of the harvest, that
he will send forth labourers into his harvest."
Matthew 9:36-38

As it was in Jesus' day, so it is today. There is a plenteous harvest in the earth. This great harvest is the people who are
perishing and destined for hell because they lack knowledge
of the saving work of Christ. They are bound by sin and
death, full of confusion, and scattered by the winds of the
times. Truly, they are sheep who have no Shepherd. When
Jesus saw the lost multitude of His day, He said, *"The harvest*
truly is plenteous."

GOD'S PASSION FOR THE LOST

When the religious leaders of Jesus' day complained that
He visited and ate with sinners, He taught them three para-
bles that revealed God's heart of compassion toward sinners.
He taught them that God was like the faithful, compassionate
shepherd who left his flock to seek the one lost sheep until it
was found [Luke 15:1-7]. He taught them that God was like
the woman who sought diligently for her one lost piece of silver and then rejoiced when it was found [Luke 5:4-10]. And

1

He revealed that God was like the loving father in the parable of the prodigal son who watched daily for his son's return. When the son returned, the father gave him the best robe, a ring for his finger, shoes for his feet, and a great feast of celebration to demonstrate his great joy [Luke 15:11-32].

In the parable of the one lost sheep, Jesus revealed God's intense concern for the precious lives yet missing from His kingdom. He said,

> *"What man of you, having an hundred sheep, if he lose one of them, doth not leave the ninety and nine in the wilderness, and go after that which is lost, until he find it? And when he hath found it, he layeth it on his shoulders, rejoicing. And when he cometh home, he calleth together his friends and neighbors, saying unto them, Rejoice with me; for I have found my sheep which was lost.*
>
> *Luke 15:4-6*

The man in this parable was willing to leave his ninety-nine safe sheep to go after the one that was lost. When he found the lost sheep, he called his friends and neighbors together to rejoice with him.

This parable reveals the strong passion God has for the lost; for even one sheep outside His fold. He is more concerned for one lost sinner than for ninety-nine righteous that are safe. This reality becomes very clear when we read Jesus' interpretation of the parable. He said,

> *"I say unto you, that likewise joy shall be in heaven over one sinner that repenteth, more than over ninety and nine just persons, which need no repentance."*
>
> *Luke 15:7*

According to Jesus, heaven rejoices MORE over one lost sinner that is found than over ninety-nine righteous already in the kingdom. This does not mean that God does not love the saved. We are indeed precious in His sight. But we are found. We are safe in the fold; our eternity secure. The heavenly

2

Father's greatest concern is for the multitudes of sinners that have not been saved. He is deeply concerned about the harvest!

It is very easy for Christians to become like the religious leaders of Jesus' day. We get caught up in our own little worlds and forget about what really concerns the Father and the Lord Jesus. But though we may get caught up with a thousand "spiritual" distractions, God does not change. His will is always the same and His desires remain constant. He is the Lord of the harvest and the patient husbandmen Who is waiting for the precious fruit of the earth [James 5:17]. He is not willing that any should perish [I Timothy 2:4; II Peter 3:9].

The heart of God concerning the lost is clearly revealed in these words of Jesus,

> *"...I am not come to call the righteous, but sinners to repentance...I am not sent but unto the lost sheep of the house of Israel...For the Son of man is come to seek and to save that which was lost."*
>
> *Matthew 9:13; 15:24; Luke 19:10*

THE HUSBANDMAN IS WAITING FOR THE HARVEST

> *"Be patient therefore, brethren, unto the coming of the Lord. Behold, the husbandman waiteth for the precious fruit of the earth, and hath long patience for it, until he receive the early and latter rain."*
>
> *James 5:7*

The *"precious fruit of the earth"* James was referring to is the multitude of people in the earth who have not come into the kingdom of God. The heavenly husbandman is patiently waiting for this precious fruit to be harvested. In fact, the second coming of the Lord is delayed because God is waiting for the precious fruit of the earth! He is waiting patiently for the precious lives that have been purchased by Jesus' precious blood. The Holy Spirit confirms this truth through Peter's writings saying,

> *"The Lord is not slack concerning his promise* [of coming again]...*but is longsuffering to us-ward, not willing that any should perish, but that all should come to repentance."*
>
> II Peter 3:9

The Lord is not delaying His coming for any other reason except that He is not willing that any person should die in their sins and spend eternity in hell. He is longsuffering toward the human race, waiting as long as possible so that as many as possible come to repentance and salvation.

Sometimes when I am travelling, I stop at fast food restaurants and get something "to go." On more than one occasion I have paid for a meal and travelled ten or fifteen miles down the highway only to discover that the hot apple pie I ordered and paid for was missing. I never bother to go back because the hot apple pie is not worth it. If, however, I had purchased a three hundred dollar suit and after leaving the store discovered that the sales person failed to include the pants with the suit coat, I would definitely go back and collect the pants.

God made a tremendous investment in the earth when He gave His Son. He paid for the ransom of every man, woman, boy and girl. The precious blood of Jesus was shed to purchase lives that could never be redeemed with silver or gold. Because of that tremendous investment, God will not close this age until every person that can possibly be harvested into His kingdom is. He has made an incredible investment and will not conclude this age until He has received ALL He has paid for.

LIFT UP YOUR EYES

Referring to the harvest field of lost souls, Jesus spoke

4

these words to His disciples,

> *"Say not ye, There are yet four months, and then cometh harvest? behold, I say unto you, Lift up your eyes, and look on the fields; for they are white already to harvest."*
>
> *John 4:35*

Jesus admonished His disciples to open their spiritual eyes and be aware of the season they were in. Somehow they had failed to realize that a great spiritual harvest was ripe. Perhaps they were caught up with their own programs, their own needs, their own failures, or their own thoughts and hopes. While they had their eyes fixed upon themselves, they missed the fact that fields of souls were waiting to be harvested.

What Jesus said to His disciples many years ago is true of the season we are in now. It is time for the harvest. The fields are ripe and ready. The harvest is not for the next generation; it is not in the next decade. There are not yet *"four months"* to harvest. *The fields are already white unto harvest!*

Part of understanding the workings of God is to know that He is a God of times and seasons. There are times of visitation; times of special operations. Jesus wept over Jerusalem because although they were religious and had the scriptures, they did not recognize the time of their visitation [Luke 19:44].

I encourage you to lift up your eyes and see that there is a great harvest ripening in the earth in this very hour. Quit thinking only about your own needs. Quit thinking only about your own wants or your own dreams. Look upon the fields and you will see that harvest time is near. It is the season of rain. It is time for a mighty outpouring of the latter rain of the Holy Spirit. It is a time when many fields are crying out for laborers. And it is time for us to be about our Father's business. *It is time for the harvest!*

Is there any way to participate in this great harvest? Can you make a difference in the reaping of precious fruit? If so, what can you do? What part can you play? And how can you get started? That is what *Praying for the Harvest* is all about.

A PRAYER ASSIGNMENT TO THE CHURCH

In order for there to be an abundant harvest of lost souls there must be cooperation between God and man. In fact, every spiritual result in the earth transpires through this working together. Believers are as essential to a successful harvest as is God Himself. We are co-laborers together with Him. Because our role is so essential, we must learn how to fulfill it.

Jesus revealed one very significant aspect of our involvement in the harvest when He told His disciples,

"...*The harvest truly is plenteous, but the labourers are few;* **Pray ye therefore**..."

Matthew 9:37-38

Notice that when Jesus saw the plenteous harvest, He did not instruct His disciples to go forth and labor in the fields. He did not tell them to recruit workers. He did not tell them to sit still and watch God work. In response to the great harvest waiting in the fields and the shortage of laborers, Jesus said, *"Pray ye therefore."*

In essence, Jesus said to His disciples, "Do you see what I see? I see multitudes that are lost and need to be harvested. But there is a shortage of laborers. Because of this great need, I want you to pray."

Jesus saw the harvest of His day, recognized that there was a shortage of effectual laborers and commissioned His disciples to become involved through prayer. Prayer is Jesus' *first command* and must, therefore, be every disciples' *first response* in participating in the harvest. **One of the most**

important ways to participate in the harvest is through prayer!

"Oh no," you say, "please don't ask me to pray. Anything but that! I'll work; I'll pay tithes; I'll help someone else. I'll even go to a foreign land and preach. But prayer is just not my thing. Please don't ask me to pray."

Don't get under condemnation if you have an aversive response to prayer. It is really quite normal. The flesh and the mind are often uninterested in spiritual disciplines; sometimes they recoil at them. And prayer is both a discipline and a sacrifice.

Jesus' disciples had to deal with this very issue. They wanted to learn to pray—*"Lord, teach us to pray,"* they said. When it came to actually praying, however, they chose to sleep instead. It was in the context of this familiar incident in the garden of Gethsemane that Jesus uttered a statement that is still true today. He said, *"the spirit indeed is willing, but the flesh is weak"* [Matthew 26:41].

What Jesus said to His disciples is a reality we must all deal with. Although we are often willing to pray, much of the time our flesh does not want to pray. It would rather please itself or just be lazy and sleep. We must, however, have a readiness not only to will, but also to perform what we have purposed [II Corinthians 8:11].

Praying For The Harvest

Since Jesus commissioned disciples to pray for the harvest, we must learn to pray. We must be taught, as were Jesus' disciples, *how* to pray and *what* to pray. Only then can we fulfill our responsibility in prayer concerning the harvest.

In *Praying for the Harvest* I am going to encourage you to become involved in the harvest through prayer. First, I will teach you what effective prayer is and show you from the

Word of God that dynamic results can be achieved by praying simple, effectual prayers. Then I will teach you three specific Bible prayers to pray concerning the harvest. These simple, but effectual prayers will prepare the harvest for reaping, cause effectual laborers to be thrust forth into the harvest fields, and prepare you to be effective as you labor in your own field.

Praying for the Harvest is a prayer assignment. Although you may not like to pray and may not know what to pray, I am sure you want to cooperate with God and be part of causing Him to rejoice by participating in the harvest. I hope that by teaching you what effectual prayer is and giving you a specific prayer assignment, I will motivate you to fulfill the responsibility the Lord of the harvest has given you. I believe you will complete this assignment of *Praying for the Harvest*.

Prayer is one of your primary responsibilities concerning the harvest. ***Pray Ye Therefore!***

Section One

Lord, teach us to pray

Luke 11:1

And it came to pass, that, as he was praying in a certain place, when he ceased, one of his disciples said unto him, Lord, teach us to pray, as John also taught his disciples.

CHAPTER
ONE

WHY DON'T BELIEVERS PRAY?

O f all the spiritual activities believers are called to be involved in, praying is one of the most difficult to cultivate and maintain. Although the New Testament is filled with exhortations about the life of prayer, few believers ever develop an effective prayer life.

There can be many deterrents to the life of prayer. A deterrent is any object, attitude, or way of thinking that hinders the performance of an activity or task. Some deterrents to prayer are as simple as laziness, lack of discipline, or preoccupation with other things. Other deterrents may include wrong ideas about prayer that have been developed through wrong teaching or bad experiences in prayer. Because the advancement of the kingdom of God and the fulfilling of His plans and purposes depends to a significant extent upon the effective praying of believers, it is important that we alleviate whatever deters us from praying.

Perhaps it has been difficult for you to develop a life of prayer. What are the reasons? Have you been deterred from praying because you are lazy? Have you been deterred from praying because you do not know how to pray or what to pray? Have you been deterred from praying because of teaching you've heard about prayer? Have you been deterred from praying because of how you've heard others pray?

In this chapter, we are going to answer the question, "Why don't believers pray?" We will discover some of the main deterrents to prayer and present Biblical answers to basic misconceptions. The deterrents I will address are by no means exhaustive, but represent some of the primary reasons believers do not pray. Let's look at some of them.

I Don't Know How To Pray

During His three plus years of ministry, Jesus spent considerable time praying. It was not unusual for Him to spend the whole night in prayer [Luke 6:12] or to arise early in the morning to pray [Mark 1:35].

One day, He was praying in a certain place and His disciples were with Him. When He finished praying, His disciples, probably troubled about their own life of prayer after listening to Him pray, said, *"Lord, teach us to pray, as John also taught his disciples"* [Luke 11:1]. Jesus answered them with these words,

> *"When you pray, say, Our Father which art in heaven, Hallowed be thy name. Thy kingdom come. Thy will be done, as in heaven, so in earth. Give us day by day our daily bread. And forgive us our sins; for we also forgive every one that is indebted to us. And lead us not into temptation; but deliver us from evil."*
>
> *Luke 11:2-4*

The instruction Jesus offered His disciples in response to their request to be taught to pray gives us great insight on *how* to teach prayer. Rather than teaching His disciples the mechanics of prayer or offering them a lengthy discourse on effective prayer, He simply taught them one prayer to pray.

Jesus taught His disciples *how to pray* by teaching them a specific prayer and giving them a place to start.

Perhaps, like the disciples, you have been deterred from praying because you did not know *how* to pray or *what* to pray. Because you did not know how or what to pray, you had no assurance that your prayers would be answered. Like many others, you said, "I would pray if I knew how!"

Let me encourage you, "Keep reading!" I am going to follow the pattern Jesus used when He taught His disciples to pray. I will teach you three specific prayers to pray concerning the harvest. These prayers will be a great starting point for you when you pray about the harvest and will definitely bring answers from the Lord!

GOD'S WILL IS ALREADY DETERMINED

Sometimes, because of unbiblical teaching, Christians suppose that if God has a certain will concerning a situation, it will automatically come to pass. They believe that God is in control of everything and whatever happens, therefore, must be or must have been His will.

I call this "whatever will be, will be" theology, or fatalism. This kind of thinking is not at all unlike Islamic theology which says, "If Allah wills it." In the context of this faulty thinking, prayer would be futile. If, in fact, God has already decided His will concerning something and it is going to come to pass, nothing able to impede it, assist it, or alter it in any way, what would be the use in praying?

If you think that God is in control of everything and that every event which happens is His will, now would be a good time for you to stop reading this book. After all, if God's will is already determined and cannot be affected, there is no point in learning anything or praying about anything!

Unfortunately, many believers have wrong thinking concerning the sovereignty of God. Although God is sovereign, He has limited Himself in this dispensation. One of the primary ways He has limited Himself is by giving a free will to angels and to mankind. Satan and one third of the angels exercised their free will and turned away from God. Satan is now the "god of this world" and he and his demon-spirit cohorts have a legal right to maneuver in this world. Man also exercised his free will and fell out of relationship with God into spiritual death. Since the time of Satan's rebellion and man's fall, multiplied millions of events have occurred in this earth that are not, by any means, the will of God.

God is not in control of everything or everyone. There are things that are not His will that happen and there are things that are His will that do not happen. In other words, sometimes what God wills is not what happens.

The primary way to discover God's will is by examining His Word. His Word reveals His will. Once God's will has been determined, believers can cooperate with His will themselves through faith and obedience and can also be part of bringing His will to pass through prayer. No doubt, the significant role of prayer in bringing God's will to pass in earth is the reason Jesus taught His disciples to pray, *"Thy will be done, as in heaven, so in earth"* [Luke 11:2].

Very often the will of God comes to pass only **after** God's people determine His will and then petition Him in prayer to perform His will. The Word of God is filled with testimonies of situations and peoples' lives that were impacted and altered by the power of God **after** prayer had been made to Him.

MY PRAYERS WON'T MAKE A DIFFERENCE!

Perhaps you have not developed a life of prayer because you are not convinced that your prayers will make a difference. You are not sure that anything will change if you pray. But think about this: If your prayers made no difference in the outcome of events, then God's invitation to pray would be a farce and your response in prayer would be nothing more than an exercise in religious futility!

What would have happened if the early church thought prayer made no difference and failed to pray for Peter's release from prison [Acts 12:5]? I can tell you what would have happened! Peter would have been killed and the believers would have said, "Well, I'm sure God had a reason for taking Peter home at this time."

God does not ask His people to pray just to keep hair from growing on their kneecaps. He asks His people to pray because true, heartfelt "kneeology" will impact cities, countries, and the world and will help bring His will to pass in the earth! The reason God's people are called to prayer and the reason I am encouraging you to pray is because your prayers **will** make a difference in the outcome of people's lives!

If you do not pray, however, there will most definitely be **no** results. *"You have not because ye ask not"* is the simple and profound Bible reason that promises of God go unfulfilled and situations that are not His will are left unchanged.

Paul had such confidence in the heartfelt prayers of the Philippian believers that he told them he **knew** he would be delivered from jail *"through your prayer"* [Philippians 1:19]. And he had such a sense of the important role of prayer in bringing the will of God to pass that he told the Colossians, the Ephesians, and the Philippians that he prayed for them without ceasing [Colossians 1:9-10; Ephesians 1:17-19; Philippians 1:9]. I doubt very much whether this man with such deep and comprehensive knowledge of God and of spiritual things would have invested long hours in prayer for these people unless he was sure that his prayers would affect the outcome of their lives!

In Ezekiel, God said that He looked for a man who would stand in the gap and pray so that destruction would be averted. He could find no intercessor, however. And so destruction was poured out. Notice what God said,

> *"And I sought for a man among them, that should make up the hedge, and stand in the gap before me for the land, that I should not destroy it: but I found none."*
>
> *Ezekiel 22:30*

God is not necessarily looking for whole groups to pray. He is looking for one person! One praying person can radically alter the results of the harvest. If you pray, God will hear and answer. If you pray, God **will** move!

Don't let religious thinking deter you from praying. Your prayers WILL make a difference! God needs you to pray His will. He needs you to take hold of Him in prayer and stand in the gap for the harvest!

LONG, HARD PRAYER IS NECESSARY

Another hindrance to prayer is the religious idea that in order to get results in prayer, you have to pray long and hard. Some Christians think, as did the Pharisees of Jesus' day, that they will be heard for their many words. This kind of thinking is completely out of agreement with Jesus' teaching on prayer and with almost every Bible example of prayer. **Long prayer must not be equated with effectual prayer!**

In His powerful teaching in Matthew six, Jesus addressed the issue of prayer saying,

> *"...when thou prayest, enter into thy closet, and when thou hast shut thy door, pray to thy Father which is in secret...But when ye pray, use not vain repetitions, as the heathen do: for they think that they shall be heard for their much speaking. Be not ye therefore like unto them..."*
>
> *Matthew 6:6-8*

In this scripture, Jesus remarked about a people who thought they would be heard for their much speaking. He said, "Don't be like them!" And He followed this remark by teaching the simple, short Lord's prayer [Matthew 6:9-13].

Unfortunately, some Christians have been led to believe that if they don't "get in there" and really "bombard heaven" until they get a "breakthrough," they will not get results. Sometimes, Pentecostal and charismatic believers are the worst in this area. They have been programmed to trust in the length and volume of their prayers rather than trusting in the God to Whom they pray! The New Testament makes it very clear that believers have access to the Father by the Spirit and in the name of Jesus [Ephesians 2:18; John 16:26-27]. No breakthrough of brass heavens or demonic resistance is necessary. The breakthrough has already been made!

If you wrongly assume that you must pray long and hard to break through and get results, you may never pray at all! That kind of thinking is a mental mountain that could keep you forever on the wrong side of effectual prayer. Friend, much speaking does not guarantee much results!

When the disciples wanted to learn to pray, they said to Jesus, *"Lord, teach us to pray"* [Luke 11:1]. They wanted to know how to communicate with God and receive answers. Jesus did not respond to their request with a fifteen hour discourse on prayer, but taught them **one specific prayer** to pray. The prayer He taught is often called the Lord's prayer. It is prayed to the Father and is very simple, very precise, very short, and very effectual!

I am not giving you license to cop out, be lazy, and only pray short prayers. On the other hand, however, what Jesus taught concerning prayer is very significant. By teaching His disciples the simple Lord's prayer, He clearly demonstrated that effectual prayer cannot be equated with long prayer. It is not long prayers that produce results, but heart-felt prayers directed to the Father Who hears and answers prayer!

Elijah's Short Prayer

Do you remember the time Elijah challenged the false prophets of Baal to a duel to determine whose god was God? The god who answered by fire would be the one true God.

The false prophets of Baal cried out all day to their gods in a desperate attempt to get an answer. They jumped about, screamed, and even cut themselves, but no answer came and no fire fell [I Kings 18:26-29].

Note the marked contrast of Elijah's prayer. It was short, simple, and laden with faith! He prayed,

> *"...Lord God of Abraham, Isaac, and of Israel, let it be known this day that thou art God in Israel, and that I am thy servant, and that I have done all these things at thy word. Hear me, O Lord, hear me, that this people may know that thou art the Lord God, and that thou hast turned their heart back again."*
>
> *I Kings 18:36-37*

Let me ask you a question, "How long do you think it took Elijah to pray that prayer?" Read it aloud. Did it take you more than ten seconds? I doubt it. But this simple, short prayer worked! Immediately following Elijah's short prayer the fire of the Lord fell [I Kings 18:38]!

I do not bring this story to your attention to imply that every prayer should only be ten seconds long. The point I want to emphasize is this: Short prayers can produce great results! The key to effectual prayer is not to pray long. The key to effectual prayer is to start where you can and pray fervently according to the will of God.

MY FLESH IS UNWILLING

I had a friend in college who liked to do unusual things. One uneventful evening, he decided to put a whole apple in his mouth. That was a mistake! He could not get the apple out! Fortunately, his dilemma was short-lived. He was able to maneuver the apple into position to make a bite. Finally, he was able to remove the apple from his mouth. I can guarantee you just one thing that resulted from this near-critical incident: My friend never put another whole apple in his mouth!

You may have had a similar experience in prayer. Perhaps you became enthused about prayer, set your timer and took off. Unfortunately, you bit off more than you could chew and your experience was not completely pleasant. Perhaps you "watched and prayed," but mostly watched the clock! Perhaps you kept up your commitment for a short season, but then quit. A negative experience like this could easily deter you from endeavoring to pray again.

The discipline of prayer can be likened to physical exercise. For example, the fact that you cannot lift 200 pounds of weights does not mean that you cannot lift weights. Your mind might be willing to lift that amount, but your flesh is not able. Rather than trying to lift too heavy a weight and becoming frustrated and quitting, choose a weight you **can** lift. Begin where you can and work your way up.

Similarly, if you do not run on a regular basis, don't try to run five miles on your first outing. Condition yourself. Go a distance that stretches you, but don't destroy your own incentive with a completely negative experience!

Prayer must be approached in a similar way. In your heart, you may want to pray, but your flesh does not want to pray. Jesus taught that the spirit is willing, but the flesh is weak [Matthew 26:41]. That is a spiritual truth concerning prayer that you may as well accept. If you understand that your flesh is weak and does not savor spiritual activity, you can adjust your initial effort in prayer and begin at a level you can handle and look forward to doing again.

In order to become a person who prays, you must train your flesh and condition your mind. Do yourself a favor, however, by starting with a reasonable amount of prayer time. Don't overdose on the first day and then decide that praying is so miserable, you don't want to do it again. Give yourself a break, but not an excuse. Be disciplined, but don't be stupid. Start with short times of prayer and grow from there.

I'M NOT AN INTERCESSOR

Another reason some Christians do not pray is because of false concepts of intercession. Often, intercession is presented as an activity only attainable by the spiritual elite who really know how to "get out there" in the Spirit. I have even heard phrases like "upper level strategic spiritual warfare" to describe supposed elite-level intercession. This kind of thinking deters many believers from praying because it makes intercession seem unattainable.

Intercession, however, is not mystical or mysterious. It is not only for the spiritual elite. Intercession is actually straightforward and factual. The bottom line is this: If you can determine the will of God and have a true desire to participate in bringing His will to pass, you can be an effectual intercessor.

What Is Intercession?

The word "intercession" comes from the Greek *entunchano* and means, "to fall in with" or, "to meet with in order to converse" or, "to plead with someone, either for or against another."

When we intercede, we fall in with God. We find His will and agree with Him in prayer. Intercession means to go in the same direction God is going through prayer. Simply put, intercession is the spiritual activity of locating the will of God and petitioning Him in prayer to fulfill it.

When we intercede, we meet with God to converse. We approach Him in prayer to talk over His Word and His will.

We make a presentation of His will to Him and await an answer. Intercession is coming to God for the purpose of discussing what He is going to **do** about a situation He has already spoken about.

When we intercede, we plead with God for or against another person. We do what Abraham did when he pleaded for the deliverance of Sodom and Gomorrah. He said to God, *"Shall not the Judge of all the earth do right"* [Genesis 18:25]? And then he asked God to spare the city if there were fifty righteous, then forty-five, then forty, and on down to ten. When he came to ten, he stopped pleading with God [Genesis 18:33].

Intercession is, very simply, petitioning God on the behalf of another. It is earnestly petitioning Him to act for another person's benefit. It is taking the place of another through prayer and pleading their case as a lawyer before God. Intercession is praying on another person's behalf what they do not know to pray for themselves.

Much of our intercession concerning the harvest will consist of pleading with God for the salvation of the lost. We make intercession for them because they do not know **to** and do not know **how to** pray for themselves.

Intercession Is Not Praying In Tongues

Some believers spend a majority of their time "interceding in other tongues" because they either think that praying in tongues **is** intercession or they think that praying in tongues is the best way to make intercession. At some "intercessory-prayer meetings" everyone prays in other tongues with no determined prayer-plan. If you asked many of them, "What did you accomplish in prayer?" they could not tell you. Personally, I suspect that not much is accomplished in this kind of "intercession."

I will make this statement concerning the purpose of praying in tongues and then support it with teaching from the New Testament: The overwhelming weight of New Testament teaching concerning praying in other tongues reveals that it is first and foremost for the personal edification of the person doing the praying.

First Corinthians fourteen contains very clear teaching about praying in other tongues. There we read,

> *"For he that speaketh in an unknown tongue speaketh not unto men, but unto God: for no man understandeth him; howbeit in the spirit he speaketh mysteries."*
> *I Corinthians 14:2*

> *"He that speaketh in an unknown tongue edifieth himself..."*
> *I Corinthians 14:4*

> *"For if I pray in an unknown tongue, my spirit prayeth, but my understanding is unfruitful."*
> *I Corinthians 14:14*

These scriptures from I Corinthians fourteen do not teach that when someone prays in an unknown tongue, he is interceding for another person. These scriptures reveal, rather, that praying in tongues is for the benefit of the individual who is doing the praying. The one who prays in an unknown tongue prays out of his spirit to God about mysteries, although his mind is unfruitful. The one who prays in tongues *"edifieth himself."*

Another familiar New Testament scripture says,

> *"But ye, beloved, **building up yourselves** on your most holy faith, praying in the Holy Ghost."*
> *Jude 20*

In verse 19, Jude had written about individuals who were not living in the Spirit, but were walking after their own lusts. They were becoming more and more carnal. Believers, however, were to be growing in God, advancing in strength, and building themselves up. How would they do this? By praying in the Holy Ghost. The person who prays in the Spirit, who prays in other tongues, builds up himself!

A familiar passage from Romans says,

> *"Likewise the Spirit also* **helpeth our infirmities:** *for we know not what we should pray for as we ought: but the Spirit itself* **maketh intercession for us** *with groanings which cannot be uttered."*
>
> *Romans 8:26*

Paul said that the Holy Spirit *"helpeth our infirmities."* These words could be translated, "takes hold together with us against our infirmities." Who does the Holy Spirit help when we pray? He helps us! He helps the one who is praying. This scripture does not teach that the Holy Spirit helps us to pray for other peoples' infirmities. It teaches that the Holy Spirit **helps us** with **our** infirmities.

When we pray in tongues and groan in the spirit the Holy Spirit works with us against our weaknesses. He takes hold with us and prays concerning areas of our lives that need to be strengthened and built up. As we pray with *"groanings which cannot be uttered"* the Holy Spirit indeed is making intercession, but He is making intercession for us. He helps us to pray for ourselves concerning weaknesses that we don't know how to pray about as we ought.

It is possible, of course, that the Holy Spirit may lead us to intercede for other individuals or other situations in other tongues. This can happen and I believe it is valid. Paul told the Ephesian believers, for example, to pray *"always with all prayer and supplication in the Spirit"* [Ephesians 6:18]. Their prayers in the Spirit [in other tongues] were to be for *"all saints."*

Though praying in tongues may help you intercede for others, however, that is not its primary purpose. The primary purpose of praying in other tongues is for you to fellow-ship with God yourself, to receive insight yourself, to pray concerning your own infirmities, and to edify or build up yourself. Don't equate praying in tongues with intercession.

Just think about this: If praying in other tongues was the only way to get powerful results in intercession, how did any of the Old Testament intercessors accomplish anything in prayer? Or, for that matter, how did Jesus obtain results in prayer?

Most of your intercession should be done in your native tongue. Interceding only in other tongues not only limits the effects of your intercession; it also intrudes upon the primary purpose of praying in other tongues.

Intercession Is Not Spiritual Warfare

Intercession is not what some term "spiritual warfare." Certainly, there is a time to take authority over demons. Believers can cast devils out of people because Jesus gave us authority to do so. This activity, however, is the exercise of delegated spiritual authority. It is not an exercise in persistent prayer. True, Biblical intercession is prayer made to God, not prayer made against territorial demons.

True intercession is pleading with God about His will! There is no record that Jesus did spiritual warfare against demons in prayer. There is no record that Paul did spiritual warfare against demons in prayer. There is no record that Peter did spiritual warfare against demons in prayer. There is no record that John did spiritual warfare against demons in prayer. In fact, there are **no** Bible examples where any of God's people wrestled in prayer against the devil, demons, strong men, or territorial spirits.

The Bible teaches very clearly, of course, that believers have authority to cast demons out of people. It teaches nothing, however, about believers praying offensively against demons who hold a position of rule in the spirit realm.

Do not equate intercession with warfare against the devil or demons. In so doing, you misrepresent intercession. If you truly had authority over principalities in the heavenlies, you could command them once and they would obey. In fact, if you truly had that level of authority, you could bind the devil himself once and for all!

And while I am on this subject, let me say this: You do not have to shout when you cast out demons. In fact, shouting is an indication that you lack authority. Parents that shout at their children have not properly established their authority. Teachers that shout at their students reveal a lack of authority. And believers that shout at demons reveal that they do not comprehend their place of authority in Christ.

And neither do you have to shout at God to get results. He is your Father. His eyes are upon you and His ears are open to your prayers [I Peter 3:12]. The Father Himself loves you, Jesus said [John 16:27]. So you can pray in Jesus' name and the Father will hear and answer.

Intercession Is Not Groaning Or Birthing

It is also important to understand that intercession is not groaning or birthing in the spirit. Yes, you may groan when you pray. The Holy Spirit may lead you that way and use you that way. Yes, you may travail as did Paul for the churches in Galatia [Galatians 4:19]. **But do not equate intercession with groaning!** Although you may groan at times in intercession, intercession is not exclusively groaning. Do not assume that just because you groan, you are getting results. Can you see this? Intercession simply means to make request to God on the behalf of another.

Do not be deterred from praying because of a misunderstanding concerning intercession. Intercession is not primarily done by praying in other tongues. Intercession is not spiritual warfare. Intercession is not necessarily groaning and birthing. Yes, let me reiterate, the Holy Spirit may lead you to pray these ways, but don't make a precedent of every leading of the Spirit. Your praying must be based on the Word of God and the precedents established therein.

An Example Of Intercession

Abraham was an effectual intercessor. His pleading with God for the salvation of Sodom and Gomorrah is a beautiful example of the power of intercession. Notice the way he talked with God,

> *"And Abraham drew near, and said, Wilt thou also destroy the righteous with the wicked? Peradventure there be fifty righteous within the city: wilt thou also destroy and not spare the place for the fifty righteous that are therein? That be far from thee to do after this manner, to slay the righteous with the wicked: and that the righteous should be as the wicked, that be far from thee: shall not the Judge of all the earth do right?"*
>
> *Genesis 18:23-25*

God responded to Abraham's intercession in the affirmative, saying,

> *"...If I find in Sodom fifty righteous within the city, then I will spare all the place for their sakes."*
>
> *Genesis 18:26*

Abraham continued bargaining with God for the preservation of Sodom and Gomorrah until he arrived at the figure of ten righteous. We read,

> *"And he said, Oh let not the Lord be angry, and I will speak yet but this once: Peradventure ten shall be found there. And he said, I will not destroy it for ten's sake."*
>
> *Genesis 18:32*

What was Abraham doing as he asked God to preserve these cities? He was interceding! "But," you say, "I thought intercession had to be long and loud and with crying and groaning and to really get results, I had to pray in other tongues."

No, my friend. Your concept of intercession is based on what you have seen others do rather than on Biblical precedents. Abraham's prayer is a dynamic example of intercession. He made a very simple, very specific request to God in his own language and received a swift response. He did not pray long. He did not pray in other tongues. He did not groan or war with the devil. It did not take him hours or require shouting and demonstration. Abraham's intercession required only a knowledge of God, a compassion for the people, and a vocal request in agreement with the heart of God. He simply asked God to do what was right.

Were Abraham's prayers effectual? Unequivocally, Yes! God listened to Abraham and heeded his request. Perhaps Sodom and Gomorrah would have been spared if Abraham had continued on in intercession. We know, however, without a doubt, that Abraham was effectual as far as he attempted to go.

You don't have to be *deep* or part of some *spiritual elite* to be an effective intercessor. Intercessors simply plead the facts before God. They remind Him of His character and His Word. When you present your case to God clearly and accurately, based on His Word, He will respond. He will watch over His Word and perform it!

Deterrents Removed

Several years ago, my brother invited me to go deer hunting. I agreed and we hiked out to a place he had chosen. After waiting forty-five minutes a large buck came into view and began to feed. My brother handed me the rifle and told me to shoot. I had never shot a rifle and did not know where to aim or even how to aim.

After some simple instructions, however, I laid down in the cold snow and sighted up through the scope. The deer was around 250 yards away. That is a long shot for a beginner! After I got everything lined up, I squeezed the trigger. The deer did not take another step; I dropped him where he stood. I had a perfect shot!

Did you know your prayers can be the same? If you will sight up according to the Word of God and take a calculated shot, you **will** get results! You can get supernatural results by praying simple, Bible-based prayers. Don't be hindered or deterred from praying because of misconceptions about prayer. You can make request to God and change the complexion of cities and nations. You can make a difference in the harvest!

CHAPTER TWO

WHAT IS EFFECTIVE PRAYER?

If you are like me, you don't want to spend your time praying if nothing is going to result from your efforts. That would be a waste of precious time and an exercise in futile religious activity. As far as I am concerned, there is no use mouthing empty words that produce no change just to satisfy some kind of religious guilt. I don't want to waste time in prayer; I want to redeem the time! I want to pray effective prayers.

Prayers that are effective are prayers that cause the power of God to be released into the situations we are praying about. If we pray about something and God's power is not released, then nothing changes and our prayer time was ineffective. Only when God's power is released into the situation we are praying about will there be results. And only when we pray effective prayers will God's power be released. So if we want to achieve results in prayer, we must learn what effective prayer is and begin to pray that way.

What kind of prayer will bring results? What kind of prayer will affect peoples' lives with the power of God? What kind of prayer will make an impact upon the harvest; upon millions of lost souls? What kind of prayer is effective?

EFFECTUAL, FERVENT PRAYER

In the book of James, we learn about the kind of prayer that causes the power of God to be released into the situations we are praying about. James wrote,

> "...The effectual fervent prayer of a righteous man availeth much."
>
> *James 5:16*

The Amplified Bible renders this scripture in a way that should stir every heart to prayer. It says,

> "...The earnest (heartfelt, continued) prayer of a righteous man makes tremendous power available—dynamic in its working."
>
> *James 5:16 Amp*

The kind of prayer that makes the tremendous, dynamic power of God available is called **effectual, fervent prayer**. If effectual, fervent prayer causes the release of God's dynamic power, then it is absolutely essential that we learn how to pray this kind of prayer.

Effectual Prayer

The English word "effectual" comes from the Greek verb *energeo* and means "to put forth power." In James 5:16, the verb *energeo* is in the present participle form. It denotes an inworking of God that brings revelation of His will and results in prayer that is motivated by and in agreement with the revelation received. In other words, when God reveals His will to someone and they pray *motivated by* and *in agreement with* His revealed will, then tremendous power will be released and results will be forthcoming! **Effectual prayer**

30

begins with a revelation of the will of God and concludes with His will being accomplished by His power!

The apostle John was referring to effectual prayer when he wrote,

> *"And this is the confidence that we have in him, that, if we ask any thing according to his will, he heareth us: And if we know that he hear us, whatsoever we ask, we know that we have the petitions that we desired of him."*
> *I John 5:14-15*

When believers pray according to God's will, they can be sure God hears them. And, as John said, if they know God hears them, they also know that they have the petitions they prayed about. God hears and answers prayers that are in agreement with His will!

The first "if" believers must comply with in prayer is to ask according to God's will. *If* we ask according to God's will, we know He heard us. Then, *if* we know God heard us, we can be sure that we have the answers we desired.

Now let's reverse this. How can we be sure we have what we prayed for? We can be sure *if* we know that God heard us when we prayed. But how can we be sure God heard us when we prayed? We can be sure He heard us *if* we asked according to His will. Effectual prayer begins with knowing the will of God. But how can we know the will of God?

We can know the will of God by knowing the Word of God. God's Word and God's will are one. Through His Word, He clearly reveals what is and what is not His will. If we can understand God's Word, we can determine His will. If we can determine His will, we can ask according to His will. And if we ask according to His will, we can be sure that our prayers will be heard and answered!

When the will of God is revealed and we pray according to that revealed will, our prayer IS an effectual prayer! When

31

we pray effectual prayers, they WILL be heard and answered!

So if you ask, "How can I pray a prayer that will cause God's power to be released?" I will tell you to pray an effectual prayer. And if you ask, "But how can I pray an effectual prayer?" I will tell you to pray a prayer that is according to God's will. And if you respond, "But how can I pray a prayer that is according to God's will?" I will tell you to pray according to the Word of God. **Effectual prayer is birthed out of and in agreement with God's will as revealed in His Word.**

Fervent Prayer

In order for the power of God to be released through prayer, believers must not only pray effectual prayers; they must also pray fervently. James stated clearly that effectual, fervent prayers cause the dynamic power of God to be released. He wrote,

> "...effectual **fervent** prayer...availeth much."
> James 5:16

The English word "fervent" comes from the Greek *zeo*. *Zeo* means "to be hot" or "to boil." It means to be tenacious in spirit. It means heartfelt and earnest.

The best definition I can think of for "fervent" is this: You've got to mean it! To be fervent does not necessarily mean to be long, to be loud, or to be physically or emotionally expressive. To be fervent simply means that you must want an answer! You must be attached in your heart to the request you are praying about. It has to be burning in you!

To be fervent in prayer means to keep on praying insistently until you get results. As the Amplified Bible says, *"the earnest (heartfelt, continued) prayer of a righteous man makes tremendous power available"* [James 5:16 Amp].

We can see an example of fervent prayer in the story of Elijah when he went to the top of Mount Carmel to pray for the rain. The Bible says that he cast himself down on the earth and put his face between his legs [I Kings 18:42]. That is the way eastern women travailed in birth. Elijah was travailing fervently for the rain! He kept on praying and kept on praying until he saw a rain cloud appear on the horizon.

Jesus confirmed the importance of persistence in prayer in His parable of the man who went to his friend's home at midnight to get bread for another friend. The man who needed bread kept knocking and asking and knocking and asking until he received **all** he needed! Jesus taught that the man received what he asked for and more, not because of a relationship, but because of his importunity [Luke 11:8]. He received because of his persistence and fervency!

After teaching this parable about persistence in prayer, Jesus told His disciples that they should,

> "...Ask and **keep on asking,** and it shall be given unto you...knock and **keep on knocking,** and the door shall be opened to you. For whoever asks and **keeps on asking** receives...and to him who knocks and **keeps on knocking** the door shall be opened."
>
> *Luke 11:9-10 Amp*

Jesus also taught about the necessity of fervency and persistence in prayer in His parable about the widow and the unjust judge [Luke 18:1-8]. In this parable, a widow came to a certain judge day after day making the same request. For a time, the judge refused to grant her request. Eventually, however, through persistence, the widow wore him out and he granted her request. The judge did not grant the widow's request because of a relationship, but **because of her persistence** [Luke 18:15]!

Jesus taught His disciples this parable to reveal the importance of persistence and fervency in prayer. He said, *"that they ought always to pray and not to turn coward—faint, lose heart and give up"* [Luke 18:1 Amp]. **Fervency in prayer means to always pray and never give up!**

EXAMPLES OF EFFECTUAL, FERVENT PRAYER

Prayer must be both *effectual* and *fervent* in order to be effective. You can pray fervently—with much zeal and feeling —but if your prayer is not effectual—in agreement with God's will—you cannot be guaranteed results. Or you can pray an effectual prayer—one in agreement with God's will—but if you are lethargic and not persistent, you cannot be guaranteed results.

The Greek translation of the phrase, *"effectual fervent prayer,"* from James 5:16 could be rendered, "to pray with prayer," or more literally, "an inworking, heartfelt supplication consistent with conformity to the mind of God." **Effectual, fervent prayer means to pray in agreement with the revealed will of God and mean it!**

Effectual, fervent prayers produce results. When you know the will of God and continue steadfast and fervent in prayer, God's power will be released. ***Persistence breaks resistance!***

Elijah's Prayer For Rain

Immediately following his teaching in James 5:16 about effectual, fervent prayer, James gave an illustration of effectual, fervent prayer. No doubt this illustration was strategically chosen by the Holy Spirit as a pattern for believers to follow. We read,

> *"Elias was a man subject to like passions as we are, and he prayed earnestly that it might not rain: and it rained not on the earth by the space of three years and six months. And he prayed again, and the heaven gave rain, and the earth brought forth her fruit."*
>
> *James 5:17-18*

34

First, it was God's will that it not rain for three and a half years. Elijah prayed in agreement with God's will and it did not rain for three and a half years. Then it was God's will that it rain again. The Bible says,

> *"And it came to pass after many days, that **the word of the Lord came to Elijah** in the third year, saying, Go, shew thyself unto Ahab; and I will send rain upon the earth."*
>
> I Kings 18:1

Again, Elijah prayed in agreement with God's revealed will. He simply agreed with the word of the Lord in prayer. He asked God to perform what He had already declared to be His will. I Kings 18:42 says,

> *"...And Elijah went up to the top of Carmel; and he cast himself down upon the earth, and put his face between his knees."*
>
> I Kings 18:42

It was time for the rain according to the word of the Lord so Elijah set himself to pray. He prayed effectually—according to the revealed will of God—and fervently—with his head bowed between his knees, typical of the way eastern women travailed in birth. He kept praying and sending his servant to look until the rain clouds began to gather in the sky!

Elijah's prayer was *effectual* because it was based on the revealed will of God. And we know his prayer was *fervent* because James tells us that he prayed earnestly. And it is obvious that Elijah's prayer was *effective* because it began to rain! Elijah prayed effectual, fervent prayers both when he prayed that it would **not** rain and when he prayed that it **would** rain after three and one half years of drought.

Elijah's effectiveness in prayer was not because of his prophetic office. In fact, the Holy Spirit was very careful **not** to mention his prophetic office, emphasizing, rather, his humanity. Elijah *the man* prayed an effectual, fervent prayer

35

that caused the power of God to be released and the rain to fall!

Other New Testament Prayers

Let's look at several other New Testament scriptures to complement what we have learned about effectual, fervent prayer.

Paul wrote to the church at Philippi when he was in jail. Although he was imprisoned, he was rejoicing because he expected to be delivered through their prayers. He wrote,

> *"For I know that this shall turn to my salvation* **through your prayer**, *and the supply of the Spirit of Jesus Christ."*
> *Philippians 1:19*

Perhaps Paul was confident he would be delivered through the prayer of the Philippians because of his experience of being supernaturally delivered from the Macedonian prison after he and Silas prayed and sang praises [Acts 16:26-27].

Perhaps Paul was confident he would be delivered through the prayer of the Philippians because of what occurred when Peter was imprisoned and the church prayed for him. Herod had imprisoned Peter and was planning to behead him, but the church kept on praying. The Bible says,

> *"Peter therefore was kept in prison:* **but prayer was made without ceasing** *of the church unto God for him."*
> *Acts 12:5*

This is a great Biblical pattern of praying to get results! The church *"prayed without ceasing."* That is fervency! They prayed *"unto God."* That is where intercession is directed. And they prayed *"for him."* They prayed for Peter and specifically for his release.

Did their prayers avail much? Was the power of God released into that situation? Yes! God sent an angel and supernaturally delivered Peter. The early church prayed an effectual, fervent prayer, God's power was released, and their request was answered!

Whenever the church, that is **you**, will pray according to God's will and pray fervently, the power of God will be made available to the situation or to the person you are praying about. And that power will work dynamically to alter the situation!

In the book of Colossians, we find a New Testament man who exemplifies the activity of effectual, fervent prayer. Paul wrote about this man with these words,

> "Epaphras...always labouring fervently for you in prayers, that ye might stand perfect and complete in all the will of God. For I bear him record, that he hath a great zeal for you..."
>
> *Colossians 4:12-13*

In Epaphras, we find a model of an effectual, fervent prayer warrior. He had great zeal and was praying that the will of God would be accomplished in the Colossian believers' lives. His effectual, fervent prayers would cause the dynamic power of God to be released to those he was praying for.

Knowing God's will is the basis for effectual prayer. Agreeing with God's will with a heartfelt desire that His will come to pass produces fervency in prayer. *Effectual, fervent prayer is whole-hearted agreement with God! And effectual, fervent prayer causes a release of His power!*

THREE EFFECTUAL PRAYERS

In the chapters ahead, I am going to teach you three effectual prayers to pray concerning the harvest. These prayers are Bible prayers and are, therefore, according to the will of God.

Because they are according to the will of God, they are effectual. Two of these prayers are prayers that God **specifically** said to pray. Friend, if God asks you in His Word to pray a prayer, you can be assured that it is an effectual prayer! It will produce results if you pray it and mean it! **God will definitely answer prayers that He asks you to pray!**

The three prayers I am going to teach you are prayers every believer can pray. You do not need to be a prayer warrior to pray them. You do not need to be a prayer expert to pray them. You do not need to pray in other tongues to pray them. All you must do is pray fervently from your heart and these three effectual prayers will cause supernatural results in the harvest!

As you learn to pray the kind of prayers James wrote about—*effectual, fervent prayers*—you will have a tremendous part in releasing the dynamic power of God to make an impact upon the harvest. And you will be taking an important step of obedience in fulfilling Jesus' admonition to, *"Pray ye therefore."*

Section Two

Ask ye of the Lord rain

Zechariah 10:1

Ask ye of the Lord rain in the time of the latter rain; so the Lord shall make bright clouds, and give them showers of rain, to every one grass in the field.

CHAPTER
THREE

THE HUSBANDMAN IS WAITING FOR THE RAIN

According to James, the coming of the Lord is being postponed because the husbandman is waiting patiently for the precious fruit of the earth. By the inspiration of the Holy Spirit, he wrote,

> *"Be patient therefore, brethren, unto the coming of the Lord. Behold, the husbandman waiteth for the precious fruit of the earth, and hath long patience for it, until he receive the early and latter rain."*
>
> James 5:7

The "husbandman" James wrote of is God. The English word "husbandman" comes from the Greek *georgos*. *Ge* means "land or ground" and *ergo* means "to do." A "husbandman" is "one who has something to do with the ground." This is how closely God identifies Himself with the precious fruit of the earth. By calling Himself a husbandman, He is saying, "I care deeply for the world and for the fruit that is in it and will do all that I can to ensure a plentiful harvest."

The "precious fruit of the earth" James wrote of refers to the unsaved multitudes who have not yet been harvested into the kingdom of God. These lost souls are scattered and fainting. They are bound in sin and bound for hell because they have not yet accepted the free gift of salvation which Jesus died to procure. It is for the harvest of this precious fruit that the heavenly husbandman is waiting.

When James said that the husbandman "hath long patience" for the precious fruit of the earth, he did not mean that God is sitting idly by waiting for something to happen. God is patient, rather, in these two ways. First, He is patient in the sense that He is postponing the end of time and delaying final judgement until as many sinners as possible are reaped into His kingdom. Second, He is patient in the sense that He is actively and steadily pursuing the precious fruit of the earth. Peter said,

> *"The Lord is not slack concerning his promise, as some men count slackness; but is longsuffering to us-ward, not willing that any should perish, but that all should come to repentance."*

> *II Peter 3:9*

The husbandman has not forgotten His promise of coming again, but He is delaying as long as possible so that as many lives as possible may be saved. How long, however, will the heavenly husbandman wait? James wrote,

> *"...the husbandman waiteth for the precious fruit of the earth, and hath long patience for it, **until** he receive the early and latter rain."*

> *James 5:7*

The husbandman will wait for the precious fruit of the earth **until** He receives the "early and latter rain." The "early and latter rain" refers to the outpouring of the Holy Spirit upon the harvest fields of the world. These rains of the Spirit ready the hearts of the lost, convict them of sin, and prepare them to be reaped into God's kingdom.

The heavenly husbandman is waiting **until it rains** because the precious fruit of the earth cannot be harvested without an outpouring of the rain. Until the early and latter rains fall, the husbandman will continue to delay His return. So how long will the Lord wait before He comes again? He will wait *until* He receives the early and the latter rain.

By the inspiration of the Holy Spirit, James revealed the deeply significant relationship between the early and latter rain and the harvest of the precious fruit of the earth. He made it clear that in order for there to be a harvest of the precious fruit of lost sinners, the rains of the Holy Spirit must fall upon the harvest fields. Is there any way for us to help ensure that the rain of the Spirit falls on the harvest fields of the earth?

Preparing The Fields Through Prayer

Usually, when we think about how to bring in the harvest of lost souls, we think about how to conduct effective evangelism programs. We think about strategies, tactics, and methods for getting people to church. We think about doing crusades and motivating believers to witness. We think about sending missionaries to other nations. There is something else we must consider, however, when contemplating our strategy for bringing in the harvest.

According to James, the heavenly husbandman is not waiting for the precious fruit of the earth until Christians develop better evangelistic programs. And He is not waiting for the harvest until some magical moment in time when people will be swept into the kingdom. The heavenly husbandman is waiting for the harvest **until** the outpouring of the early and latter rain. He is waiting for the precious fruit of the earth until when? *Until it rains!*

Perhaps you never realized the significant relationship between the early and latter rain and the harvest of precious fruit. Perhaps you never considered that some fields may not be ready for the seed of God's Word. Perhaps you never considered that some harvest fields are not, at this time, ripe unto harvest and ready for reapers. Here is the truth of the matter: **The harvest fields of the world cannot be prepared and the harvest of precious fruit cannot be reaped without the rain of the Holy Spirit.**

In this section, we will discover the very significant relationship between the harvest of the precious fruit of the earth —the salvation of sinners—and the rain—the outpouring of the Holy Spirit. We will study the early and latter rain mentioned in James five and examine the typology presented in the Old Testament. We will learn that without the rain of the Holy Spirit there will be no spiritual harvest.

After learning about the early and latter rain and discovering its essential relationship to the harvest, we will learn one effectual prayer to pray which will cause the rain of the Holy Spirit to fall upon the earth to prepare the precious fruit for harvest.

CHAPTER
FOUR

RAIN IN THE OLD TESTAMENT

In order to understand what James meant when he wrote about the early and latter rain, we must look to the Old Testament. It is there that the New Testament rain of the Holy Spirit is foreshadowed and it is from there that James borrowed his terminology. When we look to the Old Testament, we discover several important references to the natural early and latter rains and learn about their critical role in preparing the natural harvest.

THE RAIN GUARANTEED A HARVEST

The promise of abundant rain for the production of a bountiful harvest was an arrangement God made with Israel if they would keep His commandments in the land of Canaan. He said,

> "Then I will give you **rain in due season,** and the land shall yield her increase, and the trees of the fields shall yield their fruit. And your threshing shall reach unto the vintage, and the vintage shall reach unto the sowing time:

and ye shall eat your bread to the full, and dwell in your land safely."

Leviticus 26:4-5

God promised to give Israel rain in due season. This promised rain of heaven would cause the land to yield its increase and the trees to yield their fruit. The resulting harvest would be so plenteous that it would carry them to the time of their next planting!

God's promise of rain and the resulting abundant harvest can also be found several places in Deuteronomy. In one place, we read,

> *"The Lord shall open unto thee his good treasure, the heaven to **give the rain** unto thy land in his season..."*

Deuteronomy 28:12

In another place, God said,

> *"For the land, whither thou goest in to possess it, is not as the land of Egypt, from whence ye came out, where thou sowedst thy seed, and wateredst it with thy foot...But the land, whither ye go to possess it, is a land of hills and valleys, and drinketh water of the rain of heaven: A land which the Lord thy God careth for: the eyes of the Lord thy God are always upon it, from the beginning of the year even unto the end of the year. And it shall come to pass, if ye shall hearken diligently unto my commandments which I command you this day, to love the Lord your God, and to serve him with all your heart and with all your soul, That I will give you the rain of your land in his due season, **the first rain and the latter rain,** that thou mayest gather in thy corn, and thy wine, and thine oil."*

Deuteronomy 11:10-15

It would be different for Israel in the land of Canaan than it had been in Egypt. In Egypt, they had to irrigate by human

46

effort in order to produce a harvest. The water they pumped with their feet flowed down canals they dug with their hands.

In Canaan, however, God promised to watch over the land. If Israel was obedient, He would water their land with the rain of heaven. It would be supernaturally irrigated! He would care for it and His eyes would always be upon it. When the early and latter rains came in due season the land would be nourished and the people could gather in their corn and wine and oil.

THE EARLY AND LATTER RAINS

In the previous scripture the Lord referred to the *"first rain and the latter rain."* The first, or former, rain—*moreh* in Hebrew—was "the spring rain" or "a sprinkling rain." These were the light showers that prepared the ground for seed and brought forth the early growth of the crop. The spring rains usually fell in October and brought the seed out of the ground beginning the growth process which would later culminate in a profitable harvest.

The latter rain—*malqush* or *geshem* in Hebrew—was the "heavy rain" or the "gathered rain." This rain fell shortly before the harvest and produced the final spurt of growth making the harvest ripe, full, and plentiful.

The relationship between the early and latter rain and an abundant harvest is obvious: The right rain in the right season guaranteed an abundant harvest! The corn would be gathered in. The wine and the oil would be abundant. Grass would come up in the fields and the people would eat and be full!

Joel chapter two gives us further insight into the relationship between the early and latter rain and an abundant harvest. There we read,

> *"Fear not, O land; be glad and rejoice: for the Lord will do great things...Be glad then, ye children of Zion, and rejoice in the Lord your God: for he hath given you **the former rain** moderately, and he will cause to come down for you the rain, **the former rain, and the latter rain** in the first month. And the floors shall be full of wheat, and the fats shall overflow with wine and oil. And I will restore to you the years that the locust has eaten..."*
>
> *Joel 2:21-25*

The first sentence of this passage says, *"Fear not, O land; be glad and rejoice: for the Lord will do great things."* What was the great things the Lord was going to do? He was going to send the rain! He was going to pour out of His heavenly treasure and nourish the fields. He was going to send the former and the latter rain to the earth. And when the earth received the former and latter rain the threshing floors would be full of grain. The fats would overflow. And there would even be a restoration of the harvest that had been destroyed by the locust! Then the land would be glad and rejoice!

No Rain, No Harvest

Notice what happened, however, when the rains of heaven were withheld from a field. God spoke these words to rebellious Israel,

> *"And also I have withholden the rain from you, when there were yet three months to the harvest: and I caused it to rain upon one city, and caused it not to rain upon another city: one piece was rained upon, and the piece whereupon it rained not withered."*
>
> *Amos 4:7*

Notice that God withheld rain from some fields and cities and caused it to rain in other fields and cities. The harvest fields that received no rain withered and no harvest was reaped from them.

And notice these disheartening words from Jeremiah about a lack of rain,

> *"...they were ashamed and confounded, and covered their heads. Because the ground is chapt, **for there was no rain in the earth,** the plowmen were ashamed, they covered their heads."*
>
> *Jeremiah 14:3-4*

The ground in this scripture was chapt and hard because there was no rain in the earth. The fields were not soft and moist, prepared to receive seed and produce a harvest. The plowmen didn't even want to plow their fields. They were ashamed and confounded and covered their heads. Without the softening work of the early rain there was no reason to plow the fields and certainly no reason to sow seed.

These Old Testament scriptures reveal the significant relationship between the early and latter rains and the resulting abundant harvest. God, being a husbandman and caring for His people, kept His eye upon the promised land of Canaan and guaranteed heavenly rains if the people would walk in His commandments. He would send the early and latter rain and there would be an abundant harvest. **No rain meant no harvest, but the right rain in the right season guaranteed an abundant crop.**

CHAPTER
FIVE

THE RAIN OF THE SPIRIT

The Old Testament early and latter rain is clearly a type and shadow of the New Testament outpouring of the Holy Spirit. The prophet Joel helps reveal this connection in his address to the children of Zion. He declared that there had been a moderate outpouring of the early rain, but that there would be a much greater outpouring of the latter rain. Notice his prophetic words,

> *"Be glad then, ye children of Zion, and rejoice in the Lord your God: for he hath given you the former rain moderately, and he will cause to come down for you the rain, the former rain, and the latter rain in the first month. And the floors shall be full of wheat, and the fats shall overflow with wine and oil. And I will restore to you the years that the locust hath eaten..."*
>
> *Joel 2:23-25*

To whom was Joel speaking in this prophetic utterance? Was he speaking to the people of his own time or to people of a future time? Was he speaking of natural rain and a natural harvest or was he speaking of another kind of rain and another kind of harvest?

As Joel prophesied, he was, in a sense, caught in a time-warp. He prophesied concerning his present time, concerning the church age, and even prophesied up to the close of the church age and the beginning of the millennial reign. What he prophesied concerning the early and latter rain referred not only to natural rain and the resulting natural harvest, but also to the outpouring of the rain of the Holy Spirit in the church age and the harvest of souls it would produce!

When Joel prophesied, he was speaking not only to Israel, but also to the church. He exhorted us, the *"children of Zion,"* to be glad and rejoice because there was coming an outpouring of rain! This outpouring would produce a great harvest, even redeeming the precious fruit of the earth that had been stolen.

That the Old Testament early and latter rain is a type of the New Testament outpouring of the Holy Spirit becomes even clearer when we note that what Joel prophesied in Joel 2:21-25 concerning the early and latter rain was immediately followed by the clear promise of the outpouring of the Holy Spirit. In verse 28, he prophesied,

> *"And it shall come to pass afterward, that I will pour out my spirit upon all flesh..."*
>
> Joel 2:28

When the world received its initial outpouring of Holy Ghost rain on the day of Pentecost, Peter said, *"this is that which was spoken by the prophet Joel"* [Acts 2:16]. Peter confirmed that the outpouring of the Spirit on the day of Pentecost was a direct fulfillment of what Joel had prophesied. It is clear, then, that the early and latter rain Joel prophesied of referred not only to natural rain in the Old Testament, but also to the New Testament outpouring of the Holy Spirit on the harvest fields of the world.

Let's look at one more Old Testament scripture that connects the early and latter rain of the Old Testament to the outpouring of the Spirit of God upon the earth. The prophet Hosea said,

> *"Then shall we know, if we follow on to know the Lord: his going forth is prepared as the morning; and he shall come unto us as the rain, as the latter and former rain unto the earth."*

Hosea 6:3

Before the great Second Coming when the Lord will return to the earth in power and great glory, He will come to the earth as the early and latter rain. Before He comes in judgement to separate the goats from the sheep, He will come as the rain in the outpouring of the Spirit. Before the close of this age, He will come in the outpouring of the Spirit to the great harvest fields of the earth and draw to Himself as abundant a harvest as possible!

The former rain of the Holy Spirit has come moderately, but there is coming a combination of both the former and latter rain. This outpouring of the Spirit will not be moderate, but will be a deluge! The floors will be full, the vats will overflow, the years of destruction will be restored, and precious fruit will be harvested into God's eternal kingdom!

NEED FOR THE RAIN OF THE SPIRIT

In the same way that natural rain is absolutely essential to a natural harvest, so the rain of heaven, the outpouring and moving of the Holy Spirit, is essential to a spiritual harvest. **Without the rain of the Holy Spirit there will be no harvest of souls.**

The church has too often done as Israel did when they were in Egypt. We have attempted to water the spiritual fields through human effort. But nothing can produce crops like the true rain of heaven! It is full of heavenly conviction, revelation, and life and is powerful in producing results. No human institution or human effort can bring forth the kind of rain that is needed to prepare the spiritual fields for harvest. Listen to this question Jeremiah asked,

> *"Are there any among the vanities of the Gentiles that can cause rain? or can the heavens give showers? art not thou he, O Lord our God? therefore we will wait upon thee: for thou hast made all these things."*
>
> *Jeremiah 14:22*

No initial or lasting spiritual results in the harvest can be produced by human effort. Only God can send the rain that produces spiritual harvest. No matter what we try in the natural, no matter what special projects or invented gimmicks, we cannot produce the rain of the Spirit. We must give up our programs, plans, and natural human efforts and wait upon God for the rain!

WHAT DO THE RAINS ACCOMPLISH?

What do the early and latter rains accomplish? First, the early rains soften the earth to receive the seed; they prepare the fields for sowing. When there is no rain of the Holy Spirit, the ground of peoples' hearts is dry and hard. Consequently, when the seed of God's Word is scattered on these fields there is little results. Because the seed cannot get into the ground, the devil steals the potential for harvest. Hard hearts need the early rains to soften them for plowing and seeding. When hearts are prepared by the early rains of the Spirit, the seed of God's Word can be deeply planted and a harvest can be expected.

Do you recall what we learned from Jeremiah about what happens when the early rains are withheld from a field? Notice these words again,

> *"...they were ashamed and confounded, and covered their heads. Because the ground is chapt, **for there was no**

rain in the earth, *the plowmen were ashamed, they covered their heads."*

Jeremiah 14:3-4

The ground Jeremiah spoke of was chapt and dry because there was no rain in the earth. The fields were not prepared to receive seed. Without the softening work of the early rain there is no reason to sow seed.

I'm sure you are familiar with the parable of the sower and the seed from Mark four. Some seed fell by the wayside, on hard ground that was not prepared. This seed didn't even get into the ground before it was stolen by the devil [Mark 4:15]. Hard ground cannot receive seed. Early rains are needed, therefore, to prepare the ground.

The early rains also help in the initial development of the crop, bringing forth the early growth that pushes up through the earth. If there is no rain after the seed is sown, the young crop will die in the field, wilted by the scorching sun.

The work of the latter rain is to complete the development of the harvest. The fields are not ready and the sickle will not be put to the harvest until the fruit is ripe [Mark 4:29]. Only when the latter rains have prepared the fields white unto harvest will laborers be sent forth to reap!

The early and latter rains are essential to an abundant harvest. They not only prepare the ground to receive seed, but are necessary in both the initial and final stages of the growth of the harvest. Without the rains, the fields cannot produce a harvest. *The husbandman must wait for the precious fruit of human lives until He receives the early and the latter rains of the Spirit.*

UNPREPARED FIELDS

Not every field is ready to be harvested or even to be planted. What Jesus spoke to His disciples about the readiness of the harvest of His time cannot be broadly interpreted to mean that a harvest is always ready in every place. There was a harvest ready in Jesus' time and in that geographic location because of the advance ministry of John the Baptist. John had been preaching the Word of God and the Holy Spirit had been moving to prepare hearts for the ministry of Jesus.

In Acts 16, we find an incident that may well represent an occasion when a field was not ready for planting or harvest. Paul and Silas had been travelling and preaching together and wanted to extend their boundaries into Asia. They made plans to go there, but the Holy Ghost forbade them. We read,

> "...[they] *were forbidden of the Holy Ghost to preach the word in Asia.*"
>
> *Acts 16:6*

After the Holy Spirit forbade Paul and Silas to preach in Asia, they travelled to Mysia and attempted to go into Bithynia. The Bible says, however, that *"the Spirit suffered them not"* [Acts 16:7]. Isn't that unusual? Jesus commanded His disciples to go into all the world and preach the gospel, but the Holy Ghost forbade Paul and his company to go and preach the Word in these particular fields. Why would the Holy Spirit forbid them to go to Asia or Bithynia?

I am convinced that the fields of Asia and Bithynia were not yet ready for the gospel message. They would be at some point in the future, for at a later time the Bible says that all Asia heard the Word [Acts 19:10]. At that particular time, however, the fields of Asia and Bithynia were not ready for the seed of God's Word. Note the obvious leadership of the Lord of the harvest, however, as He directed Paul and his company into a ready and waiting field. The Bible says,

> "*And a vision appeared to Paul in the night; there stood a man of Macedonia, and prayed him, saying, Come over into Macedonia, and help us. And after he had seen the vision, immediately we endeavoured to go into*

*Macedonia, assuredly gathering that the Lord had called us
for to preach the gospel unto them."*
Acts 16:9-10

In this vision, Paul received clear direction from the Lord
to go to the field of Macedonia and preach there. Macedonia
was a field calling for help. It was ready for the seed of the
gospel. It was a field ready for harvest. And Luke reports
that, *"immediately we endeavoured to go."*

Not long after Paul and the others arrived in Macedonia,
they spoke the gospel, planted seed, and reaped one of the
first converts from this harvest field. Luke reported,

> *"...we sat down, and spake unto the women which
> resorted thither. And a certain woman named Lydia, a sell-
> er of purple...which worshiped God, heard us: **whose heart
> the Lord opened**, that she attended unto the things which
> were spoken of Paul. And when she was baptized..."*
Acts 16:13-15

Lydia was ready for the Word! The Spirit of God had been
at work. The early rain had been falling. Her heart had been
opened by the Lord. Because her heart was ready, Paul was
able to plant and reap at almost the same time!

Later, Paul cast a spirit of divination out of a young girl
and he and Silas were jailed. At midnight, however, they
prayed and sang praises. The prison shook with the power of
God and the prison doors opened. Only a short time later the
keeper of the prison was reaped into the kingdom along with
his household [Acts 16:25-34]. Macedonia was a ready field!

At a later time, Paul travelled to the city of Corinth and
began to minister there. As in many other places, he met very
strong resistance. This city, however, was going to be a longer
stop for Paul than other cities had been. The Lord appeared to
him in a vision and said,

> *"...Be not afraid, but speak, and hold not thy peace: For*

*I am with thee, and no man shall set on thee to hurt thee:
for I have much people in this city."*

Acts 18:9-10

When Jesus told Paul, *"I have much people in this city,"* He
was not referring to believers, but to a harvest of sinners yet
waiting to be reaped! The city of Corinth was a ready field!
And Paul remained there for one year and six months.

FIELDS READY FOR HARVEST

In the agricultural area where I grew up, the farmers
understood the importance of timing in planting and reaping.
The fields had to be prepared by rain and plowed open before
the seed was planted. If there was no spring rain the farmers
would wait to plant.

The farmers also knew when to harvest. In all my early
years, I never saw a combine [a harvesting machine] in a field
at the beginning or in the middle of the growth season. There
was no use going into the field if the crop was not ready to be
harvested. But when the crop was ripe, the farmers worked
around the clock to harvest it.

Concerning the way the kingdom of God works, Jesus
said,

> *"...So is the kingdom of God, as if a man should cast
> seed into the ground; And should sleep, and rise night and
> day, and the seed should spring and grow up, he knoweth
> not how. For the earth bringeth forth fruit of herself; first
> the blade, then the ear, after that the full corn in the ear.
> **But when the fruit is brought forth, immediately he
> putteth in the sickle, because the harvest is come."***

Mark 4:26-29

The sickle is put in **only** when the harvest is ready; when
the fruit is ripe. The Amplified Bible translates a portion of
this scripture in a very interesting way. Verse 29 says,

58

"But when the grain is ripe and permits, immediately he sends forth [the reapers] and puts in the sickle, because the harvest stands ready."

Mark 4:29 Amp

It is only when the grain is ripe and permits that the reapers are sent forth with their sickles to secure the harvest. Sometimes, in our concern about *how to* harvest the lost, we fail to realize that there is no use sending forth reapers until the harvest is ready. And how does the harvest become ready? It becomes ready when the early and latter rains are falling!

The rain of heaven, the outpouring of the Holy Spirit, plays an essential role in developing and preparing a ripe and ready harvest. **The harvest fields of precious fruit must be prepared by the rain of the Spirit!**

Do you remember the critical revelation James brought forth by the Holy Spirit? He said,

"Behold, the husbandman waiteth for the precious fruit of the earth...until he receive the early and latter rain."
James 5:7

The heavenly husbandman is waiting for the precious fruit of the earth, but He is also waiting for the early and latter rains. Until it rains, He will have to wait!

Thank God, we can do more than cast the seed of His Word on the ground and hope. We can also pray for the rains of the Holy Spirit. **We can ask for the rains of heaven which prepare the ground for seed and the fields for harvest!** Let's learn now how to pray for the rain.

CHAPTER

SIX

ASKING FOR THE RAIN

Believers play a tremendous part in causing the early and latter rains of the Spirit to be released. Our prayers ascending to heaven are like the moisture that evaporates from the earth and forms the clouds. When enough moisture has evaporated, the clouds become heavy and it begins to rain!

In the same way, when effectual, fervent prayer is going forth from different places, from different churches and individuals, it will not be long until the clouds begin to gather as they did when Elijah prayed for the rain! When you see the clouds on the horizon, you know it is time for the "abundance of rain!"

In Zechariah 10:1, God instructed us to ask for rain. He said,

> "Ask ye of the Lord rain in the time of the latter rain;
> so the Lord shall make bright clouds, and give them show-
> ers of rain, to every one grass in the field."
>
> *Zechariah 10:1*

In this scripture, God instructed us to ask for the rain and revealed that our asking will cause a release of the showers of heaven. The rains that fall from heaven help prepare the harvest in the fields. When we *ask* for rain the Lord *will send* the rain!

When, however, are we to ask for rain? Zechariah 10:1 says that we are to ask in the time of the latter rain. But when is the time of the latter rain? Are we in that season? Is now the time to pray for the rain?

THE TIME OF THE LATTER RAIN

The particular time period called *"the time of the latter rain"* is actually the whole church age. This season of time extends from the day of Pentecost—which marked the first local deluge of the Holy Spirit—until Jesus comes again.

The time of the latter rain is the dispensation when the Holy Spirit is poured out in the earth, moving in the hearts of men, convicting them of sin, and revealing salvation through Jesus Christ. In this season of the latter rain thousands of souls can be reaped in a day, just as happened on the day of Pentecost. Joel was prophesying of the time of the latter rain when he spoke these words,

> *"Be glad then, you children of Zion, and rejoice in the Lord, your God; for He gives you the former or early rain in just measure and in righteousness, and He causes to come down for you the rain, the former rain and the latter rain..."*
>
> *Joel 2:23 Amp*

The time of the latter rain began in Jerusalem on the day of Pentecost with the first outpouring of the Holy Spirit. Although this outpouring was indeed a manifestation of the latter rain in the time of the latter rain, it was only the first deluge of the Spirit and was localized in one city.

What occurred in Jerusalem on the day of Pentecost was only the beginning of the season of the latter rain. If you follow through the book of Acts and read church history, you will discover that there have continued to be localized outpourings of the rain of the Spirit. In Acts 10, for example, the household of Cornelius received an outpouring of the Spirit.

Even today outpourings of the Holy Spirit are occurring in different places. Although we are in the time of the latter rain, however, it is **not** raining in some fields. The outpouring of the latter rain, you see, is not automatic. If you want rain to fall on certain fields, you must pray!

WHY PRAY FOR RAIN IN THE TIME OF RAIN?

Why does God instruct us to ask for rain in the time of the latter rain? It seems a bit strange to ask for rain when we are in the rainy season. If it is, in fact, the rainy season and God wants it to rain, why doesn't He just send the rain?

I cannot give you a full theological dissertation about *why* our prayers make a difference when what we are asking for is already the established will of God. What I can say is this: God would not instruct us to do anything that was merely an exercise in futility. He would not ask us to pray for the rain just to keep us religiously busy. **The reason we are instructed to ask for rain in the time of the latter rain is because our asking makes a difference in whether it rains or not!**

Jesus said, *"Ask, and you shall receive."* James confirmed this saying, *"ye have not, because ye ask not."* If we do not ask, we will not receive. However, when we pray effectual, fervent prayers tremendous power will be released that is dynamic in its operation. When we ask for the rain, as God's Word instructs, then it will rain!

Let's read this instruction and promise from Zechariah once more,

> *"Ask of the Lord rain* [matar] *in the time of the latter...rain* [malqush]. *It is the Lord Who makes lightings,*

63

which usher in the rain and give men showers [geshem] *of*
it, to every one grass in the field."

Zechariah 10:1 Amp

When we ask for the rain [*matar*] in the season of the gathered rains [*malqush*] the Lord will answer by pouring out the
heavy rain showers [*geshem*] of the Holy Spirit upon the dry
and dying harvest fields of the world. Wherever these rains
fall there will be open hearts, revival in the fields, and a
tremendous harvest!

We *are* in the season of the latter rain. This *is* the time,
then, to ask for and expect a deluge of the rain of heaven! We
have received a moderate outpouring, but it is time for a
greater outpouring of the latter rain; the heavy gathered rains!
This is the rain which brings the fruit to full readiness for harvesting!

We are in the time of the latter rain! Now is the time to ask
for local showers and for a total outpouring of the Holy Spirit
in the earth. *Ask ye of the Lord rain!*

ELIJAH'S PRAYER FOR RAIN

One of the great teachings on effective prayer in the Bible
is found in James five. There we find both an excellent teaching on prayer and an example of effective prayer that relates
specifically to the prayer we are learning concerning the outpouring of the Holy Spirit. James taught,

> *"...The effectual fervent prayer of a righteous man*
> *availeth much. Elias was a man subject to like passions as*
> *we are, and he prayed earnestly that it might not rain: and*
> *it rained not on the earth by the space of three years and six*
> *months. And he prayed again, and the heaven gave rain,*
> *and the earth brought forth her fruit."*

James 5:16b-18

Elijah effected in the natural realm through prayer what we want to effect in the Spirit realm through prayer. In response to his prayer for rain the heavens opened, the clouds gathered, the rains were poured out upon the earth, and fruit came forth! **Effectual prayer made the rains come forth and the rain made the fruit come forth!**

The bringing forth of fruit began with Elijah's revelation of the will of God. In fact, the reason he was able to pray an effectual, fervent prayer was because God had revealed His will to him. He told Elijah, *"I will send rain upon the earth"* [I Kings 18:1]. Elijah simply prayed according to God's will and prayed fervently! That is why he had such tremendous results. He asked for rain in the time when it was God's will that it rain!

The fact that Elijah prayed for rain **after** God told him that He was going to send rain reveals the importance of agreement with God in prayer. Although God had established His will in heaven, Elijah's prayers brought God's will to pass in the earth. Basically, Elijah prayed, *"Thy will be done on earth."* This illustration of effective prayer from the life of Elijah underscores the tremendous importance of cooperating with the will of God through prayer.

When Elijah prayed earnestly for the rain, the heavens gave forth rain and the earth brought forth her fruit. The bringing forth of fruit for harvest always follows the outpouring of the rains of heaven. And the outpouring of the rains of heaven always follow effectual, fervent prayer for rain. What is going to happen when you pray earnestly for rain? There will be an outpouring of the Holy Spirit upon the harvest fields and there will be a harvest of precious fruit!

"But," you say, "Elijah was a prophet. He had greater power with God than the average man. He held a divine office." Notice, however, that in James 5:17 the Holy Spirit took careful pains **not** to mention Elijah's prophetic office. In fact, the Holy Spirit purposely disassociated Elijah from his prophetic mantle and emphasized that Elijah prayed as a man subject to the same passions we are. Listen to what the Word of God says,

> *"Elias was a man subject to like passions as we are, and he prayed earnestly that it might not rain: and it rained not...And he prayed again, and the heaven gave rain..."*
>
> *James 5:17-18*

Who prayed earnestly that it might rain and it rained? Was it Elijah the prophet or Elijah the man? James said that it was Elijah the man who prayed and obtained an answer. Elijah the man was subject to the same human passions we are! He made mistakes and he had weaknesses. In fact, on one occasion, after he had contested the prophets of Baal and won a great victory, he wanted to die [I Kings 19:4]!

My friend, James 5:17-18 is not the testimony of a prophet's effectual praying. It is the testimony of a human being who knew and agreed with God's will in prayer and obtained results. The outpouring of rain was the result of a man praying an effectual, fervent prayer!

There is little doubt that the Holy Spirit inspired the example of Elijah the man and his effectual prayer for the rain as an encouragement to all of us that we can pray effective prayers and get results!

You Can Pray Effective Prayers

So who can pray effectual, fervent prayers that make great power available and bring results on the earth? Believers can pray these powerful prayers! Men who fail can pray these powerful prayers. Women who make mistakes can pray these powerful prayers. Young men who are subject to temptation can pray these prayers. Normal people can pray these prayers and get powerful results!

We are all subject to human feelings, to mistakes and emotions, just as Elijah was. But don't **not** pray! *You can pray effectual prayers that make the outpouring of the rains of the Holy Spirit available to the dry and dying harvest fields of lost souls!*

It is no coincidence that James' teaching on prayer and his illustration of Elijah's prayer for the rain are in the same chapter of God's Word as his teaching about the husbandman waiting for the precious fruit until He receives the rain. This fact reinforces the profound relationship between the harvest, the rain, and our effectual prayers. *Effectual prayer brings forth the rain, and rain brings forth the harvest of precious fruit!*

NOW is the time for the rain. It IS God's will that the Holy Spirit be poured out on the spiritual harvest fields just as it was God's will that it rained in Elijah's time. The husbandman is waiting for the harvest **until** He receives the rain. But prayers bring the rain! You can pray for rain according to the will of God and the rain will begin to fall!

Before Elijah began to pray for the rain, he told Ahab, *"Get thee up...for there is a sound of abundance of rain"* [I Kings 18:41]. Elijah could hear the sound of rain with his spiritual ears before it began to rain in the natural realm.

Do you hear that sound? Do you hear the sound of the abundance of rain? Do you realize it is the season of the latter rain of the Spirit? Then get up to the mountain of prayer and begin to pray!

Do you want revival? Do you want people to be saved? Do you want the harvest to come in? **Then ask for the rain!** Lift up your eyes upon the fields, recognize the need for rain in order to prepare them, understand it *is* God's will that it rain, and **"Pray ye therefore!"**

Remember this: You cannot plow and plant with the hope of a harvest if there is no rain. So you must pray for your fields. You must ask for the rain. This is the **first way** for you to be involved in preparing the harvest in your field. *Prayer brings the rain of the Spirit and the rain of the Spirit produces the harvest of precious fruit that God is waiting for!*

CHAPTER
SEVEN

PRAY YE THEREFORE

When we ask for the rain, our desire is to receive the results of that outpouring—an abundant harvest. Certainly, the outpouring of the Holy Spirit is exciting. However, the Lord of the harvest rejoices more over one soul harvested into His kingdom than over ninety-nine who move in the Holy Ghost! Our *goal* is harvest and the *means* is the rain of the Spirit.

How do we pray for the rain? By praying this simple, but effectual prayer: *"Lord, send the rain."* This simple prayer is an effectual prayer because it is a Bible prayer. It is in agreement with the Word of God and the will of God. In fact, it is a prayer that God told us to pray. As you pray this prayer with a heartfelt concern for the precious fruit of the earth, the refreshing early spring rains and the heavy gathered rains, the revival rains of heaven, will begin to fall upon the fields you pray for.

When you pray for the rain, you are simply asking God to fulfill His Word. You are asking Him to pour floods upon the dry grounds. You are asking Him to pour out His Spirit on the people in your field. You are asking Him to fulfill the word He spoke through the prophet Joel when He said, *"I will pour out my spirit upon all flesh."* When you pray for the rain, you are asking the Lord to move by His Spirit upon the harvest fields of the earth. You are asking Him to send an outpouring of the Holy Spirit upon your countries, your states, and your cities.

PRAYING FOR SPECIFIC FIELDS

On the day of Pentecost there was a mighty outpouring of the Spirit in Jerusalem. It rained in that city because the disciples were praying every day in that city. Isn't it curious that it *poured* in Jerusalem when people *prayed* in Jerusalem? *If something is happening in the upper room something will be happening on the city streets!*

It is possible, you see, to have local showers. This truth is foreshadowed in the Old Testament in these words from Amos,

> *"And also I have withholden the rain from you, when there were yet three months to the harvest: and I caused it to rain upon one city, and caused it not to rain upon another city: one piece was rained upon, and the piece whereupon it rained not withered."*
>
> *Amos 4:7*

God can cause it to rain upon one city and cause it not to rain upon another. That is why you must pray for rain in your field.

Perhaps you wonder what field you should pray for. Of course, you must follow the leading of the Holy Spirit. If you feel impressed, for example, to pray for Russia, Mongolia, or Finland, then obey God and pray for those fields. But if you do not have a leading to pray for a particular field, make sure you pray for your own!

What is your field? Your field is the area of the world where you live. New York City, for example, could be called

70

a field. Or a whole country could be called a field. Your field is where you live!

THE RESULT OF ASKING FOR THE RAIN

What will happen when you ask for the rain? Zechariah 10:1 says,

> *"Ask ye of the Lord rain in the time of the latter rain; so the Lord shall make bright clouds, and give them showers of rain, to every one grass in the field."*
>
> *Zechariah 10:1*

When you **ask** for the rain, God will **send** the rain. He will give *"showers of rain"* and these showers will produce *"grass in the fields."* The final result of your prayers will be a harvest of precious fruit.

Isaiah 45:8 is descriptive of what will happen when you pray. It says,

> *"Drop down, ye heavens, from above, and let the skies pour down righteousness: let the earth open, and let them* [the rain and the ground] *bring forth salvation, and let righteousness spring up..."*
>
> *Isaiah 45:8*

Notice how the Amplified Bible renders this scripture,

> *"Let fall in showers, you heavens, from above, and let the skies rain down righteousness [the pure, spiritual, heavenly-life possibilities that have their foundation in the holy being of God]; let the earth open and let them, skies and earth, sprout forth salvation, and let righteousness germinate and spring up (as plants do) together; I the Lord have created it."*
>
> *Isaiah 45:8 Amp*

Read the above scripture again from the Amplified Bible. What a powerful request! We need the showers of heaven;

71

that heavenly-life that has its foundation in God. When it rains, righteousness will spring forth. The Lord has created this working. He has ordained both in the natural realm and in the spiritual realm that the rain and the ground work together to bring forth fruit.

When the heavens *"drop down,"* when it rains, the ground will be softened for the seed of God's Word. Good seed planted in good ground with the timely rains of heaven assures a good harvest. When the Holy Spirit is poured out, men's hearts will be opened and salvation will spring forth!

Perhaps your field seems like a desert in its spiritual condition. In the desert, seed often lies dormant for months; sometimes for years. One rain shower, however, can cause the desert to look like a watered garden. This can happen in your fields!

Some fields have had the seed of God's Word sown in them, but the rain of the Spirit is needed before the seed can develop and ripen for harvest. God can make the wilderness *"a pool of water, and the dry lands springs of water"* if you will pray [Isaiah 41:18]. Listen to His promise,

> *"For I will pour water upon him that is thirsty, and floods upon the dry ground: I will pour my spirit upon thy seed...And they shall spring up as among the grass, as willows by the water courses."*
>
> Isaiah 44:3-4

God said He would pour water upon the thirsty and floods upon the dry ground. He also said that He would pour out His Spirit upon our seed. This "seed" refers specifically to the offspring of Israel, but could also refer to the Seed of God's Word that has been sown in human hearts! When it rains, this good Seed will germinate and take root in people and they will spring up and become trees of righteousness!

I know that the prayer, *"Lord, send the rain,"* sounds simplistic. It does not seem that praying this simple prayer could

72

actually bring results. But remember: *"You have not because you ask not."*

Our God is not deaf. Neither will He withhold what He Himself wants to do. We must ask simply and fervently with faith. Our effectual, fervent prayers will make the rains of heaven available to lost and dying harvest fields!

God will watch over His Word to perform it. It is His will to pour out His Spirit upon the people in your city and nation. **So ask God to fulfill His Word by pouring out the rain of the Spirit upon your field! Ask ye of the Lord rain!**

SPECIFIC PRAYERS TO PRAY

Here are several prayers you can use as a pattern to help you start praying for the outpouring of the rain of the Holy Spirit:

> *Lord, I ask You to send the rain. Pour out Your Spirit upon the earth. Send the rain and prepare the fields for the seed of Your Word. Pour out the heavy rains of the Holy Spirit so that the harvest is abundant and full!*

Here is a prayer to pray for your city:

> *Lord, I ask for the rain of the Holy Spirit to fall in my city. May there be a mighty outpouring! May hearts be prepared and made hungry for the Word of God. Pour out Your Spirit in this wilderness so that the precious fruit of the earth may come to harvest. Cause this wilderness to become a beautiful watered garden by the rains of heaven.*

Section Three

℘ray that laborers be thrust forth into the harvest

Matthew 9:38

*Pray ye therefore the Lord of the harvest, that
he will send forth labourers into his harvest.*

CHAPTER
EIGHT

PLENTEOUS HARVEST, FEW LABORERS

In this section, we will learn our second effectual prayer. Like the first prayer we studied, this prayer is simple, but will bring powerful results because it is according to the will of God. In fact, this is a prayer Jesus asked His disciples to pray concerning the harvest. Whereas the first prayer we learned pertained to the preparation of the harvest, this prayer concerns those who will go forth to gather in the prepared harvest. This prayer is for laborers to be sent forth.

When Jesus saw the multitudes of lost souls, He declared that the harvest was plenteous. He also declared, however, that there was a shortage of laborers to work in the harvest fields. Because of this shortage of laborers the full and ready harvest could not be gathered in. Notice this important scripture,

> "But when he saw the multitudes, he was moved with compassion on them, because they fainted, and were scattered abroad, as sheep having no shepherd. Then saith he unto his disciples, The harvest truly is plenteous, but the

labourers are few; Pray ye therefore the Lord of the harvest,
that he will send forth labourers into his harvest."
Matthew 9:36-38

The shortage of laborers is a very serious problem. Even if fields are completely ripe, they cannot be harvested without laborers. Someone, some human being, must go and reap the harvest. God does not preach, the Holy Ghost does not preach, and Gabriel and Michael do not preach. The work of preaching the gospel and reconciling sinners to God has been committed to believers [II Corinthians 5:18-20]. Believers plant and water the seed of God's Word. Believers bear witness to a lost and dying world. Believers reap the harvest!

The great tragedy of a shortage of laborers is that ripe and plentiful harvests will never be harvested. Without spiritual laborers to bring in the spiritual harvest, sinners will die and go to hell. No matter how perfect the rain, how rich the soil, how incorruptible the seed sown, or how developed the crop, if there are no laborers, there will be no harvest gathered in! The consequence of a shortage of laborers is the same as the consequence of having no rain: **There will be no harvest!**

Today, just as in Jesus' day, there is a shortage of effectual laborers—men and women who are called and supernaturally equipped to do the work of harvesting souls. This is a monumental problem, for at this very moment the harvest fields of the world are becoming ripe. Jesus was referring to ready harvest fields when He said,

"Do you not say, It is still four months until harvest
time comes? Look! I tell you, raise your eyes and observe
the fields and see how they are already white for harvest-
ing."
John 4:35 Amp

In this hour, many of the harvest fields of the world are ripe. There are not *"four months until harvest."* The fields are white already! Some of the white harvest fields will not be harvested, however, unless effectual laborers are raised up to go forth and reap. There **must be,** in this hour, a raising up and a thrusting forth of effectual workers into the ripe harvest fields. Supernaturally called, equipped, and sent laborers must go forth NOW because when it's time to harvest, it is time to harvest!

CHAPTER
NINE

SENT FORTH LABORERS

B ecause of the shortage of laborers available to reap the harvest of His day, Jesus asked His disciples to pray. He said,

> "Pray ye therefore the Lord of the harvest, that he will **send forth** labourers into his harvest."
>
> Matthew 9:38

The most common word used concerning the sending forth of individuals with a divine commission is the Greek *apostello*. This word means "to be sent forth into a service" or "sent forth with a commission." Jesus used a different word, however, when He asked His disciples to pray that the Lord of the harvest would "send forth" laborers. In this request, He used the Greek *ekballo*.

The word *ekballo* is very strong. It comes from two Greek words: *ek*, which means "out of" or "away from" and *ballo*, which means "to thrust, to cast, to pour, to put into, or to insert." *Ekballo* means "to drive out" or "to send forth" and implies the notion of violence. It is most often translated "cast out" as in the context of ousting demon spirits. It means to strongly thrust some thing or some person out of one realm into another realm.

The word *ekballo* is used in Mark 1:12 concerning the operation of the Holy Spirit in driving Jesus into the wilderness following His baptism in the river Jordan. That verse says,

> *"And immediately the spirit driveth* [ekballo] *him into the wilderness."*
>
> *Mark 1:12*

By the Spirit's strong thrust, Jesus was motivated and directed to his first destination after being anointed with power for service.

The meaning of *ekballo* creates a forceful image concerning the sending forth of laborers. When the Lord of the harvest sends forth a laborer, that laborer will not just stumble out or casually wander into a harvest field, but will be **thrust out** *[ekballo]* by the Lord of the harvest. He will be launched out, poured into, sometimes driven, to the place the Lord has ordained.

When the Lord of the harvest *ekballo*'s a laborer, He deals in such a way that those being thrust forth are under a very strong influence to do His will. Only the Lord of the harvest has this divine ability to deal with the hearts of men and thrust them forth into the harvest. And only divinely thrust forth laborers will be effectual in their work!

WHAT DOES IT MEAN TO BE SENT FORTH?

To be sent forth into service does not mean to be sent somewhere by a local church, a seminary, or some other Christian organization. Those who are only sent forth by a human institution will not be divinely equipped. They will fade in the heat of the work or pass out in battle. They will grow weary as they attempt to produce spiritual results by the arm of the flesh. Their efforts may very well be in vain.

The true sending forth of laborers is the work which the Lord of the harvest does in causing individuals to be strongly thrust forward toward a particular ministry and place. This sending forth might include special manifestations such as visions and prophecies, but is primarily that something particular and individual that the Lord does by His Spirit in the hearts of chosen laborers.

In Matthew 10:1-5, we find a pertinent example of what it means to be sent forth. In these verses, Jesus was sending forth His twelve disciples. We read,

> *"And when **he had called** unto him his twelve disciples, **he gave them power** against unclean spirits, to cast them out, and to heal all manner of sickness and all manner of disease...These twelve **Jesus sent forth**..."*
> *Matthew 10:1, 5*

First, Jesus *called* twelve men that He had selected. These men were not selected by a role of the dice, but according to a very specific purpose. Then Jesus *gave power* to these twelve chosen men so that they could accomplish what they were called to do. Then Jesus *sent forth* these men to their specific fields of labor.

To be sent forth includes a divine calling, a supernatural empowering, and a specific mission/destination. When the Lord of the harvest "sends forth" a laborer, He calls them, equips them, and thrusts them forth!

BEING SENT AND BEING EFFECTIVE

There is a very significant relationship between being sent and being effective. The significant relationship is this: Divinely sent laborers are supernaturally empowered for their tasks! This truth is exposed in Romans 10:14-15 where Paul wrote,

*"How then shall they call on him in whom they have not believed? and how shall they believe in him of whom they have not heard? and how shall they hear without a preacher? And **how shall they preach, except they be sent?**"*

Romans 10:14-15a

Did you notice the last question, *"How shall they preach except they be sent?"* As much as it is true that sinners cannot believe on Jesus without hearing the Word and cannot hear the Word without a preacher, it is true that no one can preach effectively unless he is sent. No one can effectually proclaim the gospel unless they are sent! But, praise God, the inverse is also true. If a believer is truly sent, he will be equipped to effectively proclaim the gospel! He will get results!

When the Lord of the harvest thrusts someone forth to labor, they WILL be empowered to labor! The initial requisite for being able to proclaim the good news and labor effectively in the harvest field is to be sent forth by the Lord of the harvest!

The Lord of the harvest is the One who calls and equips laborers and then thrusts them forth into pre-determined fields. Those whom He sends forth, He also empowers and directs. **The laborers He sends forth, then, are always sent forth with divine equipment and divine direction!**

DESIGNATED FIELDS

The Lord of the harvest sends different laborers to different fields. Because He is the Lord of His harvest, He knows *who* to send, *where* to send them, and *when* to send them. Realize that as you pray for laborers to be thrust forth, Jesus will call and send specially designated laborers to the fields you pray for.

After Jesus had called, equipped, and sent forth the first twelve apostles, He appointed seventy others to go before

Him into the cities where He would come. To these seventy laborers, He said,

> "...The harvest truly is great, but the labourers are few: pray ye therefore the Lord of the harvest, that he would send forth labourers into his harvest. **Go your ways**..."
>
> Luke 10:2-3

Jesus instructed the seventy laborers to, "Go your ways," and sent them out by twos into the many different places He would go. Notice that He did not tell them, "Go your way," as if each were going to the same place, but, "Go your ways," indicating that each had a different direction and a different destination. Different laborers were sent to different places.

The apostle Paul was very conscious of this concept of specific laborers being designated for specific fields. Writing of his own territory of labor, he said,

> "But we will not boast of things without [outside] our measure, but according to the measure of the rule which God hath distributed to us, a measure to reach even unto you. For we stretch not ourselves beyond our measure, as though we reached not unto you: for we are come as far as to you also in preaching the gospel of Christ: Not boasting of things without [outside] our measure, that is, of other men's labours..."
>
> II Corinthians 10:13-15

The "measure" that God had distributed to Paul was the predetermined territory he was sent to work in. The Greek, *metron*, actually means, "a portion measured off from the whole." Paul was only sent to a portion of the whole harvest field of the world.

In verse 15, Paul made it clear that by his "measure" he meant the specific field of labor he was assigned to. Outside his measure, on the other hand, was beyond his proper limit, geographically and spiritually, and in another man's sphere of labor. Paul recognized his own field of labor and was very careful not to go beyond its limits.

The Amplified Bible renders Paul's words in a very clear way. It says,

> "We...will not boast beyond our legitimate province and proper limit, but will keep within the limits [of our commission which] God has allotted us as our measuring line, and which reaches and includes even you. For we are not overstepping the limits of our province...We do not boast therefore beyond our proper limit, over other men's labors...still within the limits of our commission..."
> II Corinthians 10:13-15 Amp

The NIV renders Paul's words in a way that clearly confirms the fact that God designates specific fields of labor to specific laborers. It says,

> "...we will confine our boasting to **the field God has assigned to us**, a field that reaches even to you."
> II Corinthians 10:13 NIV

Paul's field of labor extended to the Corinthian church. He was sent to them and he was an apostle to them. There were other churches in other places, however, that did not fall within his apostolic territory. For example, the church in Rome was not established or overseen by Paul. He did have a desire to minister to them, however, and wrote these words to them informing them of his desire,

> "...from Jerusalem, and round about unto Illyricum, I have fully preached the gospel of Christ...But now having no more place in these parts, and having a great desire these many years to come unto you...I will come to you."
> Romans 15:19, 23-24

TIMELY FEET

Laborers must go to the right fields in the right seasons.

And the Lord of the harvest knows when both the harvest fields and the laborers are in their prime season for the greatest results. Notice these wonderful words Paul quoted from the prophet Isaiah,

> *"And how shall they preach, except they be sent? as it is written,* **How beautiful are the feet** *of them that preach the gospel of peace, and bring glad tidings of good things!"*
> Romans 10:15

The word "beautiful" used in the King James Bible veils a tremendous insight concerning the timely directing of the Lord in thrusting forth laborers. The word translated "beautiful" comes from the Greek *horaios* and means, "that which is in season" or "the time when something is at its loveliest or at its best." *Horaios* refers to something being timely or coming in the right season.

Isn't it interesting that, *"how shall they preach, except they be sent"* and *"How beautiful* [timely] *are the feet of them that preach"* are found in the same scripture? Those who are truly sent by the Lord to preach in particular harvest fields have timely feet. In other words, they come to the right place at the right time! They come at the right season to reap the harvest of a particular field. Laborers who are truly sent by the Lord of the harvest have "timely" feet.

I remember hearing the testimony of a young missionary from the United States who was travelling in the Philippines. Together with a local pastor, she walked six hours to reach a remote village. This village had no radios, no television, no luxuries and had never really heard the gospel. When the missionary and the pastor arrived, there was a large opening already cleared by the villagers for their meeting. The pastor and missionary were surprised. Who knew they were coming? A bowed over woman approached this young missionary and with weeping told her that she had been praying for years that God would send a laborer to speak to them. This village was ready and the ministers sent there truly had beau-

87

tiful feet. They came in the timing of God to a village ripe for harvest.

Perhaps you think, "Why didn't God just send someone from the Philippines to that village? It would have been much easier." I don't know why the Lord sent that particular missionary to that particular field. I am not the Lord of the harvest. But I do know this: **Jesus is the Lord of the harvest and He knows which laborers to thrust forth into each particular field at just the right time.**

Notice this occurence from Paul's ministry,

> *"Now when they had gone throughout Phrygia and the region of Galatia, and were forbidden of the Holy Ghost to preach the word in Asia, After they were come to Mysia, they assayed to go into Bithynia: but the Spirit suffered them not."*
>
> Acts 16:6-7

Paul was divinely directed **not** to go to Asia or Bithynia to preach the Word. Perhaps danger awaited him there. Perhaps the harvest was not yet ripe in that field. Perhaps both of these things were true. In any case, the Lord of the harvest kept Paul from going to these fields.

The Lord of the harvest saw, however, that His harvest in Macedonia was ready for the gospel message. That evening, He gave Paul a vision of a man in Macedonia standing up and saying to come and help them. Paul and his company determined that the Lord was speaking to them and proceeded to the harvest field of Macedonia. There they preached Christ and reaped souls [Acts16:9-34].

At a later time, Paul travelled to the city of Corinth. The Lord of the harvest directed him to stay there because that field was ready to be reaped. He told Paul, *"I have much people in this city"* [Acts 18:10]. The Lord of the harvest instructed Paul to stay and reap in Corinth because that field, clearly seen in the spirit realm by Jesus, was white unto harvest!

A few years ago, a couple I know quite well left a church they had been pastoring for fourteen years to pioneer a church in a city in Russia. After being in that Russian city for a season, they discovered that three people had been praying intently that the Lord would send them a seasoned pastor of middle age with a family. The Lord answered the specific prayer of that "field" by thrusting forth this seasoned, middle-aged pastor and his family to their city!

Although being sent to that city and that foreign nation has not been easy for that pastor and his family, they have no doubt that the Lord of the harvest sent them there. Much fruit has already been reaped and much more fruit will yet be reaped!

The Lord of the harvest calls, equips, and sends forth specific laborers to preach in specific places at specific times. Know, then, that when you ask Him to thrust forth laborers into a particular field, laborers that are specially chosen and specifically equipped by Him **will** be sent to those fields!

CHAPTER
TEN

THREE SENT FORTH LABORERS

In the previous chapter, we learned that the Lord of the harvest thrusts forth the right laborers into the right fields at the right times to reap the harvest. In this chapter, we will examine three sent forth laborers and learn more about what it means to be sent forth by the Lord.

JONAH — A SENT FORTH LABORER

In the Old Testament, the word of the Lord came unto a man named Jonah and directed him to a specific city ready for repentance. The Bible says,

> *"Now the word of the Lord came unto Jonah...Arise, go to Nineveh, that great city, and cry against it; for their wickedness is come up before me."*
>
> *Jonah 1:1-2*

Jonah was not interested in this particular assignment. Not only did he refuse God's command. He actually ran in the opposite direction. We read,

"But Jonah rose up to flee unto Tarshish from the pres-ence of the Lord, and went down to Joppa; and he found a ship going to Tarshish: so he paid the fare thereof, and went down into it, to go with them unto Tarshish from the pres-ence of the Lord."

Jonah 1:3

Jonah was resisting the sending forth of the Lord. In fact, twice in this passage we read that he was fleeing from the presence of the Lord. Apparently, the divine influence of God's presence was so strong upon him, he could hardly resist. He wanted to get away from that influence. We will discover, however, that it was almost impossible for Jonah **not** to go to the harvest field of Nineveh.

After Jonah's ship left port the Lord caused a mighty storm to rise up so that the men in the ship feared for their lives. They believed that one of the passengers had provoked God and were urgent to discover who it was. Since no one would confess, they cast the lot. Through the casting of the lot it was determined that Jonah was the cause of the storm. He was thrown overboard and left to drown. God, however, pre-pared a great fish and directed it to swallow Jonah, thus pre-serving [though somewhat uncomfortably] his life.

In this wretched condition, Jonah decided to repent and obey God's directive to go to Nineveh and preach repentance. He said, *"I will pay that that I have vowed"* [Jonah 2:9]. Apparently, at some time in the past, Jonah had vowed to the Lord that he would do His will. After Jonah determined to keep his vow, God spoke to the fish and it vomited Jonah up on the shore.

Notice that the fish did not spit Jonah up in Nineveh. God did not force Jonah to go there. Neither will He force other laborers into their fields. He calls and strongly influences laborers to go, but each must say "Yes" to Him of their own will and then go.

After the fish spit up Jonah, God presented him with the same commission He had presented to him the first time. We read,

> *"And the word of the Lord came unto Jonah **the second time**, saying, Arise, go unto Nineveh, that great city, and preach unto it the preaching that I bid thee."*
> *Jonah 3:1-2*

This time Jonah obeyed God's directive and *"arose, and went unto Nineveh, according to the word of the Lord"* [Jonah 3:3]. Immediately upon arriving in the city, he preached the message of repentance God had commanded him to preach. He declared: *"Yet forty days, and Nineveh shall be overthrown"* [Jonah 3:4].

I suspect that Jonah did not preach this message with great enthusiasm or love. He did not want to be in Nineveh and he did not want that city to repent. The results of his preaching, however, were outstanding! How could this be? **It was because Jonah was the laborer sent by God to that field to preach that message.**

The people of Nineveh believed Jonah's preaching and began to repent. Before long, the king heard Jonah's message and he repented. Then the king decreed a fast in the whole city and commanded everyone to repent from their evil ways. God saw their repentance and withheld the judgement He was planning to send.

Jonah should have been ecstatic about the results of his preaching. What a breakthrough! What results in an evil city! What a testimony to include in his next newsletter! Jonah, however, was angry because God granted Nineveh repentance! He did not want Nineveh to be spared; he did not want their judgement to be stayed.

Jonah, you see, was not a completely willing laborer. When God first called him to go to Nineveh, he ran. And when the Ninevites repented, he was mad. Perhaps you ask,

"Why didn't God raise up a different laborer, maybe someone from Nineveh or at least someone who had a heart for Nineveh?" I don't know. I'm not the Lord of the harvest, are you? All I can conclude is that Jonah was the right laborer with the right message for that field.

The Lord of the harvest does not always gently lead laborers into His harvest. Sometimes He has to *thrust them forth.* In Jonah's case, God prepared the storm, the throw of the dice, and even the fish in order to bring Jonah to the place where he would say "Yes" to God's directive. God did not force Jonah to go. But He directed even the circumstances to help Jonah become willing!

Sometimes, when called laborers see the task prepared ahead for them, they may want to say, "No, Lord, the task is too difficult." Often, chosen laborers do not feel equipped for their assignments. And sometimes laborers simply do not want to go to the fields where God is sending them.

The Lord of the harvest has a unique ability, however, to thrust forth laborers into His harvest. And that is why we, the body of believers, *must pray* to the Lord of the harvest concerning this thrusting forth of laborers. He has a unique way of getting the attention of even the most unwilling laborers. He has a way of speaking that bypasses the mental realm and stirs the deepest recesses of men's beings. And He has a way of preparing even circumstances, if necessary, to cause each laborer to come to the point where his answer is, "YES"! As we pray, the Lord of the harvest will call, equip, and thrust forth supernatural laborers.

PAUL — A SENT FORTH LABORER

When Jesus revealed Himself to Paul on the road to Damascus, He appeared in a very supernatural way and for a very specific purpose. Paul's own testimony of his conversion reveals this purpose. He reported that Jesus told him,

*"...I have appeared unto thee **for this purpose, to make thee a minister and a witness**...Delivering thee from the people, and from the Gentiles unto whom now **I send thee**."*

Acts 26:16-17

Jesus told Paul that He had appeared unto him for *"this purpose."* His purpose was to make him a minister and send him forth to reap a Gentile harvest. In calling and equipping Paul, Jesus was fulfilling His responsibility as Lord of the harvest.

Paul's writings concerning himself always strongly reflect his consciousness of his divine calling. He realized that Jesus appeared to him for the purpose of sending him forth into the harvest field. Paul often referred to himself this way,

"Paul, an apostle, (not of men, neither by man, but by Jesus Christ..."

Galatians 1:1

The Amplified Bible renders these words of Paul this way,

"Paul, an apostle—special messenger appointed and commissioned and sent out—not from [any body of] men nor by or through any man, but by and through Jesus Christ, the Messiah, and God the Father Who raised Him from among the dead."

Galatians 1:1 Amp

Paul was a *"special messenger appointed and commissioned and sent out"* by Jesus Christ, the Lord of the harvest. He was divinely called, divinely equipped, and divinely sent.

In Galatians two, Paul testified of how the Lord of the harvest worked in him and in Peter. He wrote,

"...For he that wrought effectually in Peter to the apos-

95

*tleship of the circumcision, the same was mighty in me
toward the Gentiles."*

Galatians 2:8

The Amplified Bible renders Paul's words this way,

*"For He Who motivated and fitted Peter and worked
effectively through him for the mission to the circumcised,
motivated and fitted me and worked through me also for
[the mission to] the Gentiles."*

Galatians 2:8 Amp

The Lord Jesus not only called and sent forth Paul. He
also called and sent forth Peter. Jesus called both of these
men, equipped them, and sent them forth to their respective
fields of labor. Paul went forth divinely equipped as a laborer to the Gentiles. Peter went forth divinely equipped as a
laborer to the Jews.

The same Jesus worked mightily in Paul and in Peter, but
He thrust them forth to different fields. Think about it. Paul
was a highly educated Jew, but the Lord of the harvest sent
him to the Gentiles. Peter was a simple fisherman, but the
Lord of the harvest sent him to the highly educated Jews. We
would have done it the other way. But we are not the Lord of
the harvest! Jesus knows best! Can you see how important it
is to let the Lord decide? **Pray that He will call, equip, and
thrust forth the right laborers into His harvest!**

PHILIP — A SENT FORTH LABORER

Philip was the only man specifically designated in the
New Testament as an evangelist [Acts 21:8]. As far as we
know, he began his spiritual life as a simple disciple. Because
he was faithful and full of faith and of the Spirit, however, he
was one of seven men chosen in the church at Jerusalem to be
a deacon to the widows [Acts 6:5].

The next time we read of Philip is in Acts eight. Apparently, he was forced out of Jerusalem along with other disciples because of the intense persecution [Acts 8:1-4]. He travelled down to the city of Samaria and preached Christ there. He was very effective in his preaching and also worked miracles, cast out demons, and healed the sick [Acts 8:6-7, 13].

Up to this point it seems that the Lord of the harvest was dealing with Philip internally; just speaking to his heart. Nothing supernatural or out of the ordinary had happened to make him stand out as specially sent forth.

Later, however, while Philip was yet in Samaria, something notable did occur. We read,

> *"And the angel of the Lord spake unto Philip, saying, Arise, and go toward the south unto the way that goeth down from Jerusalem unto Gaza, which is desert."*
>
> *Acts 8:26*

An angel of the Lord of the harvest was sent to bring a special assignment message to Philip. His message directed Philip to a very specific place. He was to go on the road which ran from Jerusalem to Gaza. Although it is very likely that Philip had questions about why the Lord of the harvest was sending him from the ripe and ready harvest field of Samaria to the desert of Gaza, he was obedient and *"arose and went"* [Acts 8:27].

On that same road was a chariot bearing an Ethiopian eunuch of great authority. He had been to Jerusalem to worship and was returning to his own country. When Philip saw that chariot the Holy Spirit spoke to him and said,

> *"...Go near, and join thyself to this chariot."*
>
> *Acts 8:29*

In response to this clear directive, Philip ran! When he came near to the chariot, he heard the eunuch reading from the prophet Isaiah about a *"sheep to the slaughter"* and a *"lamb dumb before his shearer"* [Acts 8:32]. He asked the eunuch if he understood what he was reading. The eunuch replied that he could not understand unless someone would guide him. So Philip joined the eunuch in his chariot, began in the scriptures where he had been reading, and preached Christ to him. The eunuch believed Philip's preaching, was saved and baptized, and returned to his own country rejoicing [Acts 8:30-39]!

Do you see what transpired here? The Holy Spirit had been working in the eunuch's heart. The eunuch had been to Jerusalem and, no doubt, heard about all that was happening there. The seed of God's Word had been sown in his heart and he was hungry for the truth. The eunuch was ripe unto harvest! But how would this precious fruit be gathered into God's kingdom? A laborer was needed.

The Lord of the harvest, ever vigilant and watchful over His harvest, saw the Ethiopian eunuch. And the Lord of the harvest, aware of His own team of laborers, selected Philip and thrust him forth to the ripe harvest. Philip went to the field specified by the Lord and gathered in precious fruit for the glory of God. Heaven rejoiced that day over the one sinner that was saved!

A great harvest was reaped on the day Philip preached to the Ethiopian eunuch! A strategic "precious fruit" was harvested into the kingdom of God! Bible scholars tell us that the Ethiopian eunuch evangelized his country! You see, in one well orchestrated spiritual event, the Lord of the harvest both reaped precious fruit and called to Himself another laborer for another ready and waiting harvest field!

CHAPTER ELEVEN

THE NEED FOR YOUR PRAYERS

It is the prerogative of Jesus to call, equip, and send forth laborers into His harvest. But when will He call, equip, and send? He will call, equip, and send when we pray! How, then, can we be involved in the thrusting forth of supernaturally effective laborers into ripening harvest fields? **"Pray ye therefore!"**

Jesus, very aware of the need of the harvest and very aware of the inability of individuals to call and equip themselves, said to His disciples,

> "...The harvest truly is plenteous, but the labourers are few; Pray ye therefore the Lord of the harvest, that he will send forth labourers into his harvest."
>
> *Matthew 9:37-38*

The Greek word translated "pray" in Jesus' instruction "pray ye therefore" is *deomai*. It means, "to see the need and then make that need known by petitioning and supplicating until that need is met." When Jesus instructed His disciples to pray, He was telling them to see the harvest, recognize that there was a shortage of laborers, and petition Him until the situation changed. Prayer will change the situation of a short-age of effectual laborers for the harvest fields!

Notice that Jesus did not tell His disciples, "The laborers are few, so could you please go?" He did not tell them, "The laborers are few, so could you recruit workers." Rather, in view of the shortage of laborers, Jesus said, *"Pray ye therefore."* His use of the word "therefore" in the instruction "Pray ye therefore" forever associates the activity of prayer with the desperate need for divinely called, equipped, and sent forth laborers.

THE LORD OF THE HARVEST

Jesus not only instructed His disciples to pray. He also instructed them Who to pray to. He said,

> *"Pray ye therefore the Lord of the harvest..."*
> *Matthew 9:38*

The disciples were to address their prayer for laborers to the Lord of the harvest. Who is the Lord of the harvest? It is Jesus Himself! By calling Himself "Lord of the harvest," Jesus revealed His ownership of and deep concern for the harvest. The disciples are not lord over the harvest. The church is not lord over the harvest. And the devil is not lord over the har-vest. By calling Himself "Lord of the harvest" and referring to the harvest as "his harvest," Jesus was saying, "The harvest is Mine. It is my concern and my responsibility."

Jesus told His disciples to pray that the Lord of the harvest would *"send forth laborers into his harvest."* In this short phrase there is encapsuled a truth that stretches from Genesis to Revelation. That truth is this: It is the Lord's prerogative to call, equip, and send forth men and women to the assign-ments He has prepared for them.

Think for a moment of the great names you know from the Bible. Names like Moses, Abraham, Joseph, David,

100

Samuel, Jonah, Samson, Paul, Peter, and John. Every one of these individuals was called, equipped, and sent forth by God according to His own purpose and plan.

Jesus did not instruct His disciples to pray that laborers would be sent forth, but to pray that **He would send forth laborers**. By instructing the disciples to ask Him to do the work of calling, equipping, and thrusting forth laborers, Jesus revealed His divine responsibility and divine ability to accomplish that assignment.

As the Saviour Who died for the world, Jesus became deeply involved with the harvest. Now He will also be intimately involved with the process of sending forth workers into His harvest. He is not going to hire cheap labor and He is not going to send forth workers without the very best equipment. Rather, He will personally call, personally equip, and personally send forth supernatural laborers into His harvest!

Jesus is Lord of the harvest. The harvest is His harvest and His responsibility. He is the One Who sends forth laborers. Recognizing Jesus' role as Lord of the harvest gives us a foundation of understanding that will help us pray confidently what He has instructed us to pray.

RESPONDING WITH PRAYER

The harvest fields of this generation are crying out for deliverance; for a message of truth and love. They are crying out for help like the Macedonian man.

In order to reap the harvest of souls, effective laborers must be sent forth. Only the Lord of the harvest, however, can call, equip, and thrust forth empowered laborers into His harvest fields. If He is the only One who can send forth laborers, what can we do? What part can we play?

Too often the church responds only in natural ways to

great spiritual needs. We make this very mistake concerning the sending forth of laborers into the harvest. We try to get involved in ways that we are neither called nor qualified to handle. For instance, we might exhort other believers to do the work we think they should do. We might start schools of "higher education" in an attempt to train ministers. We might attempt to emotionally energize one another through hype or guilt. We might ask questions like, "How can we do more? What other programs could we institute? Who should we send?" We wrongly suppose that if we can motivate enough workers or develop just the right program, we will win the lost.

The **initial response** believers must make, however, when they realize the immensity of the harvest and the shortage of laborers is to pray to the Lord of the harvest and ask Him to send forth laborers into His harvest. If you desire laborers to be thrust forth into their respective fields to harvest lost souls and advance the kingdom of God, then become involved through prayer.

It is the privilege and responsibility of every Christian to pray, asking the Lord of the harvest to thrust forth supernatural laborers. Since Jesus requested prayer in view of the problem of a shortage of laborers, we can be sure that our prayers will be effectual in changing the situation of the shortage of laborers.

So let Jesus be Lord of the harvest. You just pray the effectual prayer in Matthew 9:38. As you do your part in prayer, Jesus will do His part as Lord of the harvest. He will answer your prayers by strongly influencing laborers both internally and externally, bringing them to the place where they are willing and obedient to go to the harvest fields where He directs. When they go forth, they will go supernaturally endowed with gifts from on high! They will come at the right time and reap a harvest of souls!

CHAPTER TWELVE

PRAY YE THEREFORE

We have learned in this section that although the harvest fields are prepared by the rain of the Holy Spirit, laborers are needed to reap the harvest. These laborers must be called, equipped and sent forth by the Lord of the harvest in order to be effective. You can have a powerful part in the thrusting forth of effective laborers through your effectual prayers.

Asking the Lord of the harvest to send forth laborers is an effectual prayer because it is according to the will of God. It is a prayer that Jesus said to pray. This prayer is not long, intense, or deeply intellectual, but it will produce a powerful response from the Lord of the harvest because it is according to His will!

There are two general ways you can pray concerning laborers going into the harvest fields. First, you can pray for a specific field that you know needs laborers. Perhaps there is a specific nation on your heart. Perhaps your own city is desperate for laborers. Any harvest field that touches your heart should command your prayer!

Perhaps your own family is the harvest that needs to be reaped. What can you do for them? They do not seem interested in listening to you. You've said all you know to say and there is no response.

At this point, you can definitely "Pray ye therefore." This is what Jesus said to do when He looked upon a harvest field that needed laborers. He understood that it was not physically possible for Him to minister to the whole multitude. If He could have helped them, He would have. But Jesus said, "Pray ye therefore."

If you have family or friends that are unsaved and they won't listen to you, then pray to the Lord of the harvest. Ask Him to look upon them, determine who they will listen to, and stir up a laborer to go to them and speak the Word of God in a way they will receive.

Second, you can pray for a specific person you know is called to go forth into the harvest field, but is standing still. Don't bug that person with your constant harping about working for God. Your words may produce condemnation, frustration and even resentment. The calling of God is different. It is sweet, but strong! Don't try to tell others to do something for the Lord. There is no benefit in dealing with their heads or emotions! Rather, "Pray ye therefore" to the Lord of the harvest about that person and petition Him to supernaturally call, equip and thrust them forth into the right field at the right time.

THE RESULTS OF PRAYING FOR LABORERS TO BE SENT FORTH

In Matthew 9:36-38, Jesus saw the harvest and the shortage of laborers and instructed the disciples to pray. Immediately following this passage the Holy Spirit records that the Lord of the harvest did exactly what He had just instructed His disciples to pray about. Matthew 10:1-6 records that He called the disciples He had chosen and gave them power. After calling and empowering them, He sent them forth, commanding them where to go. We read,

> "And when he had **called** unto him his twelve disciples, he **gave them power** against unclean spirits, to cast them out, and to heal all manner of sickness and all manner of disease...These twelve **Jesus sent forth**, and commanded them, saying, Go not into the way of the Gentiles, and into any city of the Samaritans enter ye not: But go rather to the lost sheep of the house of Israel."
> *Matthew 10:1, 5-6*

Matthew 10:1-6 is a Holy Ghost inspired "visual aid" of what will happen when believers follow Jesus' instructions to ask Him to send forth laborers. He will call those He has chosen, give them power, and send them forth with divine direction to their specific fields!

Have great confidence that the Lord of the harvest will thrust forth laborers into the fields you pray for. These laborers may come from the other side of the world or may come from a different church in your community. Where they come from is not your concern.

When you pray for laborers to be sent forth the Lord will hear and answer because it is His will! He asked you to pray, didn't He? He asked you to see the need and petition Him, didn't He? Do you think He will not hear and answer? The Lord of the harvest **will hear** and **will answer** by calling, supernaturally equipping, and thrusting forth laborers to the fields you speak out in prayer. So be listening for great harvest reports from the fields you pray for. They will surely come!

SPECIFIC PRAYERS TO PRAY

Here are several prayers you can use as a pattern to help you start praying for laborers to be thrust forth:

Lord of the harvest, I ask You to send forth laborers into Your harvest fields. Motivate men and women to go forth. Stir up their hearts to do the work. Call them, Lord. Get a hold of their hearts. Deal with them supernaturally. Speak to them by the Holy Spirit and anoint them with power! Call them, equip them, and thrust them out into fields ready for the message of the gospel.

Here is a prayer you can pray for a specific field:

Lord, prepare laborers for _____. You see that field, Lord. You see the tremendous need there. Manifest Yourself to someone as You did to Paul. Call them, equip them and thrust them forth to reap precious fruit. Give them great boldness. Grant unto them a voice and an effectual door of utterance to reach the harvest in that place.

Here is a prayer to pray for your family:

Lord of the harvest, You know my family needs to be saved. I have tried to witness to them, but it seems I am too close. Stir up a special laborer for this special field. Send an anointed, beautiful laborer to my family to speak Your Word and harvest them into Your kingdom.

Section Four

ℜraying for yourself

Acts 4:29-30

Lord...grant unto thy servants, that with all boldness they may speak thy word, By stretching forth thine hand to heal; and that signs and wonders may be done by the name of thy holy child Jesus.

CHAPTER
THIRTEEN
———

THE POWER TO BE A WITNESS

The first two prayers we studied are interrelated. We learned first how to pray for the rain of heaven—the outpouring of the Holy Spirit. The heavenly Father answers this prayer by pouring forth the rain of the Holy Spirit upon the harvest fields we pray for. And the rain of the Holy Spirit causes an abundant growth of precious fruit.

In conjunction with praying for the rain, we learned to ask the Lord of the harvest to thrust forth laborers into His harvest fields. Jesus responds to this prayer by calling, equipping, and sending forth laborers to reap the plenteous harvest. Just as He did with the first sent ones, Jesus equips and empowers modern day sent ones.

These first two prayers cause the harvest to be prepared and laborers to be called, equipped, and thrust forth into it. Now we must learn to pray for ourselves so that we can be effectual witnesses in the places God has set us.

Before I teach you how to pray for yourself, I want you to realize something important. Although others may pray for you, no one will be as interested in and as dedicated to your life as you are. If you will not invest into your own life through prayer, do not expect others to pray for you. You need to lift up your own eyes upon the harvest, see the great need, and get yourself ready to work in the harvest field!

THE WHOLE GREAT COMMISSION

In the 40 days between Jesus' resurrection and His final ascension, He instructed His disciples concerning their future ministry. Luke said that He gave *"commandments unto the apostles whom he had chosen"* [Acts 1:2]. One of the most familiar and famous of Jesus' commandments during this time period was the commandment He spoke immediately prior to His final ascension to heaven. At that time, He commissioned His disciples with these words,

> *"...All power is given unto me in heaven and in earth. Go ye therefore, and teach all nations, baptizing them in the name of the Father, and of the Son, and of the Holy Ghost: Teaching them to observe all things whatsoever I have commanded you: and, lo, I am with you alway, even unto the end of the world..."*
>
> *Matthew 28:18-20*

These words of Jesus are commonly recognized as the Great Commission. In this commission, Jesus instructed His disciples to go into the world and make disciples from all nations. This commission, preached as a popular text for generations, has stirred many believers to go into the world with the good news of salvation.

There is, however, an essential part missing from the Great Commission as it is recorded in Matthew 28. Although the other part of Jesus' commission is recorded in another gospel, it is vital and must be considered. The other part of the Great Commission is found near the end of Luke's gospel. Immediately prior to His ascension, Jesus said,

"And, behold, I send the promise of my Father upon you: but tarry ye in the city of Jerusalem, until ye be endued with power from on high."

Luke 24:49

In this part of the Great Commission, Jesus qualified His command to go into all the world with His instruction to *"tarry...until ye be endued with power."* The word "tarry" means "to sit" or "not go forth." The essence, then, of what Jesus commanded His disciples immediately prior to His final ascension to heaven was this: *Go into all the world and minister, BUT do not go until you are empowered from on high!*

Although Jesus commanded His disciples to go into the harvest fields and preach the gospel, He also commanded them **not to go** until they were filled with the power of the Holy Spirit! He instructed His disciples—not suggested, but instructed—**not** to leave Jerusalem, but to wait for the out-pouring of the Holy Spirit [Luke 24:49].

It was, in fact, this vital part of the Great Commission that Luke recalled in Acts one when he wrote these words,

*"And, [Jesus] being assembled together with them, commanded them that they should not depart from Jerusalem, **but wait for the promise of the Father**, which, saith he, ye have heard of me. For John truly baptized with water; but ye shall be **baptized with the Holy Ghost** not many days hence."*

Acts 1:4-5

DISTRACTED WITH JESUS' SECOND COMING

Immediately following Jesus' instruction to wait for the promised outpouring of the Holy Spirit, the disciples asked Him when the prophesies of scripture concerning the restoration of the kingdom to Israel would be fulfilled. They asked,

111

"Lord, wilt thou at this time restore again the kingdom to Israel?"

Acts 1:6

Notice how Jesus answered His disciples' concern about end time events. He said,

"It is not for you to know the times or the seasons, which the Father hath put in his own power. But ye shall receive power, after that the Holy Ghost is come upon you: and ye shall be witnesses unto me..."

Acts 1:7-8

In this answer to His disciples, Jesus used the word "But" to strike a contrast between being concerned about times and seasons and receiving the power of the Holy Spirit. He instructed His disciples where to focus their attention. It was not their business to know about the times or seasons. BUT, they were to be concerned about being filled with the power of the Holy Spirit and witnessing the message of salvation to the world! Again, Jesus directed His disciples' attention to the outpouring and empowering of the Holy Spirit.

Many believers in this hour are like Jesus' disciples. They are overly concerned with times and seasons. "When is Jesus coming again," they ask? "Why is His return delayed," they wonder? The thing believers of this hour should be most concerned about, however, is how to **become** and **stay filled** with the power of the Holy Ghost so that they can reap the harvest of lost souls!

Our business is to be about the Father's business. And the Father's priority business is the harvest! So don't waste too much time and energy trying to determine when Jesus will come again. I can tell you when He will come. He will come when the early and latter rains have fallen, when the gospel has been preached to every people group, and when the precious fruit of the earth has been reaped.

If believers continue to be over concerned about when Jesus is coming again, He will never come. But if believers are filled with the Holy Ghost and out reaping the harvest, it won't be long until Jesus splits the Eastern sky!

Jesus' Last Words

When I was young, my parents would sometimes slip over to the neighbors or the relatives for evening coffee. They often left us boys with instructions concerning studies, cleaning up, and what to do with the dog. If there was an instruction especially important for us to remember, they would repeat it on their way out the door.

Jesus did something similar. In the last few days before His final departure, He taught His disciples things that were essential for them to know in order to be effective in the New Testament. His most important words were reserved for the moments immediately prior to His final departure. The **very last words Jesus spoke** before He ascended to heaven were,

> *"But ye shall receive power, after that the Holy Ghost is come upon you: and ye shall be witnesses unto me both in Jerusalem, and in all Judæa, and in Samaria, and unto the uttermost part of the earth."*
>
> *Acts 1:8*

Immediately after Jesus spoke these words, *"He was taken up"* [Acts 1:9]. The disciples were now on their own. What were they going to do? Were they going to proceed directly to the harvest fields? Were they going to begin immediately to preach the good news? No, they remembered the instructions of Jesus and,

> *"...returned they unto Jerusalem from the mount called Olivet...And when they were come in, they went up into an upper room...These all continued with one accord in prayer and supplication, with the women..."*
>
> *Acts 1:12-14*

The disciples—all of them—tarried in Jerusalem in obedience to the instructions of Jesus. They continued in prayer with one mind in the upper room until they were endued with the power of the Holy Spirit from on high. **It was Jesus' commandment to tarry until endued with the power of the Spirit that the disciples remembered and obeyed after He ascended**.

TARRY UNTIL YOU ARE ENDUED WITH POWER

The consequence of being empowered by the Holy Spirit was that the disciples did, in fact, fulfill the Great Commission to go into all the world! They testified boldly and powerfully, demonstrating Jesus' resurrection and the power of His name in Jerusalem, Judæa, Samaria, and unto the uttermost parts of the earth. **It was the power of the Holy Spirit that made them effectual!**

There are many in this hour who are going into all the world to testify of Jesus, but are not endued with power. Yes, believers are commanded to go, but NOT UNTIL they are filled with Holy Ghost power. If you go out to the harvest fields without power, you will be in disobedience to the Great Commission! The bottom line is this: **There is no use going to the harvest fields without Holy Ghost power!**

You have authority to go to the world and preach the gospel because Jesus commissioned the church to go into the world and preach. But remember that Jesus also told His disciples, *"Tarry...until ye be endued with power from on high."* **An absolutely essential part of the Great Commission was, and is, to tarry in prayer until endued with power from on high!**

I exhort you to do what the early disciples did. Be willing to go to the world, but don't go without the power! Tarry until! Then when until is past, GO AND TELL!

CHAPTER
FOURTEEN

EMPOWERED FOR SERVICE

All throughout the Bible men and women who were called by God to do works of service were empowered by His Spirit to do those works. When the anointing of the Holy Spirit came upon these individuals, they were supernaturally empowered — changed, as it were, into different men — and enabled to do great exploits for God. By the anointing of the Spirit, they ministered the power and the voice of God to their own generations.

In the Old Testament, men like Moses, David, Saul, Samson, Gideon, Joseph, Ezra, Jeremiah, Elijah, Elisha, and Isaiah were stewards of God's anointing and vessels of His power. These chosen and anointed vessels fulfilled the will of God by the anointing of the Holy Spirit which rested upon them.

In the New Testament, God also calls individuals to special works of service. Some are called to be apostles. Some are called to be evangelists. Some are called to healing ministries. Some are called to work miracles. Some are called to do practical works of service.

It is also true in the New Testament, however, that the whole body of Christ is called to do the works of Jesus. All believers can witness the gospel to the lost. All believers can lay hands on the sick. And all believers can pray and expect God to hear and answer in mighty ways. Every believer, then, including you, should be available and ready to be used by God in the ministry of the Word and the Spirit.

An absolutely essential factor in being used by God in New Testament ministry is the empowering of the Holy Spirit. If believers are not Spirit-filled and Spirit-empowered, they will not be able to accomplish the will of God in reaping the harvest.

In this chapter, we will look briefly at the ministry of Jesus, the ministry of the early church, and the ministry of a few individuals in the early church to demonstrate that they accomplished their ministries by the power of the Holy Spirit. Then we will emphasize the fact that we, too, must be Spirit-empowered in order to be effective in reaping the harvest.

JESUS WAS EMPOWERED BY THE HOLY SPIRIT

From a very young age, Jesus knew what His ministry would be. In fact, He referred to being about His Father's business when He was only twelve years old [Luke 2:49]. Jesus was also deeply acquainted with the scriptures and personally developed. The Bible testifies this of Him when He was only twelve years old,

> *"And the child grew, and waxed strong in spirit, filled with wisdom: and the grace of God was upon him...And Jesus increased in wisdom and stature, and in favour with God and man."*
>
> *Luke 2:40, 52*

Although Jesus knew His mission, was well acquainted with the scriptures, and was personally prepared, He had to be endued with the power of the Holy Spirit in order to be

116

effective. Before He was empowered by the Spirit, He performed **no** miracles, healed **no** sick people, cast out **no** devils, and preached **no** messages. It was not that Jesus did not **want** to do these things. It was that Jesus **could not** do these things! Why couldn't He preach, teach, heal, or work miracles? He could not do these works because He had not yet been empowered by the Spirit.

When the time drew near for Jesus to begin His public ministry, He needed a baptism of power. He went to the river Jordan and submitted Himself to be baptized by John. When He came out of the water something tremendous happened. Matthew records these words,

> *"And Jesus, when he was baptized, went up straightway out of the water: and, lo, the heavens were opened unto him, and he saw the Spirit of God descending like a dove, and lighting upon him."*
>
> *Matthew 3:16*

When Jesus came out of the Jordan river the heavens opened and the Spirit of God descended upon Him. He was endued with power from on high just as He later told His disciples they would be. But why did Jesus need this baptism of power? Wasn't He the Son of God? Wasn't He the Messiah? Didn't He have a divine mission?

Yes, Jesus was the Son of God and called with a divine mission, but He had laid aside all His godly attributes and came to the world as a man. Like any other man, He had to be anointed with the Holy Spirit, for the Holy Spirit is the power and ability of God which enables men to be effective in ministry; both in ministering the Word of God and in ministering the power of God. *The Holy Spirit is the Agent of Accomplishment!*

When Jesus began His ministry at age thirty, He quoted these words from the prophet Isaiah concerning Himself,

"The Spirit of the Lord is upon me, because he hath anointed me to preach the gospel to the poor; he hath sent me to heal the brokenhearted, to preach deliverance to the captives, and recovering of sight to the blind, to set at liberty them that are bruised, To preach the acceptable year of the Lord."

Luke 4:18-19

Jesus testified that His ability to effectively proclaim the gospel and do mighty works was because of the anointing of the Holy Spirit. Peter confirmed that the Holy Ghost equipped Jesus to be effectual when he said,

"How God anointed Jesus of Nazareth with the Holy Ghost and with power: who went about doing good, and healing all that were oppressed of the devil; for God was with him."

Acts 10:38

Jesus went about doing good and healing because *"God was with Him."* How was God with Jesus? He was with Him in the baptism of the Holy Spirit and power! **Without the baptism of power, Jesus, although perfect, knowledgeable, and prepared, would have been completely ineffective in ministry!**

The Word of God says that the servant is not greater than his master. And Jesus said that whoever wanted to *serve* Him would have to *follow* Him [John 12:26]. If we really want to serve the Lord Jesus in ministry, we have to follow Him as our example in ministry.

How can we expect to do even a part of the effectual work Jesus did without at least a degree of the anointing of the Holy Spirit and power He had? If Jesus could do no effectual work of Himself, then we would be fools to think we could do any effectual work by ourselves. Because we have been sent to the world with the same commission Jesus had, we must also have the same divine equipment He had. We, too, must have heaven open upon us and be endued with the power of the Holy Spirit from on high!

THE EARLY CHURCH WAS EMPOWERED BY THE HOLY SPIRIT

The disciples experienced wonderful results when they ministered with Jesus during His three years of ministry because He had given them power and authority to minister in His name [Luke 9:1-6]. Their ministry was not finished, however, when Jesus died, resurrected, and ascended on high. The disciples were to continue in ministry as per the New Testament plan of God.

Jesus had already told them that when the Holy Ghost came upon them, they would receive power to be witnesses [Acts 1:8]. The word "power" He used is the Greek *dunamis*. *Dunamis* means inherent power or the power to perform anything intended. It is from *dunamis* that we get our English word dynamite.

What was the *dunamis* power of the Holy Ghost for? What was the reason for having it? Was it to have power for power's sake? Was it just to be able to say, "I have power now because I've been baptized in the Holy Spirit?" Was it to feel some kind of special physical manifestation? No! The results intended and, praise God, produced by the *dunamis* power of the Holy Ghost was the divine ability to be witnesses! *"You shall receive power"* and *"you shall be my witnesses"* were the results of the infilling of the Holy Spirit!

Baptism For Service

Because the disciples tarried for the Holy Spirit in Jerusalem according to the commandment of Jesus, exactly what Jesus foretold happened. The Bible says,

*"And when the day of Pentecost was fully come, they were all with one accord in one place. And suddenly there came a sound from heaven as of a rushing mighty wind, and it filled all the house where they were sitting. And there appeared unto them cloven tongues like as of fire, and it sat upon each of them. **And they were all filled with the Holy Ghost, and began to speak** with other tongues, as the Spirit gave them utterance."*

Acts 2:1-4

Luke tells us that there came a sound from heaven like a rushing mighty wind. This was the outpouring of the Spirit. And **all** the disciples in that upper room [not just the apostles] were filled with the Holy Ghost and began to speak.

After being filled with the Spirit the disciples rushed forth from the upper room and began to go into all the world and preach by going first, as Jesus had instructed them, to Jerusalem. Because of the outpouring and infilling of the Holy Spirit, they had great results in the harvest! Because something happened in the upper room, something happened on the city streets!

A very key phrase from Acts two is, *"And they were all filled with the Holy Ghost, and began to speak."* The result of *infilling* is *speaking.* When the well of the human spirit is full of the Holy Spirit, it overflows through the lips. Out of believers' innermost beings flow rivers of living water, inspired words from God, the power of the Spirit [John 7:37-38]! In the initial outpouring of the Holy Spirit, the disciples spoke in languages they did not know. But even with their minds disengaged, they testified of the works of God [Acts 2:11]!

So often believers think they must have a high-powered sales pitch, a perfectly outlined testimony, a good speaking voice, or proper spiritual etiquette to bring forth fruit for God. The early disciples, however, under the influence of the Holy Spirit, testified about the wonderful works of God with their minds in neutral! They spoke in unknown languages and those that heard them said, *"we do hear them speak...the wonderful works of God"* [Acts 2:11].

The multitudes that heard the disciples' message thought they were drunk with wine because they were obviously under the influence of something. The disciples were not, however, under the influence of alcohol. They had yielded to and been filled with the Holy Spirit. And this was the key to their effectual witness!

Peter's Inspired Message

By the inspiration of the Holy Spirit, Peter preached the first gospel message to the gathered multitudes in Jerusalem, recounting the death and resurrection of Christ. The result of his Holy Spirit inspired preaching was this:

> *"Now when they heard this, they were pricked in their heart, and said unto Peter and to the rest of the apostles, Men and brethren, what shall we do?"*
>
> *Acts 2:37*

Those who heard Peter preach were *"pricked in their heart."* That is what happens when the gospel is preached by the unction of the Holy Spirit. The words spoken go past mens' minds and fly swiftly, like arrows, straight to the heart! Conviction is brought, faith arises, decisions are made, and the harvest is brought in!

Peter did not give an altar call or beg people to come forward after he preached. The people responded on their own! And on that day 3,000 of God's precious fruit were reaped into His kingdom. That was a tremendous harvest! The field in Jerusalem was obviously ripe. But how was it reaped? **It was reaped through Holy Ghost anointed speaking!**

Too often, we have tried to convince or coerce people to accept Jesus. We thought that more *persuasion* would produce more *salvation*. What we really need, however, is a greater unction of the Holy Ghost upon our simple testimony of

Christ. Our anointed testimonies will cause the hearts of men to be pierced. They will know that the message we speak is true! There will be a weight of reality about what we speak. There will be an authority in the doctrine we preach. People will sense and know that what we speak is truth. And that truth will pierce their hearts and set them free. They will ask, "What can I do to be saved?" **The baptism and anointing of the Holy Spirit is an absolutely essential factor in being an effectual witness!**

The Hand Of The Lord

When the early church in Jerusalem began to be persecuted, some of the believers were scattered to other places. The Bible says that everywhere they went, they preached Christ. Notice these words,

> *"Now they which were scattered abroad...travelled... preaching the word to none but unto the Jews only. And some of them...when they were come to Antioch, spake unto the Grecians, preaching the Lord Jesus. And **the hand of the Lord** was with them: and a great number believed, and turned unto the Lord."*
>
> *Acts 11:19-21*

The Bible says that *"the hand of the Lord"* was with these believers as they preached the Lord Jesus. The *"hand of the Lord"* is the manifestation of the Holy Spirit in or upon people. When Elijah ran faster than Ahab's chariot, it was because *"the hand of the Lord"* was on him [I Kings 18:46]. When Elisha prophesied by the Spirit to three kings, it was by *"the hand of the Lord"* upon him [II Kings 3:15].

The *"hand of the Lord"* was with the early believers as they shared the gospel. And the Bible says that *"a great number believed, and turned unto the Lord"* [Acts 11:21]. The precious fruit of the earth in Antioch was reaped by these believers because they preached the Word and the Holy Spirit worked with them.

You see, it was not only the apostles that gave compelling witness of the resurrection of Jesus by the inspiration of the Holy Spirit and harvested precious fruit. Unnamed believers also gave compelling witness of Jesus by the inspiration of the Holy Spirit and harvested precious fruit! **The early church was effective because of the empowering of the Holy Spirit!**

PAUL WAS EMPOWERED BY THE HOLY SPIRIT

In Acts chapter nine, we read of Paul's radical conversion experience. He met the Lord Jesus, heard a supernatural voice, saw a supernatural sight, and received a supernatural commission [Acts 26:13-17]. After an experience like this, Paul was ready to hit the road with the gospel message! He certainly had received the *"Go Ye"* from the Lord. Before he could go to the Gentiles with the gospel, however, Jesus instructed him to go to Damascus.

After Paul arrived in Damascus, Jesus sent a disciple named Ananias to minister to him. The Bible records that Jesus instructed Ananias to lay hands on Paul so that he would receive his sight [Acts 9:11-12]. Notice, however, that there were further instructions Jesus gave to Ananias concerning Paul. We know this because when Ananias found Paul in Damascus, he told him,

> *"...Brother Saul, the Lord, even Jesus, that appeared unto thee in the way as thou camest, hath sent me, that thou mightest receive thy sight, and be filled with the Holy Ghost."*
>
> Acts 9:17

Not only was Ananias sent by Jesus to minister restoration of sight to Paul. He was also sent to lay hands on Paul and pray for him to be filled with the Holy Ghost!

Even though Paul had an incredible experience with the Lord and was called to be an apostle to the Gentiles, he needed to be filled with the Holy Ghost before he was sent to minister! Soon after Paul was filled with the Holy Ghost, we read this testimony about him,

*"he **spake boldly** in the name of the Lord Jesus..."*
Acts 9:29

Later in the book of Acts, we read that Paul continued to speak boldly. Notice these words about him and Barnabas,

*"Long time therefore abode they **speaking boldly** in the Lord..."*
Acts 14:3

What enabled Paul to speak boldly and effectively like the other disciples? He was able to speak boldly and effectively because he had been filled by the same Holy Spirit. And through a continued lifestyle of prayer and fellowship, Paul maintained a Spirit-filled, Holy Ghost empowered, effectual ministry. In fact, Paul testified about the Holy Spirit's important role in his ministry in his letter to the Romans. There he wrote that he accomplished his ministry, both in word and deed, *"by the power of the Spirit of God"* [Romans 15:19].

You see, it is not enough to be called by Jesus. It is not enough to have an education or to know the Bible It is not even enough to have a vision from heaven! **Believers must be filled with the power of the Holy Spirit in order to be effectual witnesses!**

STEPHEN WAS EMPOWERED BY THE HOLY SPIRIT

Another New Testament disciple who spoke powerfully and worked miracles because he was filled with the Holy Spirit was Stephen. We don't know whether or not Stephen held one of the five-fold ministry offices, but we do know that he was effective. He *"did great wonders and miracles among the people"* because he was *"full of faith and power"* [Acts 6:8].

The Word of God gives us this testimony of Stephen's speaking,

124

"And they [the religious leaders] *were not able to resist the wisdom and the spirit by which he spake."*

Acts 6:10

Why was Stephen able to speak in such an irresistible manner? Was it because of speech lessons? Was it because of the Bible School training he had? Was it because he was an apostle? Was it because he was an anointed evangelist?

According to the Word of God, Stephen was simply a table-waiter, a helps minister, an ordinary disciple who was full of the Holy Ghost [Acts 6:5]. And yet the Bible says that the religious leaders, those profoundly educated in the scriptures, could not resist the wisdom and spirit by which he spoke. What was the *"spirit by which he spake?"* It was the Holy Spirit!

Because Stephen was filled and stayed filled with the Holy Spirit, he spoke with a fervor and a wisdom that could not be resisted. That, my friend, is the potential of effective witness when one is filled with and remains under the influence of the Holy Ghost. **There is a connection between what believers are full of and what comes out of them!**

SPIRIT EMPOWERED BELIEVERS

To witness the gospel effectually, believers must be filled with, inspired by, and assisted by the Holy Spirit. Some believers want to witness their faith with what they call a silent witness. That is a contradiction in terms and not at all in line with God's Word. To witness means "to speak" or "to tell what you know!" **And the Holy Ghost gives believers the divine power to tell!**

The Holy Spirit Witnesses Through Believers

In John 15:26, Jesus said that the Holy Spirit would testify of Christ. He said,

"But when the Comforter is come...he shall testify of me."

John 15:26

How does the Holy Spirit testify of Jesus? Does He speak out loud into the air? Does He write words on a wall? No. **The primary way the Holy Spirit testifies of Jesus is through the mouths of believers!**

Let's read John 15:26 and 27 together and note the relationship between the ministry of the Holy Spirit and the ministry of believers as they work together to testify of Christ,

"But when the Comforter is come...he shall testify of me: And ye also shall bear witness..."

John 15:26-27

Although the Holy Spirit can testify of Jesus directly to individual hearts, He most often speaks through filled and yielded believers. When believers speak by the unction of the Holy Spirit, their minds will be under His control. Then what Jesus told His disciples **would** happen, **will** happen. He said,

"...take ye no thought how or what thing ye shall answer, or what ye shall say: For the Holy Ghost shall teach you in the same hour what ye ought to say."

Luke 12:11-12

The enduing of power by the Holy Spirit always produces powerful speaking. This speaking is not flowery words of mens' wisdom, but is, as Paul said, a *"demonstration of the Spirit and of power"* [I Corinthians 2:4]!

If you want to witness effectually and have a part in reaping the harvest, you must be empowered by the Holy Spirit. There is no use going to the harvest fields of lost souls without it. You will not be divinely enabled to tell!

Learning the gospel message is not unimportant, but learning alone will not produce results. Speaking the Word of God by the inspiration of the Holy Spirit produces results! To

126

have something impacting to say when you get to the harvest fields, you must first go to the upper room UNTIL you are empowered!

CHAPTER
FIFTEEN
_____

MAINTAINING THE POWER OF THE SPIRIT

The disciples experienced the outpouring of the Holy Spirit in Acts two. They preached the gospel of Jesus by the power of the Spirit and thousands of people were saved, baptized, and added to the church. In Acts three, Peter healed a man who had been lame since birth. What more could the disciples want? Supernatural things were happening! Most believers would be satisfied with these kinds of results!

But there was more work to be done; a variety of work to be done. To continue in the same measure of effectualness the disciples had to continue in the same measure of the anointing of the Holy Spirit. But to continue in the same measure of the anointing of the Holy Spirit, they had to keep praying.

And so although a tremendous harvest had already been reaped and although the power of God was being manifested, the disciples gathered together in prayer to ask God to continue to work in and through them. As a company, they came together and prayed these words,

"And now, Lord, behold their threatenings: and grant unto thy servants, that with all boldness they may speak thy word, By stretching forth thine hand to heal; and that signs and wonders may be done by the name of thy holy child Jesus."

Acts 4:29-30

Notice what the disciples asked for in this verse. They asked for boldness to speak the Word of God effectually and asked for healings and supernatural miracles to confirm the Word they were preaching. And what did they get? The next verse says,

"And when they had prayed, the place was shaken where they were assembled together; and they were all filled with the Holy Ghost, and they spake the word of God with boldness...And with great power gave the apostles witness of the resurrection of the Lord Jesus: and great grace was upon them all."

Acts 4:31, 33

When the disciples asked for boldness, healings, signs, and wonders, the Lord answered them by filling them with the power of the Holy Spirit. By the Spirit, they were enabled to speak and work effectively!

HOLY GHOST BOLDNESS

When the disciples prayed for boldness to speak, they were all filled with the Holy Ghost and empowered to speak the Word with boldness! And the Bible says that they were **all** filled, not just the apostles.

The effectual, fervent prayer the disciples prayed was not long, loud, or complicated. It was, rather, a simple request in their own language that was according to the will of God. In fact, their prayer seems almost too simple to have produced the response they received from God. Because their prayer was according to His will, however, and because they prayed fervently, their simple, short prayer for boldness was answered.

God responded. The building shook with His power. The anointing of the Holy Spirit was released. Boldness was imparted. They were *"all filled with the Holy Ghost"* and went forth witnessing with great boldness and power! By the enabling ability of the Holy Spirit the disciples became effectual laborers in the harvest fields. Because of their effectual, fervent prayer, much power was made available to them that was dynamic in its working!

Being Filled And Staying Filled

I want you to notice and understand that the phrase from Acts 2:4, *"And they were all filled with the Holy Ghost, and began to speak with other tongues,"* and the phrase from Acts 4:31, *"and they were all filled with the Holy Ghost, and they spake the word of God with boldness,"* do not represent the same experience. The outpouring of the Holy Spirit in Acts two was the disciples' initial baptism in the Holy Spirit. As a result, they spoke with other tongues and witnessed effectually. Everyone who will repent and be baptized can receive this *"gift of the Holy Ghost"* [Acts 2:38; 19:6].

The experience of the infilling of the Holy Spirit recorded in Acts 4:31 was different. The infilling recorded there was the ongoing empowering of the Holy Spirit for testifying the gospel that is maintained through prayer. This experience was not a repeat of what happened in Acts two. The disciples did not "get tongues" again. Rather, they were "power maintained" by the anointing of the Holy Spirit to minister boldly and effectively.

There is an *initial evidence* and an *ongoing evidence* of the infilling of the Holy Ghost. The initial evidence is speaking in other tongues by the inspiration of the Holy Ghost. Believers can continue to exercise this personal devotional gift at will for the rest of their lives. It will be a great assistance to them

131

in devotional life. The ongoing evidence of the infilling of the Holy Ghost is the ongoing divine unction to testify boldly of Christ.

As a believer, you should walk in both of these experiences. You should be filled with the Spirit and speak in other tongues. And you should pray for boldness to speak God's Word and experience the inspiration of the Holy Spirit causing you to effectually proclaim the gospel. You must not only have the initial evidence, but also the ongoing unction! You must continue to pray for the power of the Holy Spirit. You can do no effectual testifying of the gospel without it. Silent witness must go. **You must pray to be filled with power!**

Continuing in prayer maintains the fullness of the Holy Spirit and the fullness of the Holy Spirit enables believers to be effective in proclaiming the gospel. When the gospel is effectually proclaimed, men's hearts are pierced, conviction is brought, and the harvest is reaped! We all need the ongoing empowering of the Holy Spirit in order to be effectual witnesses and effective reapers in the harvest!

The early disciples began their prayer for boldness in Acts four by saying, *"Lord, behold their threatenings."* They had been challenged by the religious leaders to disobey Jesus' commandment to preach. So they asked God to look at their situation, to look at the work which must be accomplished, and to do something to help them.

You may need to pray in a similar way. Perhaps you won't pray, "Lord behold their threatenings," but you might pray this: "Lord, look at the work which must be done in my city. Look at the many needs of the many lost. Observe those who are discrediting your name [this one really gets God's ear]. Look at those who are filling our state with violence, with pornography, with hate. And then, Lord, look at me! I am Your servant in this city. I am called to be a witness in this place to help bring in the harvest of lost souls. Behold my situation, Lord, and grant me boldness to speak Your Word!"

The ongoing empowering of the Holy Spirit to be an effectual witness belongs to every believer. It is not just for pastors, evangelists, and missionaries. So stay in prayer for yourself. Continue to pray for boldness and stay filled with the Spirit! When you are Spirit-filled, you will be able speak with boldness!

HEALINGS, SIGNS, AND WONDERS

Not only was the disciples' prayer for boldness to speak answered. Their request that the Lord stretch forth His hand and heal and do signs and wonders was also answered. In Acts five, we read,

"And by the hands of the apostles were many signs and wonders wrought among the people..."

Acts 5:12

The power of the Holy Spirit to heal and to do signs and wonders was not only manifested through the apostles. The same power was manifested through common believers as they testified of Jesus. In Acts eleven, we read,

*"And some of them...spake unto the Grecians, preaching the Lord Jesus. And **the hand of the Lord** was with them: and a great number believed, and turned unto the Lord."*

Acts 11:20-21

What was *"the hand of the Lord"* that was with these believers as they testified of Jesus? It was the power of God demonstrated by the working of His Spirit through them!

We also read these wonderful words in Mark sixteen,

"And they went forth, and preached every where, the Lord working with them, and confirming the word with signs following. Amen."

Mark 16:20

The Lord worked with His disciples as they went forth and preached His Word. He stretched forth His hand of power to bear witness with signs and wonders that what His disciples were preaching was true!

Hebrews two offers a comprehensive statement about how God worked by His Spirit through the early church. We read,

> *"God also bearing them witness, both with signs and wonders, and with diverse miracles, and gifts of the Holy Ghost..."*
>
> *Hebrews 2:4*

As the disciples witnessed of Jesus, God also witnessed by working through them in signs, wonders, and diverse manifestations of the Spirit. The demonstration of Holy Ghost power was irrefutable evidence that the Word spoken about Jesus was true!

We read this testimony of Paul and Barnabas in Acts fourteen,

> *"Long time therefore abode they speaking boldly in the Lord, which gave testimony unto the word of his grace, and granted signs and wonders to be done by their hands."*
>
> *Acts 14:3*

Do you remember what the disciples prayed in Acts four? They prayed that God would "grant" unto His servants boldness and that He would stretch forth His hand to heal and to do signs and wonders. And what did we just read about Paul and Barnabas? We read that God gave testimony to His Word and "granted" signs and wonders to be done by their hands!

The *"hand of the Lord"* being with the early church was an answer to the disciples' prayer in Acts four that God would stretch forth His hand to heal and to do signs and wonders. The way God stretched forth His hand was by the power of His Spirit being manifested through believers.

The early church asked God to stretch forth His hand to work signs, wonders, miracles, and healings because that IS the will of God. They were simply asking God and the Lord Jesus to do by the Holy Spirit what They already willed to do!

Signs and wonders are confirming testimonies that Christ is alive today! And they are, therefore, a confirmation of our testimony. When people are healed, they glorify God. This attracts attention. This raises questions. This stirs up the spiritual appetites of people.

If the disciples prayed for boldness and for healings and miracles as early as Acts chapter four when the power of God was already being manifested, I believe the twentieth century church must pray the same prayer. Like the early church, we must pray for miracles, signs and wonders. We must lift up our voice in one accord and sincerely desire the empowering of the Spirit. When we pray for wonders, we will receive wonders and people will wonder what is going on!

Praying the same simple prayer the early church prayed will keep us filled with the Spirit, enable us to speak God's Word effectively, and cause healings, signs, and miracles to be manifested! **Prayer keeps us filled and being filled makes us effective!**

A Previous Power Failure

In Mark chapter nine, we find an incident where the disciples failed in ministry. A particular man had brought his demon possessed son to them so they could cast the demon out. This should not have been a problem for the disciples because Jesus had already ordained and empowered them. In Mark, we read,

> *"And he ordained twelve that...he might send them forth to preach, And to have power to heal sicknesses, and to cast out devils."*
>
> *Mark 3:14-15*

Jesus had given His disciples *"power and authority over all devils"* [Luke 9:1]. Why, then, did they have trouble with the demon possessed boy? If they had been given power to cast out all devils, why couldn't they cast out that particular devil?

That is exactly what the disciples wanted to know! They came privately to Jesus and asked Him, *"Why could not we cast him out?"* Jesus answered them with these words,

> *"This kind can come forth by nothing, but by prayer and fasting."*
>
> Mark 9:29

What was Jesus teaching here? Was He teaching about methods of deliverance? Was He teaching that in order to cast out a particular category of demon, believers must always pray and fast first? Was He setting forth a rule that a certain amount of fasting and prayer was required in order to get certain results?

In His answer to His disciples about why they could not cast out that devil, Jesus was not teaching a particular method of deliverance, but was relating a basic spiritual principle that every disciple who wants to do the works of Jesus must understand and follow. That principle is this: If believers want to maintain a bold confidence and a dynamic demonstration of faith and power in ministry, they must first go to a certain level of dedication in their personal prayer life.

Times of fasting and prayer maintain a consciousness of the unseen realm, of the indwelling Spirit, and of the authority of Jesus' name. Times of fasting and prayer draw attention away from the flesh and make room for the presence of God. Times of fasting and prayer yield a place to God and to His power for service. Times of fasting and prayer are a declaration to God that one is available for service.

It is apparent that the disciples' experience of power failure opened their eyes to the important connection between prayer and fasting and effective ministry because after the church in Jerusalem was established, they said,

> *"But we will give ourselves continually to prayer, and*
> *to the ministry of the word."*
>
> Acts 6:4

The disciples recognized the essential relationship between prayer and the ministry of the Word. They realized that they are inseparable! And notice from the previous scripture that prayer preceded the ministry of the Word. **There can be no effectual ministry in word or deed unless prayer precedes it!**

STAYING FILLED WITH THE SPIRIT

There is a combination of words that is common throughout the book of Acts. It goes like this: *"Then* [name] *filled with the Holy Ghost said..."*

For example, in Acts four, Peter was questioned by the religious leaders about how he healed the lame man. As Peter began to reply, the Holy Spirit took over and gave him the exact words to say. In that context, we find these familiar words,

> *"Then Peter, filled with the Holy Ghost, said..."*
>
> Acts 4:8

Was this experience a second baptism in the Spirit? Was it a repeat of Acts chapter two? No. The phrase, *"Then Peter, filled with the Holy Ghost, said,"* simply reveals that the Holy Spirit was inspiring Peter to speak. The effect of his testimony upon the religious leaders proves that he was not speaking out of his own wisdom, but by the Spirit. We read,

> *"Now when they saw the boldness of Peter and John,*
> *and perceived that they were unlearned and ignorant men,*
> *they marvelled..."*
>
> Acts 4:13

Although Peter was not educated in religion or schooled in speech, he caused even the most educated men of his time to marvel at his testimony. It was because of the unction of the Spirit!

We read the same words about being filled with the Holy Ghost and speaking in Acts 13. A man named Elymas was withstanding Paul and seeking to turn another man away from the faith. The Bible records this of Paul,

> *"Then...Paul...filled with the Holy Ghost...said..."*
> *Acts 13:9-10*

What we read here concerning Paul does not represent the first time he was filled with the Holy Spirit. These words simply reveal that the Spirit of God was moving upon him and that he was yielded to, or full of, the Spirit. What he spoke, therefore, was Spirit-inspired and full of Spirit-power. Because Paul spoke by the Spirit of God, his words had a great impact.

There is a divine truth represented by the phrase, *"then [name] filled with the Holy Ghost said."* That truth is this: When a person remains filled with and yielded to the Holy Spirit, he will speak and he will speak effectually! When believers maintain a life of prayer and continue to ask God for boldness, they remain Spirit-filled and are able to give powerful and effectual witness of the gospel!

Ephesians 5:18 literally says, *"be continually being filled with the Spirit."* Believers must remain full of the power of the Holy Ghost. There is no reason to experience a power failure like the disciples did with the demonic boy. But how can we maintain a fullness of the Spirit and power? **Prayer will bring us to and keep us at that place!**

Even the apostle Paul, though divinely called and endowed for ministry, asked that prayer be made for him so that he would have utterance to speak. To the Colossian believers, he wrote,

> *"...praying also for us, that God would open unto us a door of utterance, to speak the mystery of Christ, for which I am also in bonds: That I may make it manifest, as I ought to speak."*
>
> *Colossians 4:3-4*

To the believers in Ephesus, he wrote,

> *"Praying...for me, that utterance may be given unto me, that I may open my mouth boldly, to make known the mystery of the gospel...that therein I may speak boldly, as I ought to speak."*
>
> *Ephesians 6:18-20*

Paul was not interested in being inspired to say things he didn't know. He wanted to be inspired to say things he **did** know. Paul understood that there is a difference between speaking **with** divine utterance and speaking **without** divine utterance.

Effectual work in the harvest can only be done through the power of the Holy Spirit. And the power of the Holy Spirit is received and sustained through prayer. The simple prayer of the early church kept them at a place where they *"were all filled with the Holy Ghost, and spake the word of God with boldness."* It is the will of God that we, too, give ourselves to prayer so that our ministry to the harvest is effective.

So pray for boldness. Pray for divine unction. Pray that you might give an irrefutable, convincing, heart piercing testimony of Jesus Christ. And pray that healings, signs and wonders be done in the name of Jesus.

Maintain the fire of the Spirit of God in you. Stir yourself up, as Paul taught Timothy [II Timothy 1:6]. Don't dwindle, rekindle! How? Pray For Yourself!

When you pray for boldness and healings and miracles to operate through your life, God will answer. Old fear and tentativeness will be gone. Timidity will flee and you will be filled with the Holy Ghost and power! And you will, with great power and grace, give witness of the resurrection!

CHAPTER
SIXTEEN

GETTING THE GOODS FOR OTHERS

There is a significant parable Jesus taught His disciples as part of His response to their request, *"Lord, teach us to pray."* After teaching them the simple Lord's prayer, He continued to teach about prayer with this parable,

> *"And he said unto them, Which of you shall have a friend, and shall go unto him at midnight, and say unto him, Friend, lend me three loaves; For a friend of mine in his journey is come to me, and I have nothing to set before him? And he from within shall answer and say, Trouble me not: the door is now shut, and my children are with me in bed; I cannot rise and give thee. I say unto you, Though he will not rise and give him, because he is his friend, yet because of his importunity* [persistence] *he will rise and give him as many as he needeth."*
>
> Luke 11:5-8

The man in this parable went to his friend's house to borrow bread. His friend, already settled in for the night, refused to get up. The man would not be deterred, however. He kept knocking and asking and knocking and asking until his friend rose to answer him and gave him as much bread as he need-ed!

The man asking for bread in this parable was not doing so to meet his own needs, but to meet the needs of another who had come to him on a journey. This parable, then, is not about praying for personal needs to be met, but is about persistent-ly asking the heavenly Father to give you something so that you can meet the needs of others!

You see, as you go down the path of life God has ordained for you, you will intersect with others on their life-journeys. When you meet them will you be empty handed or will you be full of the bread of heaven; full of the Word of Life? Will you be able to meet their needs like the Good Samaritan met the needs of the beaten man, or will you have to pass by, a reli-gious failure? Will you be ready to minister the Word of God as Philip was when he intersected with the eunuch, or will you have to turn away, unprepared?

The response of the master of the house in this parable should give us great encouragement. Did he give the man who asked for bread just the three loaves he asked for? No! The master of the house gave him as many as he needed! That is a full supply! A full supply from God is like the time Jesus multiplied the fishes and loaves. Every need was met with some left over! **The master gave the man who came at mid-night enough to meet the needs of his friend!**

In John 15, Jesus said that if we keep His commandments, we are His friends. If we persist in prayer, He will arise and give us not only what we ask for, but more! *He will give us enough to meet the needs of the great harvest!*

After Jesus taught this parable, He re-emphasized the importance of persistence in prayer, instructing His disciples with these words,

"And I say unto you, Ask, and it shall be given unto you; seek, and ye shall find; knock, and it shall be opened unto you."

Luke 11:9

The Amplified Bible says,

*"So I say to you, Ask and **keep on asking**, and it shall be given you; seek and **keep on seeking**, and you shall find; knock and **keep on knocking**, and the door shall be opened to you."*

Luke 11:9 Amp

The Amplified Bible's rendering of Jesus' words brings a deeper and clearer revelation of the importance of persistence in prayer by revealing more accurately the meaning from the original Greek. The words *"ask," "seek"* and *"knock"* are structured in the present imperative and signify a continuance of activity. This means that we ask and ask and ask and keep on asking until we see results! We keep seeking and seeking until we find the power we are looking for! And we knock until the door opens!

Jesus continued encouraging His disciples to persist in prayer by informing them of the results of their persistence. He said,

"For everyone who asks and keeps on asking receives, and he who seeks and keeps on seeking finds, and to him who knocks and keeps on knocking the door shall be opened."

Luke 11:10 Amp

If you don't feel equipped to minister to the harvest, you must ask for "the goods." You must go to the Father in prayer and get "bread" for those who are hungry. Ask for words to speak to those who are lost and dying. Pray for the anointing of the Holy Spirit to come upon you so that you have something to give to others on their journey through life. Persist in prayer! Just keep asking and seeking the Lord until He gives you all you need!

Don't plan to pray once and then quit. You will never be an effectual laborer in the harvest! Prove to God that you mean business. Keep on praying every day and never give up! Persistence breaks resistance. You will have what you are seeking for, knocking for and asking for if you persist!

After instructing His disciples to ask and keep on asking, Jesus gave these examples to encourage them that they would, in fact, receive what they asked for. He said,

> *"If a son shall ask bread of any of you that is a father, will he give him a stone? or if he ask a fish, will he for a fish give him a serpent? Or if he shall ask an egg, will he offer him a scorpion?"*
>
> *Luke 11:11-12*

And Jesus concluded His teaching about prayer by saying this,

> *"...how much more shall your heavenly Father give the Holy Spirit to them that ask him?"*
>
> *Luke 11:13*

Jesus connected the parable of the man asking for bread at midnight with His instruction to keep on asking and with the truth that the Father will give the Holy Spirit to them that ask!

When you persist in asking for the power of the Holy Spirit, you will receive His divine empowering for service! The heavenly Father will not give you something different or anything less than what you ask for. He will give the Holy Spirit and the anointing of power to all that ask! And when the Holy Spirit comes upon you, you will be empowered to be a witness! You will be empowered to testify about the work of Christ. You will be anointed to preach the good news to a lost and dying harvest. **You will be an effectual laborer!**

So ask for the bread of heaven—that divine Word which you can minister to others—and you will receive. Seek the power of God's kingdom—the anointing of the Spirit—and you will find it. Knock on the doors of the kingdom of God—doors of effectual utterance—and the doors of harvest will be opened. **God will dispense to you the power you need to be an effective laborer!**

CHAPTER
SEVENTEEN
───

PRAY YE THEREFORE

In this section, we learned that the empowering of the Holy Spirit makes believers effectual in witnessing the gospel and reaping the harvest. We also learned that prayer is **essential** to staying filled with the anointing of the Holy Spirit for service. Now you need to begin praying for yourself.

The best way to pray for yourself is to pray according to the examples found in the Word of God. Too often, believers pray in ways that are not according to God's Word and are not, therefore, effective. This kind of emotionally based praying may satisfy religious feelings, but it is spiritually unproductive.

Now you know, however, what prayers to pray for yourself concerning being effective in reaching the lost. As you pray according to what you learned in this section, you will be praying according to God's will. He will hear and answer your prayers and you will increase in effectiveness!

RESULTS OF PRAYING FOR YOURSELF

When you pray for yourself, as the disciples did in Acts

four, you will have the same experience they had. When you pray for boldness, the Holy Spirit will begin to move upon you in more powerful ways, enabling you to witness the gospel effectively. Expect to be filled with the Holy Ghost and speak the Word of God with boldness. Expect your speaking to be a demonstration of the Spirit and power, as was Paul's. Expect to speak with a wisdom and a spirit which cannot be resisted, as did Stephen.

Also expect the Lord to work with you, confirming the Word you speak with signs following. Expect him to grant healings and miracles to be done through your hands.

And when you pray for bread to give to those you meet on the journey of life, expect God to fill your mouth with words from heaven. **He will give you all you need to meet the needs of those you meet!**

There is a wonderful picture in the book of Psalms of what will result as you pray for yourself. Notice these words,

> *"They that sow in tears shall reap in joy. He that goeth forth and weepeth, bearing precious seed, shall doubtless come again with rejoicing, bringing his sheaves with him."*
> *Psalm 126:5-6*

The figure in this scripture is of a man who has had crop failure to the point of despair, but who goes forth to sow his precious seed again praying for a harvest. According to God's Word, this person *"shall reap in joy."* There is no doubt that he will come again rejoicing, bringing his harvest with him!

When you pray earnestly for the ability of God to work through you, results will be forthcoming. As you pray, God will increase your ability to minister His Word. Certainly, the seed of God's Word is good. But it must be planted with the water of the Spirit into the soil of human hearts! As you go forth to sow precious Seed upon the hearts of men, you should also be "weeping"—praying earnestly for the help of

148

God. Then there is no doubt that you will come rejoicing bringing your harvest with you!

SPECIFIC PRAYERS TO PRAY

The two prayers I am going to teach you to pray for yourself are taken from the scriptures we studied in this section. Because these prayers are taken from the Word of God, they are effectual! The first prayer is the prayer the early disciples prayed in Acts four for boldness, healings, and signs and wonders. The second prayer is from Jesus' teaching about prayer in Luke eleven.

Both of these prayers will make God's power available to you and His power will be dynamic in its working! How do I know this? Because these are effectual prayers. They are according to the Word of God and the will of God. Expect to be filled with the Spirit and empowered to boldly proclaim the Word of God. And expect healings and miracles to occur as God stretches forth His hand through your hands.

Prayer from Acts 4:29-30:

> *Lord, I am Your servant. I want to be effectual as a witness. I want to bear fruit in the harvest fields.*
>
> *Lord, look at my field of labor and look at my inability. Then grant unto me, Your servant, boldness to speak Your Word. Empower me to give testimony of Jesus as did the early believers—with great ability and power and with great grace upon me. I need to have the power of the Holy Spirit operating in my life. Fill me with that power. Endue me with power from on high!*
>
> *And Lord, stretch forth Your hand through my hands to perform healings and*

miracles in Jesus' name. Do signs and wonders and meet the needs of people. Work through me by Your power and confirm that the Word I speak is true.

Prayer from Luke 11:5-13:

Lord, I knock on Your door right now and will not stop knocking until heaven is opened and Your power is poured out on me. I've come to ask for the the bread of heaven, the Word of Life, to minister to those I will meet in the journey of life. Cause me to speak Your Word effectually to the hungry that they may be forever changed. May I speak as the oracles of God! Give me ALL I need to minister effectively in Your name!

Section Five

Benefits of praying these prayers

Matthew 6:33

But seek ye first the kingdom of God, and his righteousness; and all these things shall be added unto you.

Chapter Eighteen

Residual Benefits

We have already studied the specific results that will transpire from praying the three prayers we learned. Praying, *"Lord send the rain,"* will result in the outpouring of the Holy Spirit upon the harvest fields we pray for. Praying, *"Lord of the harvest, send forth laborers into Your harvest,"* will cause the Lord of the harvest to call, equip and send forth supernatural laborers to reap the precious fruit of the earth. And praying, *"Lord, grant me boldness to speak Your Word, and stretch forth Your hand to work healings and wonders through me, and give me the "goods" to give to others,"* will cause an increase of the anointing of the Holy Spirit in our own lives.

These three effectual prayers will cause a release of God's power and produce outstanding results in the harvest if you pray them fervently. In addition to these specific results, however, some extra side-benefits will result as you pray these prayers. Let's look at three of these extra benefits.

You Will Change

Jesus taught that, *"where your treasure is, there will your heart be also"* [Matthew 6:21]. Your heart will always go where you put your treasure. When you take the treasure of your time and energy and invest in the harvest through prayer, you will develop a compassion for the harvest.

As you involve yourself in the advancement of God's kingdom by praying for the rain of the Holy Spirit to fall upon the harvest, by praying for laborers to be equipped and thrust forth, and by praying for greater power in your life to be an effectual witness, YOU will definitely change. Your heart toward sinners will change. You will experience a revival in your own life! **Praying for the harvest will change you!**

Perhaps you sense within yourself a need to return to the place where seeking the advancement of God's kingdom is foremost in your thoughts and in your actions. Perhaps you sense the need to have a greater compassion for the lost. Can you look out on the multitudes without a stirring in your heart? Can you watch a drunk walk the streets and feel nothing? Can you hear testimonies of broken lives and remain unmoved? Then you must turn your heart toward the precious fruit of the earth.

It is sobering to realize that this "earth-season" is the only segment of time in the whole of eternity when you can invest your treasure of time in prayer for the precious harvest of lost souls. A decision to give the treasure of your time to the Lord by praying the prayers you have learned in this book will not only result in lives being altered for eternity. It will also cause your heart to beat with compassion for the harvest.

YOUR NEEDS WILL BE MET

In Isaiah 58, God speaks of the fasted life-style He wants His people to live. This fasted lifestyle is,

> "...to loose the bands of wickedness, to undo the heavy burdens, and to let the oppressed go free, and that ye break every yoke...to deal thy bread to the hungry...And if thou draw out thy soul to the hungry, and satisfy the afflicted

154

soul...If thou turn away thy foot from the sabbath, from doing thy pleasure on my holy day...not doing thine own ways, nor finding thine own pleasure, not speaking thine own words..."

Isaiah 58:6, 7, 10, 13

The essence of this fasted lifestyle is to set aside your own desires, your own pleasure, your own will and your own words and give yourself to the will of God. This lifestyle is called a fast because in it you separate yourself from personal desires in order to seek the Lord and do His will. And what is God's will? His will is that the precious fruit of the earth be harvested!

Praying for the harvest is definitely part of a fasted lifestyle. As I remarked in the first chapter, prayer is a spiritual discipline. When you pray for the benefit of others, you are not doing your own pleasure, speaking your own words, or satisfying your own needs. You are sacrificing your life for the benefit of others. You are drawing out your soul to the hungry and agreeing with the plans of God in prayer.

Your prayers will help to loose the bands of wickedness and undo heavy burdens. Your prayers will help to break the yokes of bondage and set the oppressed free. When you draw out your soul through prayer, great and mighty things will transpire!

As you involve yourself in intercession and pray the three prayers I have taught in this book, you can expect the promises that accompany the fasted lifestyle to be yours. Let's read about the rewards that follow this fasted lifestyle,

"Then shall thy light break forth as the morning, and thine health shall spring forth speedily...the glory of the Lord shall be thy rereward. Then shalt thou call, and the Lord shall answer...And the Lord shall guide thee continually, and satisfy thy soul in drought, and make fat thy bones: and thou shalt be like a watered garden, and like a

155

*spring of water, whose waters fail not...I will cause thee to
ride upon the high places of the earth, and feed thee with the
heritage of Jacob..."*
Isaiah 58:8, 9, 11, 14

The word that introduces these rewards is *"Then."* When
is *"Then?"* *"Then"* is after you fulfill the requirements of the
fasted lifestyle. Only "when" you do the requirements can
you "then" receive the rewards.

Go back and read the rewards of a fasted lifestyle again.
Now read them again! These are some of the promised
rewards to those who give themselves wholly to the Lord;
who sacrifice their own desires and set themselves apart to
meet the needs of others.

God is a just God. He will not ask you to sacrifice and
then fail to reward you. If you do His will, you will be
rewarded! If you are not weary in well-doing and don't faint,
you will reap in due season [Galatians 6:9]. If you commit
yourself to praying the prayers you have learned, not only
will your prayers be answered, **but your own needs will be
met!** Jesus made this reality very clear when He said,

*"But seek ye first the kingdom of God, and his right-
eousness; and all these things shall be added unto you."*
Matthew 6:33

What are the *"all these things"* that will be added to you
when you seek first God's kingdom? They are the things
Jesus had been speaking about in the previous verses; the
necessities of life like food, shelter, and clothing. God adds
these things to those who spend their time seeking for the
advancement of His kingdom. I don't know of a more powerful way to advance the kingdom of God than to pray the
prayers I have taught in this book. *When the advancement of
the kingdom of God becomes your business, then your needs
become God's business!*

My friend, one of the great things that results when you lead a fasted lifestyle and give yourself to God by praying these prayers is that you become a candidate for having every need met! So lift up your eyes and look upon the harvest. Stop worrying about your things and seek the advancement of God's kingdom. As you seek first His kingdom, all things will be added unto you!

Unity Will Develop Among The Churches

Praying the three prayers I have taught concerning the harvest will also help produce unity in your local church and unity among local churches. Unity is not produced, you see, by saying exactly the same words or holding to exactly the same doctrines. Unity is produced by having common goals. Two people can start out miles apart, but if they are moving toward the same destination, they will eventually meet. As you and others pick up the heart-beat of God for the harvest and begin to pray, unity will result.

In Genesis 11 all the people of the earth were in one geographic location and spoke one language. Because they did not want to be scattered throughout the earth, they began to build a city and a tower to keep themselves united. Notice this significant word God spoke concerning the power of unity at work among this early people,

> "And the Lord said, Behold, the people is one, and they have all one language; and this they begin to do: and now nothing will be restrained from them, which they have imagined to do."
>
> Genesis 11:6

God said that because the people were one—of one speech and one vision—nothing would be restrained from them that they had imagined to do. Because of their unity, whatever they decided to do, they would do! That is a powerful testimony concerning the potential of a people that walk in unity!

In an orchestra, there is one instrument that all the other instruments tune to. If all the instruments are in tune with the main instrument, they will all be in tune with each other.

In a similar way, if every believer is in tune with the note God is sounding, they will be in tune with one another. The note God is sounding in this hour is, *"It's Time for Harvest."* That is His song. That is His message. Believers need to tune up with the will of God. When we do, we will be in tune with each other.

When believers pray the three prayers I have taught, they will lose their "I this, I that" mentality. The "I this, I that" mentality produces division. But as believers focus upon the harvest, reaching out in prayer from their hearts, the divisive "I" will be plucked out and they will gain the harmony that comes from having one vision.

As local churches reach out to the harvest through prayer unity and cohesiveness will develop and there will be an increase in the effectiveness of each local church and of the whole body of Christ. Notice this powerful scripture about unity from the book of Psalms,

> *"Behold, how good and how pleasant it is for brethren to dwell together in unity! It is like the precious ointment upon the head, that ran down upon the beard, even Aaron's beard: that went down to the skirts of his garments; As the dew of Hermon, and as the dew that descended upon the mountains of Zion: for there the Lord commanded the blessing, even life for evermore."*
> *Psalm 133*

It is good and pleasant for brethren to dwell together in unity. True unity among brethren is produced both by mutual love and by mutual cause. **There is no greater cause, no greater reason for working together on this planet, than to bring in the harvest of lost souls!** Individuals and local churches can disagree on church government, gifts of the

Spirit, the role of women, and other doctrines, but they cannot disagree and still call themselves Christians when it comes to the necessity of being involved in the harvest!

We cannot allow the harvest to die in the fields while we argue over harvesting methods. We cannot allow the harvest fields to become hardened and sun-scorched while we fight over scripture texts. I tell you right now that we will lose our candlesticks! It makes no difference if someone else's church does it different. Being motivated by love for God and for the harvest will produce unity.

Listen again to what unity will produce,

> *"It* [unity] *is like the precious ointment upon the head, that ran down upon the beard, even Aaron's beard: that went down to the skirts of his garments."*
>
> Psalm 133:2

The *"precious ointment"* in this scripture refers to the anointing of the Holy Spirit. **When the church is in unity the oil of the Holy Spirit will flow over every member, from the greatest to the least.**

Now notice verse three of Psalm 133,

> *"*[Unity is] *As the dew of Hermon, and as the dew that descended upon the mountains of Zion: for there the Lord commanded the blessing, even life for evermore."*
>
> Psalm 133:3

When churches are in unity the dew of the Holy Spirit will be upon them as the dew was upon the mountains of Zion. And *"it is there"* says verse three—there where the brethren are in unity—that the Lord commands blessing! **Unity makes it possible for the anointing of the Holy Spirit to be upon the body of Christ!**

The early church was together; they had all things in common. Their vision was to witness the gospel of Jesus Christ,

159

harvest the precious fruit of the earth, and make disciples of all nations. Their unity of vision is one reason they had such a tremendous outpouring of the Holy Spirit.

The body of Christ in this generation should also be in cooperation with the will of God. And His will is for sinners to be saved. God wants *"all men to be saved"* [I Timothy 2:4]. He is *"not willing that any should perish, but that all should come to repentance"* [II Peter 3:9]. The Great Shepherd is willing to leave the ninety and nine saved for the one who is lost. And heaven, says the Word of God, rejoices more over one sinner that repents than over ninety-nine that need no repentance [Luke 15:7]. Heaven is concerned with the harvest!

CHAPTER NINETEEN

CONCLUSION

God is looking for believers in this hour to stand in the gap and pray so that His will concerning the precious fruit of the earth will be fulfilled. Many, many years ago, God spoke this word through Ezekiel,

> *"And I sought for a man among them, that should make up the hedge, and stand in the gap before me for the land, that I should not destroy it: but I found none."*
>
> *Ezekiel 22:30*

At the time Ezekiel spoke this word, God found no man. I believe that in this hour, however, God will find individuals and local churches in every place—in every city, state and nation—who will stand in the gap for the lost through prayer!

Some would like to do what the apostles James and John wanted to do when a particular city rejected Jesus. They said,

> *"...Lord, wilt thou that we command fire to come down from heaven, and consume them, even as Elias did?"*
>
> *Luke 9:54*

Jesus turned and rebuked His disciples saying,

> *"...Ye know not what manner of spirit ye are of. For the Son of man is not come to destroy men's lives, but to save them."*
>
> *Luke 9:55-56*

Sometimes, when we see the unrighteousness, sin and degradation in the world, we would like people to receive their deserved judgement. We might respond like James and John did or like Jonah did concerning Nineveh. Notice, however, that this is not the spirit God is of and is not the spirit we are to be of.

Jesus came to the world, not to bring judgement, but to bring salvation. And when we consider the world, we must be of the Spirit of God. We must be concerned for and invest in the salvation of the lost.

So, rather than calling for fire upon your city, ask ye of the Lord rain. Rather than going about condemning sinners, pray for laborers to be thrust forth to bring the good news to them. Rather than talking amongst yourselves of the deserved judgement sinners are receiving, pray for boldness, healings, and signs and wonders so that you can help them escape from death into eternal life.

Believers and local churches that have left their labor of praying for the harvest must repent. There must be a change of heart, a change of mind and change of activity. It is time for local churches to go back to the work of laboring for an abundant harvest. *And that work begins with and continues in prayer!*

PRAY YE THEREFORE

The three prayers you learned in this book are effectual prayers because they are according to the will of God. It IS God's will that the Holy Spirit be poured out upon all lands!

Conclusion

It IS God's will that effective laborers go forth into the harvest! And it IS God's will that you be an effectual witness yourself!

The effectual prayers you have learned will *avail much* in your cities, counties, states and nations as you pray fervently. The fields will be rained upon by the Holy Spirit and prepared to receive the seed of God's Word. The young seed will develop and the fruit will become white unto harvest. The Lord of the harvest will call, divinely equip and thrust forth laborers into the whitened harvest fields. And you will increase in boldness—the Holy Ghost ability to effectually proclaim the gospel to your field—and will see the confirming power of God in healings, signs and wonders!

Lift up your eyes upon the harvest fields and pray! Soon you will be lifting up your eyes upon new brothers and sisters in the Lord. You will see them coming into the kingdom of God even as the father of the prodigal son saw him coming down the road back to his house. The rain of the Holy Ghost will cause righteousness to spring up from the earth. Cities will be refreshed by the sprinkling rains; they will be cleansed by the gathered, heavy rains. Dried up places will be turned into watered gardens. Laborers will be sent forth with the good news of God's love. Peace will begin to take the place of panic. Love will begin to take the place of hate. Rebellion among the young people will be replaced with zeal for the Lord of Hosts. *The three simple prayers you have learned will change the complexion of your fields if you will pray!*

The harvest is plenteous and the Lord is waiting patiently for the precious fruit of the earth.

PRAY YE THEREFORE!

Contents

Foreword

In 1931 Mrs. Emma Smythe became a friend of my family. She was then on tour, giving illustrated lectures about the Yukon. In these she included only oblique references to her own experiences. A lady to her fingertips, gentle in manner, calm of mood, it would occur to no one who met her casually that she had lived through the rigours and dangers so vividly retained in her memory. Desipte her love of fun, an underlying sadness might alert a sensitive person to the fact that she had known deep sorrow.

During the subsequent years she revealed to us the story *Yukon Lady* tells. She was always homesick for that country and always dreamed of returning, but always knew, too, that the life she describes here no longer existed except in memory. She never returned to the North, nor did she ever remarry. She lived at her old home (which she ultimately inherited) at Caron Point near Bathurst, N.B. She died there on August 3rd, 1957.

Our friendship continued to the end and her personality had its impact, in varying degree, upon three generations of my family. For this I offer thanks.

H.D.M.

Surprise

The doorbell rang and my sister Agnes went to answer it. In what seemed to me a very short time, she returned to the kitchen and I casually noticed that she seemed a bit excited.

"There's a man in the sitting room. You had better go in," she told me, in the manner of a small girl trying to withhold a piece of news she wanted to tell.

"You had better go in," she repeated.

"Can't *you* find out what he wants?" I snapped. The day was warm and I was in no humor to welcome any interruptions.

"No, I think you're the one who's wanted." And she grinned in what I thought was a decidedly silly fashion.

I gave her a withering look, laid down my work, and started for the sitting room in my most determined manner. I was going to get rid of that salesman in short order!

At the sitting room door I stopped. Before me stood Waldron Smythe, the man whom I was engaged to marry!

I had not seen him for five and a half years. I had given my promise in the days of the Klondike gold rush and shortly afterwards he had decided to join the great stampede. I had not been in favor of his going but all my objections had been quietly overruled, and in a little town in Massachusetts I had kissed him good-bye and wished him luck.

"I'll be back in two or three years," he had told me. But the two years became three, lengthened to four, then five, and five and a half. Although I was still warmly attached to him, I had by this time lost some of my enthusiasm.

And now he stood before me.

Two weeks later we were married in the little church I had always attended in my home town of Bathurst, New Brunswick, Canada. Not a cloud darkened the sky from the time the sun rose until it set. If an old adage were true I was to be happy indeed.

When discussing the future with Waldron I had shown no interest in going north.

"The matter rests with you," he told me, "but I think there is an opening for us up there."

There was no doubting his keenness for the Yukon, but I felt we could do better at home where conditions were familiar to both of us. When he agreed to this, I thought that the matter was settled.

However, one day about a week after we were married, he laid down the magazine he was reading.

"If we want to go into the Yukon this fall, we must leave here not later than September fifteenth," he announced.

I was completely taken by surprise. "Have you decided to go north?" I asked.

"It appears to be the best thing we can do," was the answer I received.

I did some rapid thinking for the next few minutes! I saw only too clearly where his heart lay. There could be no real happiness for him away from the North. And was not his happiness mine as well?

Without looking up from my sewing, I told him, "I'll be ready by that time."

A look of relief swept across his face. "Good little girl!" he cried and leaped to my side.

The call of the Yukon had him completely in its power.

On September fifteenth, 1905, in a drizzling rain, I said good-bye to the old home, kissed my sister, wrung the hand of my father (himself a pioneer of the Trail of '98), and together we went forth to a new world.

Looking back now after so many years—could I have seen into the future—would I have shunned the road I was to travel?

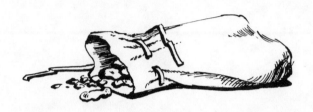

The Honeymoon

The trip across the continent at that time of year was one to gladden the heart of any Canadian and, homesick as I already was, I thrilled to it all. We left Montreal on a Sunday morning and not till the following Thursday night did the transcontinental train draw up at the station in Vancouver.

On Saturday evening we boarded the Canadian Pacific Steamer *Princess Beatrice* and on a glorious, sunny morning awoke to find Vancouver left behind and the boat well on her way up the Strait of Georgia. There followed several days of delightful steamer travel, during which we were enchanted by a school of whales at play, saw Indian totem poles and the glittering pile of Taku Glacier. North of Prince Rupert we entered Alaskan waters, calling at Juneau, the capital of Alaska. A few more hours brought us to Skagway at the head of Lynn Canal.

As I stepped from the steamer for the walk from the pier into town, I felt that the "Outside" had been left behind and the romantic life of the North was about to begin in earnest.

Already this was historic ground. During the Klondike rush there were two routes into the country. One, the Chilkoot Pass, led in from Dyea, which lies to the northwest of Skagway around a shoulder of mountain. Later, when the railroad was built through the White Pass from Skagway, Dyea was abandoned.

Skagway, itself, has changed much since the days of Soapy Smith. He was the leader of a gang of outlaws who robbed, and often murdered, the men leaving the steamers and bound for the Klondike. The miners coming out with their gold dust shared the same compliment until, one day, a returning miner found Soapy in a saloon. Drawing their guns at the same instant, each shot the other and both are buried at Reid's Falls, six miles from the town. On the mountainside, the form of a skull has been chiseled and painted white, with Soapy's name·upon it in black letters.

We left Skagway for the one-hundred-and-ten-mile run to Whitehorse the next morning. We were at last on the actual trip into the Klondike: a land where history had been made and whose name, just a few years previously, had set the whole world aflame with excitement.

There are places where the old foot trail can be seen from the train and I felt rather guilty as I saw, from my comfortable seat, the path so recently lined with laden, toiling humanity, each heart beating high with the hope of a fortune to be won. Some found their dreams came true, but the wild animals roaming over the silent mounds could tell of the destination reached by many.

It was a startling enough journey, even by train. When the line was first considered many experts said it was impossible. To survey the area the men had to be suspended by ropes from the mountain slopes. Yet so great was the traffic into the Land of Gold that the track paid for itself, mile on mile, as it was built. In July, 1900, the first train from Skagway rolled into Whitehorse.

Between the Strike in 1897 and my first journey in 1905 an era had already arrived, taken its course, and passed away. White Pass City had been a community of ten thousand people. All I saw were a few remaining logs from abandoned cabins and bare tent poles. In Dead Horse Gulch, two hundred and fifteen feet below the most northerly cantilever bridge in the world, Waldron showed me where the bodies of over three thousand horses had been left during the Stampede.

At The Summit (3000 feet) we entered Canadian territory from Alaska. Here the Union Jack and the Stars and Stripes flew side by side. Here, too, I had my first sight of the Royal North

West Mounted Police. Standing alone amid the mountain grandeur, scarlet tunic flecked with falling snow, his malemute dog at his heels, he was the personification of all I had heard of this magnificent force.

Our train was late in arriving at Whitehorse and evening was fast drawing in. The buildings of the town had been practically wiped out by a fire a short time before and the people were still housed in tents among the blackened ruins. We had our baggage transferred to the *Columbian*, the river steamer that was to leave for Dawson in the morning, and then we took a walk around what had been the town. How quiet it seemed, removed from the roar of traffic! Even the hills seemed hushed, lying like silent guardians around the little town of tents.

When we came on deck next morning the *Columbian* was just entering Lake LaBerge after having come through the Fifty Mile River, covering thirty miles of the four-hundred-and-sixty-mile trip to Dawson. I saw no sign of the crematory of Sam McGee, even though it was "on the marge of Lake Lebarge" that the awful deed was done! Here we encountered strong head winds and the boat was obliged to tie up for several hours. We moved on again about three in the afternoon and made Hootalinqua just before dark, making fast there for the night. During the next day we navigated the Thirty Mile River, which is deep, swift and crooked, and even one unused to handling boats could see that a master hand was required. When a heavy fog at evening made it necessary to tie up early once again, I could better appreciate the wisdom of the delay.

"Have you made the trip before?" the Captain asked, as I was going to my stateroom, and learning that I had not he advised me, "Be up early if you want to see the finest sight on the river. We shoot the Five Finger Rapids at break of day."

For once I was an early bird, as the clock pointed to 3:45 a.m. when I came shivering from my stateroom. Waldron had been out even earlier.

The channel here is quite wide, yet one glance showed that the water was both deep and swift. A grey mist hung above the water but the soft rays of the rising sun were doing their best to rob it of its mournful appearance. One door after another opened and the occupants of the staterooms emerged in various stages of semi-readiness. And each one tried to prevent their teeth chattering louder than those of the others! My effort was a dismal failure, my teeth beating a rat-a-tat-tat that might have served a body of troops on parade.

As the boat swept around a bend the mate, who was standing near me, said, "Look ahead, Mrs. Smythe."

Directly before us, in a straight line across the channel, rose four huge rocks which split the water into five "fingers." Only one, that on the right, was navigable for the steamer. Closer we swept and I held my breath. Something must be wrong! We were being carried directly against the first rock on the right! I watched, fascinated, forgetful of all else. Then suddenly, as though seized by an unseen hand, the vessel seemed to leap forward; there was a swift majestic sweep to one side; we sped past the rocks and glided into smooth water.

The tension broke sharply and we returned laughing to our rooms. However, our troubles were not over. There had been considerable conjecture on the trip as to conditions at Hell's Gate, a spot where the water is often dangerously low, and when we arrived we found the steamer *Dawson* fast aground in the deepest channel. There was nothing to do but tie up again and await developments.

All this tying-up and waiting had destroyed the peace of mind of one fellow passenger. Mrs. Robb had long before expressed her opinion of crew, captain and company. She would report the captain; she would have the crew dismissed; she would sue the company. She was due at a social tea in Dawson City and here she was "on a lousy steamer tied up to the shore."

When we pulled up behind the *Dawson* there were grave doubts of Mrs. Robb's survival. After lunch she flounced into the saloon where a game of cards was in progress, threw herself into a chair, and stormed, "I've thought ever since we left Whitehorse that the trip was hoodooed. Now I'm sure of it!"

"What's the trouble?" asked Mrs. Lester, another passenger.

"We've got no less than two brides on board! It's enough to make anyone sick! And I am sick!"

"Better not say too much about brides," advised Mrs. Lester, with a glance in my direction.

Mrs. Robb glared at me. "Are you one, too?"

"Is it a crime?" I asked.

"But—*are* you?"

11

"Yes."

"Hm! It's a damn wonder the ship didn't go to the bottom long ago! *Three* of them!" And out she rushed, banging the door behind her. I was so taken aback I have never been quite the same since.

In this instance we were not delayed very long. The *Dawson* gradually worked herself loose, we followed close behind, and touched in only a couple of places. During the afternoon we made good time and on reaching the White River at dusk tied up again (in spite of Mrs. Robb). This time it was to allow the crew to "wood-up," for of course wood was the fuel used.

Stewart, our destination, was only twelve miles farther, so we were astir early in the morning. I had scarcely finished breakfast when Waldron came to say we must hurry. The water was too low to allow the steamer to land and we were to be taken ashore in a dory. I had always feared the water and when I looked from the deck into the boat alongside where our baggage was already placed and realized I had to make the transfer, I thought my last hour had surely come. But the crew of a Yukon steamer thoroughly understands the meaning of the phrase "make it snappy" and I was hustled over the side and into that boat in a manner at least commendable for its speed! In terror I clutched a side of the boat in each hand and hung on, firmly resolved if the worst came to the worst to take the boat and all it contained to the bottom with me.

Yet we made the shore in safety and I stepped from the dory into an inch of snow and slush—with my rubbers carefully packed in my suitcase. I looked around for something to indicate that we had arrived at a settlement of some kind, but all I saw was a strip of gravel beach, the bank above it, and beyond this—woods.

"Where is Stewart?" I asked Waldron.

"Didn't you notice the cluster of buildings we passed just before we left the steamer?"

But just before we left the steamer my mind had been too much occupied with thoughts of a watery grave to notice anything else. Presently I heard voices and several of Waldron's friends emerged from the woods and came forward along a path to greet us. I was duly presented, but the ceremony was rudely interrupted. Our baggage had been landed and the dory returned to the *Columbian*. As it was being hoisted to the davits there was a farewell blast from the whistle and then—merciful Heaven! What *was* that noise? The earth seemed to tremble and the air was rent with the most blood-curdling "Ye-ow!—Ye-e-e-o-o-ow!"

I clutched Waldron in terror and added my shrillest screams to the bedlam, but my puny eforts were entirely lost, although alone they would have been a matter for pride.

"Don't be afraid," he reassured me, "that is only the dogs."

But I was unconvinced. "No dog ever made that noise!" I declared stoutly. My terror was not allayed until he explained that I had just heard the wolf-howl of the malemute or husky, that they were corralled, and that they always gave that cry when disturbed.

Each of the men now seized a piece of the baggage and we made our way along the trail they had come. Almost reduced to tears, I trotted disconsolately in the rear, by no means making the grand appearance befitting a bride. Scraps of the men's conversation such as "twenty cents to the pan," "ten feet to bed-rock," and so on, held no meaning for me. We came to a cabin roughly built of logs and bearing the sign: "Stewart River Grocery." One of the men, Mr. Bowen Smith, whom I later learned had been a particular friend of my father, invited us inside and as the door closed behind us I looked around.

Well! I tried not to appear conscious of the litter of excelsior, broken boxes, ashes, and other odds and ends that covered the floor. But when I looked from these to the counter I was faced with things that had never been neighbors before. On one end was a goldpan that held a pack of cards, a mouth organ, some toothbrushes and tubes of toothpaste, a strap of bells and buckles for a dog harness and several strings of brightly colored beads. Beside these was a washbasin and pitcher. The pitcher had several axe handles stuck into it and beside it in the basin was a set of dog harness and some crosscut saw handles.

While I was making this inventory, Mr. Smith had taken a chamois bag, or poke, out of his desk and from it emptied a number of large, gold nuggets. Selecting a nicely shaped one about the size of a thimble he gave it to me for luck and it is still one of my most cherished possessions. A real Klondike nugget! How I wished it had been possible not to notice the litter and the incongruity of things.

After chatting a while we continued on our way to the hotel or roadhouse and I wondered what awaited me there. The owners, Mr. and Mrs. Shand, came forward to extend a cordial welcome and my heart sank. They both wore moccasins! Very prettily beaded ones, but—moccasins. I had always loathed them. In the living room thick Hudson Bay blankets did duty for a carpet, skins of various animals served as rugs, and the walls were adorned with heads and rifles.

After a lunch Waldron left for Henderson Creek, where there were some mining claims in which he was interested. I wanted to go along, but when told I should have to walk eighteen miles, my enthusiasm cooled somewhat and I was left to occupy my time as best I could until his return a week later. Mrs. Shand understood my state of mind and put forth every effort to make me feel less lonely. The remains of her beautiful flower garden gave me a small measure of comfort. A land were flowers grew could not be wholly desolate!

Towards evening we heard the whistle of another steamer, from Dawson this time, and there was another chorus from the direction of the police barracks. Among the passengers leaving the boat there were several women and to my horror and disgust I noticed that one of them was under the influence of liquor. To escape her maudlin chatter I went to my room and remained there until the next morning. How far away the old life seemed! Could it be possible that, only fifteen days ago, I had left my laughing sisters in the old home, flowers in bloom, fruit and grain ripening in the autumn sunshine and friends gaily wishing me joy? I confess I cried myself to sleep from sheer homesickness that night.

During the week I had several callers of the male variety, all anxious to see what kind of a wife Smythe had brought in. I never knew what the consensus of opinion was, but through the long, hard years that came later I was to learn the rugged kindness of those hearts.

At the end of the week Waldron returned and we made ready for the trip to the creek. This would be the last lap of the journey and, as Mrs. Shand laughingly told me, the end of the honeymoon. The only horse the place afforded was obtained for me to ride and when he was led forth I almost collapsed. He must have weighed a ton. I had been on horseback only twice in my life and each time had dismounted suddenly and unexpectedly, so my feelings at having to ride that animal a distance of eighteen miles can be imagined. But the Yukon takes no account of human qualifications. The only way for me to get to Henderson Creek was to ride that horse—so ride that horse I must!

It seemed to me that the whole population of the village was out to witness our departure. There was a very gallant corporal of the police among the spectators who insisted on helping me to mount. His intentions were of the best but, frankly, I wished him at the bottom of the river. In spite of his gallant efforts, the expert suggestions of the bystanders, and the patience of that poor dumb brute, I remained unmounted until finally a chair was brought out. Then I was soon up, voluminous long skirts and all.

Waldron was obliged to walk, so he shouldered his rifle; we might meet a bear. The kindhearted onlookers waved, there was even a wail from the huskies to make it official, and we were off.

Shall I ever forget that ride? Across the gravel beds of sloughs that earlier in the season had been filled with water; along woodland paths carpeted thickly with autumn leaves on which the sunlight filtering through bare branches traced a cheery pattern; through groves of spruce and fir whose giant limbs shut out the sun and where a quiet twilight prevailed; we traveled all that bright October day. The shadows were lengthening when, emerging from a grove that was denser than the others, we came to a little clearing in the midst of which stood a small cabin. A friendly smoke curled from the stovepipe, there was a light in the window, and two splendid Irish terriers came bounding to meet us.

"We'll call here," Waldron announced. "The old man has invited us to stay for a cup of tea." I demurred, but just then a white-haired man hailed us from the doorway. "Don't disappoint him," Waldron begged. "He's been looking forward to this for days." So I dismounted.

The old man, a Mr. Werson, produced a sack of rolled oats for the horse and we made our way to the cabin, followed by the delighted dogs. Our host threw open the door and cried in a friendly voice, "I'm pleased to be the first to welcome you to a real Yukon miner's cabin."

The cup of tea consisted of a roast of moose meat with vegetables and gravy, baked beans, cold ham, stewed prunes, bread and butter and tea. I am afraid my appetite disappointed him but my better half did ample justice to the fare.

Darkness had fallen by the time we left, and the picture of that little cabin in a clearing on the hillside will always be with me. Our white-haired host stood silhouetted in the doorway with his dogs at his heels and around the clearing the great trees rose like sentinels, lifting their heads into the blackness and stillness of the night.

For some distance farther we traveled with only the faint light of the stars. I grew weary.

"Are we nearly there?" I questioned.

"No," he answered. "It will take some little time yet."

The moon came up and still we plodded on. Then a light appeared a long distance ahead.

"Is it the place where the light is?" I wanted to know.

"No, we must travel even farther than that."

The light was passed and still we traveled on. Suddenly, as we came around a hill, I saw smoke coming from a cabin beside the trail.

"Is it that?" I asked. But again the answer was no.

This was too much. The tears would no longer be restrained. I was so tired! "We'll never get there!" I sobbed.

"I'm sorry, dear," he soothed, "but try to keep up a little longer. We are nearly there."

I was shamefacedly drying my eyes when we rounded a sharp turn a few minutes later and came to two cabins standing side by side on the face of a hill. Light came from the windows of the larger one and Waldron cried, "Here we are!"

The door opened and his two partners—Ernest Forbes, a native of Nova Scotia, and Albert Melvin, a lifelong friend of my own family—came out to welcome us. Aching in every limb I slid from the horse. The honeymoon was over. I had arrived at what was to be my home, for the winter at least.

We went into the lighted cabin and Albert soon had lunch ready. It consisted of sourdough bread, canned peaches, dough-nuts and a delicious cup of tea. After that tiresome ride it seemed like a meal fit for a queen. When we had eaten and I had rested a bit, Waldron explained that this cabin belonged to his partners and we would occupy the smaller one alongside. So we said good night and went to it.

I saw that it had two windows and the floor had been scrubbed to the whiteness of newly dressed lumber, but it was guiltless of furniture except for an airtight heater, a washstand with basin and towels, and a homemade bunk where some gray blankets were neatly spread. Into this I crawled, too tired to care whether I ever left it or not.

Sixty Pup

When I opened my eyes again, daylight had come. For a few minutes I simply lay there, sizing up my new home. One window faced the sun, whose clear rays coming in seemed to call a bright good morning. The logs of which the walls and roof of the cabin were built were unpeeled and had been covered with cheesecloth, but this had been pulled off leaving the tacks still holding tattered fragments of cloth. It looked like a case of smallpox.

As I looked around I said to myself, "This is the Yukon. I've got here, but can I live the life?"

Then I heard a door shut somewhere near, there was a brisk step along the platform, the cabin door opened, and Waldron called, "Hi there! Albert says if you don't hurry you'll get no breakfast."

Not for worlds would I have allowed him to suspect how miserable I felt, so I made a great pretense of having just awakened, finished a hasty toilet, and hurried to the other cabin. Albert had a steaming breakfast of mush and buckwheat hotcakes, with maple syrup and coffee, and while eating this I tried to keep track of the running fire of questions he hurled at me about old scenes and old faces and to answer as many as possible. He had been away from the home town for ten or twelve years and was eager for news.

When the meal was finished he rose, and with a bow and wave of the hand, he cried, "Missus! I abdicate in your favor. Waldron tells me you are willing to do the cooking for all hands. So I hereby resign all right and title to pots, pans and dishes."

"You're taking a big chance," I told him, but he claimed he was willing to risk it.

When he and Waldron had gone out and I was busy clearing the table, Mr. Forbes asked how I was going to like living on the creek. This was a hard question and I was not going to commit myself. "I'll reserve my decision until I know more about it," I temporized.

During the morning the men discussed and planned operations for the winter. This done, Mr. Forbes started for Stewart riding my charger, Albert went to attend to affairs of his own, and Waldron and I surveyed the possibilities of rendering our cabin more homelike.

We stood at the door and for the first time I gave some attention to the location. The creek ran north and south. The hills on each side were quite high and the cabin stood on the west slope about halfway up the hillside, facing the sun. Both sides of the valley were covered with a thin layer of snow and every twig and blade of grass held a thick covering of hoarfrost. The hill opposite was in shadow, but the sun shining over the crest set all the frost-covered spears around the cabin aquiver and the slope, from where I stood to the valley below, resembled a white carpet of diamonds. Over it all brooded utter silence and I knew what Robert Service meant when he sang of "the stillness that fills me with peace." I was none too sure, though, that it filled me with peace. Infinitely beautiful, yes. But how remote it seemed, so far from—everything. How would I react to the loneliness? I knew Waldron's eye was on me so I quickly returned to the cabin and our work. At least, I would try.

Next day the horse returned pulling a two-wheeled cart on which were piled our trunks, suitcases and other luggage. This contained blinds, wallpaper, curtain material and all kinds of accessories. In a short time the cabin enjoyed a complete transformation. Waldron brought furniture from another cabin he owned, a neat little range replaced the heater, and when all was complete I viewed the result with pride.

The smallpox effect remained and our little house was still on a lonely Yukon creek, but already I had a feeling I might be sorry when the day came to leave it.

Now the real work of the winter began and I found that one day was much like another. We rose early and the creak of the windlass, as the buckets of gravel were hoisted to the surface and dumped to wait for the spring clean-up, could be heard long before the first rays of dawn appeared in the east. I can still close my eyes and hear that cheerless sound, accompanied by the lonesome hoot of an owl.

Each day the hours of daylight shortened and in November the sun dropped behind the mountain opposite and did not return to us in the valley for three months. I had never realized before what God's good sunshine really meant. That dull, somber, heavy atmosphere became so monotonous. I often looked away to the high, distant peaks which, for a shorter time each day, were flooded with sunlight and wished I could go there just to be in its glow.

Christmas passed quietly, and early in the New Year we had our first cold snap. The mercury started to drop. Thirty below zero was registered, then thirty-five—forty—fifty—sixty. If we went outside we could hear the hissing sound made by the breath freezing as it came from our lips. The coal oil took on the color of milky water and the consistency of olive oil. Water thrown out could be heard to tinkle as it hit the ground in the form of ice. The touch of wood or iron on bare flesh burned like fire. The air became thick with frost crystals and still the temperature dropped—sixty-five—seventy. While it was at that mark a miner from a place nearby paid us a visit and was astonished to find the men still working. "It's cruelty to animals!" he told them and they agreed that it was. Still the mercury continued its downward march until eighty-two, the lowest mark on the tube, was reached. Then it disappeared inside the bulb and remained there for three days.

We all concluded that the thermometer was at fault, but when the cold spell broke reports came in from different localities telling of its severity. A temperature of ninety below zero was reported from Ogilvie, a point fifty miles south of Dawson on the Yukon River, and the next issue of the *Dawson News* contained a cartoon of the telegraph operator, Wilkinson, in the act of nailing one thermometer below another in order to get a reading low enough!

While the weather was too cold to work the men amused themselves playing cards and telling tall stories, which I soon learned were for my special benefit. One day the cold spell was the topic of conversation and I saw a look of conspiracy exchanged. Then Waldron remarked casually, "Of course, no one particularly enjoys a cold snap, but it has been known to be a blessing in disguise."

"You mean the time the cold spell halted that scurvy epidemic?" another asked.

Suspicious though I was I could not help rising to the lure. "How could a cold spell do that?" I demanded.

"Haven't you heard?" inquired Waldron in well-feigned surprise. "When the Stampede was at its height the scurvy was raging. All the fresh fruits and vegetables and even drugs were gone. The doctors were at their wits end. Then a cold snap came and one of the miners had a bright idea. He lit all the candles he could lay his hands on and set them outside. When the flames froze he snipped them off and sold them for strawberries. That did it."

"I should think it would!" I snapped. Even if I had asked for it, it was a bit strong.

"It was during the same spell that the smoke from another miner's chimney froze and fell through his roof."

This was from Albert, whose face was innocent of guile. So I left for the cache to get something for tea and as the door closed behind me I heard their hearty laughter.

Life on Sixty Pup in winter was not all frost and tall stories, however. There was the intense moonlight to be enjoyed. I had never seen the like before—a steely whiteness in which every snow-wreathed tree stood like a ghostly sentinel. With not a breath of wind, millions of snow crystals sparkled like jewels.

There was also the flaming splendor of the aurora borealis, filling the night with a glory far surpassing anything seen in my eastern homeland. First, a silver curtain would be flung across the sky. Then to the silver would be added purple, violet, blue, rose, gold—all the colors of the rainbow but deeper and more vivid. The curtain would begin to wave and undulate, slowly at first but ever more quickly, until a whole section of the sky was alive with the spectacle. A crackling and hissing often accompanied the display, a weird breathtaking vision.

In addition, I had what was to me an even more novel form of amusement. Returning from a trip to Stewart, Waldron brought a pair of huskies to the creek.

"Whatever are they for?" I wanted to know.

"You must learn to drive them."

"Me!" I exclaimed, with more truth than grammar. "No, sir. Not me!" I wanted to know how, rightly enough, but was doubtful of my ability.

"There's nothing to it," he assured me. "All you need to do is swear, loud and long."

"Well, I know some of the words already," I bantered.

"You'll need to know all of them, if you drive dogs." He grinned, knowing my speech was quite unsullied.

Then he gave me a lesson or two and taught me the right (and not profane!) words of command. The tandem hitch was the popular one and no lines were used, the dogs being controlled only by the driver's voice, assisted in times of difficulty by a blacksnake whip.

These dogs were well trained so I ventured to take them out myself. As a rule all went well, but several times they sighted a rabbit and gave instant chase. Then I was thrown from the sled to land as chance favored while they continued their mad race. On more than one occasion they were captured and returned to me by an amused miner, but I persisted and in time was able to handle them quite creditably, for a woman. During the winter they helped me pass many an otherwise lonely hour.

One of them, Huskie, was a magnificent specimen of a malemute. I was terrified of him at first, remembering those frightful howls at Stewart, but we soon became fast friends. He never let me out of his sight if he could help it and when I was reading or sewing he would lie with his head on my feet.

These dogs had been given to us only while the owner was away for the winter. I had quite ceased to think about this when one day he arrived to take them home. Huskie had to be taken away by force and I was brokenhearted over losing so true a friend.

A few days later Waldron came in carrying two little black curly-haired puppies, their eyes shining like beads. He had bought them some time before and had waited until I needed them to bring them home. These really belonged to me, so I began their training early. I had them for several years and we had many good runs together. Hunter was mistaken for a bear and shot while he was chasing a rabbit. Hero was my companion through many long and lonely hours in the days to come. He always knew when my heart was heavy and would lay his head on my knee and look up into my face with a wealth of sympathy in his kind brown eyes.

The sun was now on its return journey and I watched the shadow behind the cabin creep farther and farther down the hillside every day. How glad I should be when the cheering rays came in the door. Kind-hearted Albert Melvin, realizing how the time dragged without the company of other women, offered to clear a path up the hill to a spot where I could bask in the sunshine, but I would not accept so much unnecessary labor.

"How long before it returns to us?" I had asked when the sun disappeared behind the hill in November.

"It shines in the cabin door on the fourteenth of February," I was told.

So each day was carefully checked off on the calendar and then the joke was on me in the end, for on February twelfth the sky became overcast and it remained cloudy for more than a week. When the sun shone again the shadow had passed the cabin and traveled to the bottom of the valley. The sun had come back to Sixty Pup.

As the days began to lengthen and grow warmer, I was often invited out to the dump to snipe. This meant searching among the gravel that had been brought to the surface for any pieces of gold that I might find. One day I had the novel experience of being lowered into the drift in the bucket used for hoisting and while there I received a lesson in working with woodfires.

The ground in the Yukon is always frozen as far down as it has ever been tested, so when the spot for sinking has been chosen a fire of dry wood is built. When this has burned out, the dirt thus thawed is shoveled away and another fire built, this being repeated until the layer of gravel carrying the gold is reached, if any. When the paystreak (the direction, length and depth of the gold-bearing gravel) has been located, a fire is built against the face. This is usually done in the evening and by morning it has burned out, the shaft is clear of smoke and gas, and the waste is thrown to one side while the pay-dirt is hoisted to the surface. Then the whole process is repeated as in sinking. The tunnel thus formed is called a drift and the word drifting is used instead of tunneling. Where conditions are favorable a boiler and engine are installed, the ground is thawed by steam, and the dirt handled with a gin and self-dumper.

Of all the wonder with which I came in contact while in that unique country, I think I was most impressed by the story of the mammoth. Scientists claim that this huge member of the elephant family, which we should naturally suppose belonged to a warm climate, has been extinct for more than two thousand years. Yet in that country where the ground is perpetually frozen to a depth of several hundred feet, specimens of this prehistoric animal are often found many feet below the surface. One day Waldron brought me a tooth about eight inches in length and the same in diameter which he had taken from the drift. Later, the only perfect specimen I have seen was presented to me by a miner from Thistle Creek. It weighed fifty-four pounds, was eighteen inches long, and tapered from a diameter of eight inches at the base to a fine point. This would have belonged to a mere babe-in-arms. One tusk, taken I think from Bonanza Creek, when stood on its tips allowed a man six feet tall to stand beneath the arch. One marvels at the strength required to carry a pair such as that.

The "pay" became more satisfactory and the men worked like beavers to get as large a dump as possible ready for the clean-up. Each day I spent more time sniping. Then one morning there was hurry and excitement. Through a miscalculation the drift had been carried too near some old workings filled with water. The ground dividing them had thawed and given way and the drift was flooded. The men hurried to get all the equipment out before the water rose too high and Waldron came in wet to the armpits. I later learned that he had had a narrow escape from being trapped in the drift, so swiftly had the water rushed in.

Only a short time now remained before the clean-up. So the business of making and laying the boxes, preparing riffles, and repairing flume went on apace. But at last everything was ready and I, at least, waited eagerly for the water to run. The sun had climbed higher and become stronger each day, so that by the last week of April we were getting very little darkness. This was too much for old King Winter and one morning there was a welcome gurgle in the creek. The clean-up was at hand!

The boxes had been laid end to end on a slope beside the dump. The first was the dump-box. It was much larger at one end than at the other and had concave sides. In the bottom of this, as well as in the other boxes, the riffles were carefully placed—peeled poles about five inches in diameter, fastened together at the ends with cleats. The water was channeled through the line of boxes, one man standing in the dump-box, and as the dirt was shoveled in he worked the gravel against the water, using a large fork similar to a stable fork. By this process the finer gravel was washed from the rocks which were forked out; the medium stuff was carried through the boxes and dumped beyond as tailings; and the finer gravel containing the gold settled between the riffles. After shoveling in for several days the water was turned off through the waste-gate, the riffles were lifted, and the real clean-up took place.

Albert Melvin was most anxious that I should witness this very interesting part of the work, so he stationed me near the larger end of the dump-box. So far all I could see was an accumulation of ordinary gravel in the boxes, certainly not very thrilling.

"I'll be water-boy," Albert announced. "You watch for the first trickle of water that I let through and see it hit that gravel, then pay attention to what Waldron and Forbes do with those little paddles. If the clean-up is a good one, you'll get a great kick out of it."

Then I noticed the little paddles. One man stood on each side of the dump-box and as the water flowed through they worked the gravel against it. It was astonishing to see how quickly the gravel washed away, leaving the glistening gold behind. Albert was right. It was the sight of a lifetime! I shouted with delight.

When all the gravel had been carried away the gold was gathered into a goldpan and taken to the cabin where it was thoroughly dried and the very fine sand that remained was removed by blowing. After all the dump had been handled in this way the gold-dust was weighed and divided. Both Mr. Forbes and Albert handed me a nice nugget as a souvenir. Then Albert turned to Waldron.

"Aren't you going to give the Missus a nugget, too?" he demanded.

Waldron laughed. He loved to tease me. "Give her a nugget!" he cried. "Every tooth in her head has already cost me many nuggets!"

"Hm!" commented Mr. Forbes. "If you had invested every dollar you ever made half as well, you'd have been a millionaire long ago!"

This was all very well, but we all knew our work was done and a parting inevitable. During the winter Mr. Bowen Smith, who owned the Stewart River Grocery where I had come ashore on that memorable day, had suggested to Waldron that we buy the business. He was getting old and felt that he would like to take things easier and his son, who did the freighting to and from the creeks with that famous horse, also wanted a change. So they suggested we buy them out and combine the two endeavors. Waldron favored the idea and laid the matter before me. Would I be willing to help carry on in the store, while he did the freighting? We finally decided in favor of the proposition, chiefly because the life at Stewart would be less lonely for me.

This meant preparing to leave the creek after the clean-up. At first I had thought that I should be delighted with the change, but as the winter wore away and the weather grew warm I could spend more time outdoors and a different attitude toward conditions developed. I was filled with the calm wonder of those glorious spring days. There were no winds or storms of any kind. Each day was finer and warmer than the last, until there was no darkness at all. The trees everywhere were alive with many different kinds of song birds and if I awakened during the night, no matter at what hour, I was greeted by their cheery notes. With the exception of a couple of hours near midnight, the sun shone into the little cabin through one or the other of the windows both day and night. When I stepped from the door in the morning it was like entering a garden. The ground seemed carpeted with wild flowers. It was good to be alive amid such peace and beauty and I thought with regret of leaving the place which a few months previously had filled me with an active dislike. No doubt it was a realization of these feelings that prompted Waldron to say, when we spoke of moving, "Don't bother to pack anything except your personal belongings. I can attend to the other things when I come for them with the horse. I've moved from one cabin to another often enough to know how to handle a few pots and pans."

I was glad to know that I should leave the little home as I had known it.

During that winter on Sixty Pup, Henderson Creek, I learned many things.

I learned to play cribbage.

I learned to weigh and estimate the value of gold dust.

I learned that a placer mining claim consists of five hundred feet measured along the base line and a thousand feet on each side of said line, that the claim on which gold is first found is known as Discovery and the other claims are numbered from it above or below. Thus, the claim adjoining Discovery going upstream is Number One Above, the one downstream is Number One Below.

I learned that a draw or pup is a small valley or depression in a line of hills and that it takes its name from the number of the claim on which it terminates. Therefore a pup leading into the hills from Henderson Creek on Claim Number Sixty is Sixty Pup, Henderson Creek.

I learned that there was nothing less than a quarter, or two bits, in circulation. The two bits meant a long bit (fifteen cents), and a short bit (ten cents). Relatively, fifty cents was four bits and seventy-five cents was six bits. A dollar was, rather to my surprise, simply a dollar.

I learned that the word mush can have a meaning other than that given by Webster. Colloquially, a man does not walk from here to there, he mushes. The term is also used in driving dogs instead of the familiar get-up used with a horse.

I also learned not to ask Waldron too many questions. His fun loving nature could not resist the temptation to take advantage of my greenness. Albert finally came to my rescue. "Missus," he advised, "I think when you want to know anything you had better ask me. That grinning youngster will tell you anything at all for the sake of a laugh!" Waldron's hearty, "Ha-ha-ha!" rang out. But, in self-defense, I decided to take Albert's advice.

The day of our departure arrived—a beautiful, warm, sunny morning in June. We were astir early and the little cabin was swept and dusted as carefully as ever. I said good-bye to Mr. Forbes, but Albert was to accompany us to Stewart.

We were ready to leave, but still I lingered. I went out, closed the door, then opened it and again stepped inside. I opened the cupboard and looked at the dishes, stored there as though ready for the next meal. I smoothed an imaginary wrinkle in the bed-covering and strightened the pillows just a trifle. I touched the hooks on which our clothes had hung and the nail at the head of the bed on which Waldron had hung his watch each night.

Waldron's voice called, "Waiting, dear!" A lump rose in my throat and I went out to where old Dobbin was waiting to carry me back to Stewart.

Why is there nothing permanent but change?

Weights & Measures

Yes, I rode that animal back to Stewart. This time the trip did not seem so utterly heartbreaking. The journey was on a down grade, the trail lay along a sunny slope, the day was fine, the hillsides carpeted with flowers and the air joyous with the music of birds. I carried the puppies in a sack before me on the saddle, while Waldron and Albert walked beside or behind, and we chatted of many things as we ambled along. We did not visit Mr. Werson this time. He was away and I thought the cabin looked rather lonely standing with closed doors and no smoke coming from the chimney. Neither were there any dogs bounding to meet us. So we stopped at a vacant cabin on another hillside, boiled the kettle at a campfire and ate lunch in the open, then continued on our way.

This was the season of long daylight, when we had no darkness, so the sun was still quite high when we reached the end of the wagon road. How different everything looked compared to the way it had been in the fall when I went up the creek. At that time the slough which separated Stewart Island from the mainland had been quite dry and we had traveled along its gravel bed. Now the river was in flood and the slough ran bank-full of dirty water, with here and there pieces of driftwood being carried along. It would be necessary to use a boat to get to Stewart and, as the village was about a mile upstream, I suggested that I follow the footpath along the bank to a point opposite it and wait there until the men had poled the boat up to me. Then we could all cross the slough directly to Stewart. I had no liking for being in the boat more than was absolutely necessary!

"Will you not be afraid?" Waldron asked.

I said I would not, although I was not altogether sure. But anything seemed preferable to that boat.

"Very well," he agreed, "but don't get too far ahead of us and don't walk too near the bank. Possibly the current is cutting under it and you may fall in."

So I started. All went well and I was enjoying the walk immensely when I came to a place where the trail appeared to run a little too near the bank for safety and I left it to make my way through the brush farther back. Presently I heard a twig snap and, bending down to peer through the underbrush, I saw a dim shape almost hidden among the leafy branches.

"A bear!" I breathed in terror, but had enough presence of mind to continue walking leisurely in order to avoid drawing attention to myself. By degrees I came back to the trail that now ran farther from the bank and when I reached it, thinking I had left the bear far behind and still unaware of my existence, I started to run without looking back. As a girl I had been called as fleet as a deer and had won many races in my school days. I had more reason to run now than then, so I can honestly say you couldn't see my heels for dust!

I had heard no further sound and when I thought I must surely be far enough away for safety, I stopped for breath and looked around. Merciful Heaven! Right behind me on the trail and not fifty yards away stood, not a bear, but two animals that I mistook for wolves! For one fleeting instant I had the impulse to leap into the slough. Even yet I have no idea what prevented me. A man born to be hanged will never be drowned, an old saying goes. Had I done so, I should certainly have been drowned, but I stood rooted to the spot and sent shriek after shriek ringing out on the clear air. The animals raced to within a few feet of me, sat back on their haunches, and began to wag their tails in the most friendly fashion. They seemed to like the noise! Then the mists of terror cleared from my eyes and I realized that they were really wolfish-looking huskies.

Waldron had heard the screams and, calling to Albert, "Put the boat ashore! She's fallen in!" he leaped to the bank.

"I'll watch for her in the water! And hurry!" Albert cried.

By the time Waldron broke through the brush tears had replaced the screams and I stood wringing my hands and trembling like an aspen.

"I'm sorry they frightened you, dear," he said. "They belong to the police and are really very gentle. Come, Rags! Here, Tommy!" And they came bounding to lick his hand!

When the boat came along we got safely across but I arrived at Mrs. Shand's roadhouse somewhat shaken after my scare. It seemed almost like being at home to be able to talk to another woman after not having seen one for eight months. We discussed everything from soup to nuts. The vegetables in her garden were up and growing nicely and I determined that I too would have a garden, with flowers.

It had been planned that before taking over the store at Stewart we should take a trip to Dawson City, the capital of the Yukon Territory; Waldron to attend to business matters, I to have dental work done. When we arrived at Stewart we learned that a steamer would call the next morning on her way to Dawson, so we decided (as I thought) to go on her. I left Waldron enjoying a game of cards and went to bed early. I felt that I had had a full day. But some time later he came and informed me with great delight that he and the others had arranged to join forces and go to Dawson in a small boat. It was only seventy-five miles and would be a lovely trip, he claimed. He had no fear of the water, but I lay awake all night thinking about it and was drowned over and over again. To my joy and relief there was a stiff head wind blowing in the morning and they decided in favor of the steamer after all.

The trip down was delightful and how eagerly did I watch for the first glimpse of the town. Was it possible that I was actually to see those two most wonderful of all places, Dawson and the Klondike?

While still some distance from Dawson, Waldron called to me. "If you come forward you'll be able to see the Slide before we reach Dawson," he said.

"What is the Slide?" I asked.

"Oh, before the days of the white man a great portion of the mountain slid into the valley and completely buried an Indian village. As soon as the steamer gets around that point ahead, you can see it."

Presently she rounded the bend and the calm waters of the Klondike River, the town of Dawson, and the mountain beyond with the great gash in its side, came into view.

My mind is not quite clear as to just what I expected the famous town to look like, but I believe that through my head there drifted hazily the picture of a group of rough wooden shacks, most of them built of logs, with narrow winding alleys running between them. These alleys I expected to see swarming with tall, rawboned men supposed to be miners or gamblers wearing knee-boots, hair hanging from beneath wide-brimmed hats, and long whiskers where a quantity of gold-dust was supposed to be lodged. I expected each man to carry a pick and goldpan and to have a six-gun in his belt.

What I did see was a neat little town with broad streets, electric lights, telephones and other modern conveniences. Many of the buildings were of modern type and they seemed to accentuate the quaint little log cabins that nestled beside them, some almost hidden in a mass of bloom. It was very evident that I was not the only lover of flowers who had come to this strange land.

I soon found that I was not altogether friendless myself and that though the people might be quick to resent anything that suggested a patronizing attitude from the newcomer, they were ready to extend the hand of fellowship to the stranger. As we were walking down First Avenue that afternoon I was surprised to hear my name called and to see Mrs. Franklin Steeves, whom we had met on the trip coming in, hurrying toward us with a smile of welcome. When she learned that I was to be in Dawson for a few days she insisted on taking me home with her. So Waldron was left free to attend to business and when this was done we both spent the evening with these friends. Waldron returned to Stewart the next day and I remained with them while in Dawson. After the winter of isolation on the creek this was a pleasant change and I thoroughly enjoyed the companionship. I also renewed acquaintance with Mrs. Lester and altogether spent a very enjoyable time. Even so early as 1906 Dawson was a pleasant little city in which to visit.

At the end of a week I returned to Stewart by steamer and took up my life in the Yukon in earnest. I had had no settled feeling while on the creek as I had realized that our stay there was only temporary, but this was different. We intended to locate here and once again I took stock of my environment.

Personally, I confess I would have been glad to have shaken the dust of the country off my feet. The outlook from my point of view was anything but prepossessing and I realized that "forsaking all others" can have a very literal and practical meaning.

Stewart Island is situated near the mouth of the Stewart River and is about a mile long by half a mile in width. The village is located at the upper or southern end and is the transfer and supply point for the upper Stewart as well as the various creeks along the Yukon. At that time the population consisted of four policemen, two women besides myself, and about twelve or fifteen men of various occupations and appearances, as well as transients. The telegraph office was then across the river on Split-Up Island, so named because during the big rush it often happened that a party bound for Dawson would land there and, on hearing good reports from the Stewart country, opinion would become divided. Some of the members would favor going up the Stewart and others would insist on continuing to Dawson. Often the end was the dissolution of the partnership and, in the heated argument over supplies, boats were divided and even frying pans chopped in two. Both ends of the boat would be boarded up and the owner would sail up or down river as his choice dictated. A boat launched in Whitehorse might reach its destination with the bow in Dawson and the stern in Mayo.

The store was about halfway between the roadhouse and the Police Barracks. Mrs. Shand was my neighbor on one side and while she appeared to be a woman of refinement (and I never had cause to alter my first impression) her husband was engaged in the saloon business, with all that that means in a pioneer country. My nearest neighbor on the other side, the only other woman resident of the island, was a woman commonly alluded to as Sissie. Keeping a roadhouse and running a saloon are two ancient professions, but Sissie's was even older and the facilities provided by all three made Stewart seem the perfect stopping place for the majority of the male transients that came our way. Yet had they known of my associating, no matter how simply, with my neighbor they would have looked at me askance thereafter. On the other hand I was supposed to meet on a social level those clients of Sissie's whom I frequently saw, from my window, visiting her cabin. Had I refused to do this, great indignation would have been aroused! I am still trying to figure that one out. It happened that by midsummer she left for Dawson and my immediate problem was solved.

When I arrived at the Stewart River Grocery the shavings, ashes, and so on still littered the floor, but now I could attack it with impunity. Again we undertook to render homelike what appeared to be an almost uninhabitable shack. In this case it was a Herculean task and even when we had done our best, I was not nearly so well satisfied as I had been on the creek. But Waldron was loath to spend too much of either time or money until he knew whether or not circumstances would justify it. For indeed the business seemed almost defunct. But Mr. Smith was an old man and his family was "Outside," so he had no one to take an interest in it with him. Waldron thought that by working together we could bring the business back to a paying basis and future developments proved him to be right.

"We'll make this place habitable for a year," he decided. "If worthwhile then, we'll have a new set of buildings." With this idea I was delighted for I knew that, with his customary thoroughness, a home which he built would lack no comfort or convenience that existing conditions permitted. So I set to work wholeheartedly to make the best of the material at hand. Fresh paint, new wallpaper and clean curtains were brought into play. We cut extra doors and windows, cleaned up the litter in the yard and I had flowers both inside and out wherever I could plant one.

Mr. Smith highly approved. "That looks better," he remarked and added wistfully, "If only I had had someone to help me."

But the repairs and decorations to the shack were the easiest part of the undertaking. Waldron had had some experience around a store but I had had none and when he was away freighting or otherwise engaged I was left alone to work out my own salvation. More than once I was tempted to give up. There seemed to be so much to learn.

How was I to know that German socks were what I had heard called oversocks? That granite candles were not made of granite? That silver dollar as applied to a shovel was merely a trade name for a particular kind of mining shovel and did not mean that it had been made from one of the silver dollars I had seen in circulation? And what did a man mean when he asked for a pair of mucklucks, a mattock, some rubber gaskets or a swedger? Also I must remember that men wore Stetson hats and used a Stilson wrench around a boiler. I wrestled with these and a million other problems. Although the sign described the store as the Stewart River Grocery, in catering to the business we were supposed to keep almost anything from a needle to an anchor and the work differed from that in a general store in the average town.

At that time most of our trade came from the miners on Henderson Creek. While delivering a load of merchandise, Waldron took orders for further supplies. Freight was delivered on the creek at so much per pound net. The orders were usually large, we guaranteed safe delivery, and as the trail was long and rough all goods had to be carefully packed. So I weighed and measured. I packed and unpacked merchandise of all kinds. I broke open packing cases and I nailed up others—and I did not always hit the right nail either! I checked both incoming and outgoing freight; I ordered goods and made out bills all in addition to my household tasks.

During the three months of continuous daylight people lost all sense of time. There were as many people to be seen abroad at midnight as there were at noon. Our buildings stood within a stone's throw of the riverbank and often, after having worked well into the night, I would sit for a time marveling at the calm wonder of the scene around me. While the river ran at my feet the words of Tennyson kept running through my mind, "For men may come and men may go, but I go on forever." To every place there is a definite spiritual feeling. At Stewart I was held, overpowered, even strengthened, by the steady, ceaseless, irresistible force of the mighty river.

One evening I saw a man poling a boat along close to the shore and as he passed where I was sitting he raised his hat, smiled, and spoke. I could not look into the future and know that this was my first meeting with one of the staunchest of friends. Later, he was introduced as Mr. Aish, the telegraph operator.

So the summer gradually wore away. I struggled with the perplexities of the trade and, truth must be served, made many blunders. Some of them were decidedly humorous, others almost tragic. However, Waldron was very patient and often insisted on turning near-tragedy into comedy.

Late in the season Albert Melvin came to Stewart. He had not forgotten my fear of the water and insisted on taking me out in the canoe repeatedly. At first we frequented the sloughs were the water was neither deep nor swift and as he was careful to never startle me by a quick movement, I soon became used to the motion of the boat. In time I learned to handle one as well as my strength permitted and have always felt grateful to him for this kindness. The river was our highway and, in order to get anywhere, I must travel upon it.

We were off the winter route of travel which made it necessary to lay up sufficient stock in the fall to supply the trade until the boats would run the following spring. In October Waldron went to Dawson to attend to the last details and see that nothing was overlooked. Every day orders for winter outfits were coming in from the miners and we were kept busy almost day and night.

Slush ice began to run in the river, then shore ice formed along the beaches. Each day this extended farther out. The floes thickened until no open water remained; nothing but a mass of ice moved slowly down the lane formed by the shore ice. Slowly and yet more slowly it moved. Then, on November seventh, we felt a slight tremor. The moving mass had stopped.

It was the freeze-up. We were again isolated.

Making of a Sourdough

With the closing of the river winter settled in on us in earnest. The filling of orders and the weighing of freight went on and Waldron was usually away with his load long before daylight had begun to show in the east.

Albert Melvin and his new partner, Charlie Martin, worked during the winter at cutting logs to be rafted to Dawson when summer would come. They boarded with us and, as in the previous winter, I had a family of four to care for. When baking it was very little more work to make an extra pie or some cookies. I learned that if these were put to freeze as soon as they were taken from the oven, when thawed out they would still be quite fresh, thanks to the extreme frost. This plan helped wonderfully when we were rushed.

One day a man, seeing me bring in some frozen biscuits, asked about them. I told him that if frozen while hot, when thawed out they would still be warm. For a moment he almost believed me. And then I knew that I was at home in the country. Last year they had told tall tales to me and here was I telling them to others! If I walked now with a new self-assurance, was it any wonder?

Christmas, 1906, was drawing near and Jim McLaughlin came to invite us to a housewarming on Christmas Day in the new roadhouse he had just opened at the mouth of Barker Creek. I was delighted with the idea of going, but could not see how it might be managed. The mouth of Barker Creek is twenty-five miles up the Stewart River. My previous experience in attending parties had been to don my best frock, drive perhaps a few miles, and after the fun was over to return in the early hours. But— twenty-five miles! I just could not see it. So I was rather evasive in my reply. But Jim, being a very sociable fellow, was insistent.

"Tell Waldron I said he'd just have to bring you," he ordered. "There'll be a lot of people there from the other creeks and it'll be a good chance for you to get acquainted."

When Waldron returned and I broke the news he was noncommittal. "I can't say just yet. It'll take two days and the boys are needing their outfits."

Two days to go to a party! I had never heard of such a thing. But on Christmas Eve Waldron came home early and in high spirits.

"Get your dancing pumps on!" he called to me. "We're going to a party."

Christmas morning came clear and mild. Corporal Fowell and Constable Simons of the police and Mr. Aish's friend, Mr. Dent, who was spending the winter with him, went ahead with a police dog team. Mr. Aish came with us. Owing to warm currents underneath the ice in the Stewart it cannot be trusted even in mid-winter and, in case of an accident with the horse, Waldron would have some one to help him. Luckily there was no need, for the trip was a happy one. At noon, when about half way between Stewart and Barker Creek, we came to a tent beside the trail. Here we found the other travelers with a fire going and tea made. I had brought a generous supply of lunch and when we had disposed of the greater part of it we continued on our way.

About three miles from our destination we overtook a man and his wife walking the same way and Waldron asked them to ride. The woman was—well—of ample proportions. We urged her to take the seat beside me under the robes but she declined definitely and—shades of Caesar!—she insisted on sitting on my feet. All suggestion to her to move were magnanimously waved aside. She was quite all right! I suppose she was, but when I got out of the sled both my feet were numb!

Daylight had gone before we reached Barker Creek. While still some distance out on the river we could hear voices and laughter, the jingle of bells as dog teams were being unhitched, and when we climbed the bank the scene was one to be long remembered.

The house stood about fifty yards from the bank, among tall spruce and birch from which the underbrush had been cleared away. Thick billows of white smoke belched from the chimney and went rolling skyward. Light streamed from every window of the two-story log building. Men and dogs moved about among the trees and above and behind it all the full moon rode in a cloudless sky, setting millions of snow crystals aglitter.

Our smiling host stood on the threshold waiting to receive us and during the entire time spent under his roof he proved himself to be the right man in the right place. When we drove through the trees, a laughing group surrounded us and I was lifted bodily from the sled and carried through the door which swung open at that moment. Everyone was in a holiday mood and the scene inside the building was every whit as cheery as that outside. In the large room into which we entered, garlands and festoons of evergreens with glittering tinsel abounded and, among these, lighted candles had been placed wherever safety permitted. Several lamps suspended from the ceiling completed the festive scene.

Coming upon such a spectacle after the long drive upriver, during which we had seen no human habitation whatever, seemed almost like entering fairyland. The women were in their best bib and tucker, many of the men wore the uniform of their calling—overalls and gum-rubbers—but quite a few white shirts were also in evidence, and the whole picture was enlivened by the scarlet tunics, brass buttons and yellow stripes of several Mounties. Upon our arrival we were refreshed with tea and sandwiches. Next came a season for getting acquainted and general visiting. About half past ten we sat down to a turkey dinner with all the fixings. Nothing was omitted, not even the ice cream, and by the time this was disposed of, the clock said it was past midnight. The room was then cleared, Mr. Aish produced his violin, and several hours were spent in dancing, songs and recitations.

About four o'clock we called it enough, but at daylight I was startled to hear our host shouting: "Hi, you hungry hounds! Wake up! Do you intend to lie in bed and starve to death?" He made sure that none were overlooked and in a short time a jolly crowd gathered around the table where a steaming breakfast waited.

This over, guests made ready to go their ways and Jim's parting words, "Come again soon!" followed us to the waiting sleds.

My first Yukon party was a memory. In the years spent in the land of moonlight and mystery I attended many of those social gatherings, but that one at Barker stands out most vividly. Everything seemed so quaint and unusual. Conventionality was a minus quantity, but a spirit of good-fellowship permeated all and shone in the face of everyone present.

Back at the weighing and measuring again we soon had a new proposition. The Mounties had always carried the mail to the outlying districts. Now the strength of the Force was being reduced and this activity had been given up. No mail had reached us since the last steamer and no carriers had been appointed to the task. About midwinter Waldron took a contract to carry mail once a month from Stewart Crossing. This was fifty miles up the Stewart River from us, at the point where the winter stage-line between Whitehorse and Dawson crossed the river.

Winter at Stewart proved less lonely for me than on Sixty Pup. In the first place I was much busier and enjoyed the feeling of being more a part of the firm. Several times we went across the river to the telegraph office on Split-Up Island for a game of whist with Mr. Aish and Mr. Dent. Or they came over to us and Albert Melvin and Charlie Martin joined the party. Waldron even had Mr. Aish give me violin lessons, whenever I found the time.

All this was very quiet but in the North there is always a spirit of playfulness near the surface. Sooner or later it is sure to break out somewhere. This time it happened right in Stewart. Aish, Dent, and the police boys decided to throw a party at the Barracks. It was in March and traveling was still good. They came from all the creeks around: Barker, Thistle and Henderson. Some came even from Ogilvie and the camps along the Yukon. Two small rooms were fitted up as a card room and ladies sitting room. The large barrack room was cleared for dancing. It was an extensive celebration, three days and nights being given over to entertaining the guests. This was the biggest affair yet for me in contrast to the year before! After the party broke up and things began to settle back to normal I was positively lonely for a while.

It was only later that I discovered I had acquired a reputation for being easily shocked. Perhaps I was shy or naturally quiet. More likely I was simply green. It seems, however, that one evening some scraps of conversation over a game of cards penetrated the thin partition—conversation never intended for feminine ears. I never heard them, but another did and she leaped to my defence. She was well qualified for the task, being rather an Amazon and possessing a diction more forceful than elegant herself. She rushed into the card room, shook a hammer-like fist at the men, and thundered:

"Can't you ——— men get along without swearing? Don't you know that little Mrs. Smythe is in the next room? She's a newcomer—and besides—she's a Methodist!"

Gradually the winter wore away and spring was near at hand. The freighting to the creek was finished and our stock in the store sadly depleted. By the last week in April the snow had gone and every one waited for the breakup of the ice in the river. Fed by the melting snow in the hills the river rose steadily.

I was agog with excitement. "What happens when the ice runs?" I asked Waldron.

"Anything at all can happen when the Yukon goes," he replied, which told me exactly nothing but increased my excitement.

I waited with added suspense while the river continued to rise. A wide strip of open water extended between the main ice and the banks, now green with young grass. Occasionally a slight grinding and crunching could be heard. It seemed impossible for the ice to hold much longer.

Then May seventh came clear and decidedly warm. After breakfast Waldron went to do some work in the blacksmith shop and I to take another look at the river. Was I never going to get the thrill of seeing that ice move?

Suddenly there was a report like a charge of dynamite. The earth shook and then I heard a sickening noise of ripping and tearing. The ice began to crowd against the bank and, looking beyond it, I saw the whole mass was in motion. Terrified, I fled for the blacksmith shop.

"What's the matter?" Waldron exclaimed as, breathless, I

burst through the door.

"The—the—the ice!" I stammered.

He dropped his work then and came to the riverbank with me and I watched the great mass being carried along by the current; the cakes tumbling, piling, rushing and being rushed at, the smaller ones being ground to fragments by the larger. I was witnessing forces of nature beyond the power of man to control.

So now I had really seen the breakup.

Waldron turned to me, laughing. "Now you're a real sourdough!" he cried playfully.

"A sourdough?" I echoed.

"Haven't you heard? Until you've been here a year and seen both freeze-up and breakup, you're a cheechako. After that you're a sourdough."

"But sourdough is leaven," I argued, displaying my northern knowledge. "They use it instead of yeast in making bread."

"Yes, that was the only method used during the Rush and I fancy it took most people a year to learn to use it. It has you!"

This was a nasty remark, for I never did learn to make sourdough bread. But why should I? Waldron was an expert so, when I needed to use that method, I pressed him into service.

Thy People, My People

When the river had been reported open from the foot of Lake Laberge to Dawson, we waited eagerly for the first signs of navigation. Every fall a steamer was left at the foot of this lake and fresh supplies—fruit, vegetables, eggs and other perishables—were freighted to her over the ice, to be taken to Dawson as soon as the river opened. Scows were also loaded with these commodities and their appearance was welcomed by the people living along the river. Towards spring one tired of a routine diet.

Also, we were watching for the "mosquito fleet." For reasons of economy many men preferred to buy a small boat and outfit en route, and float to Dawson. The boats were rough affairs built in Whitehorse and could be bought for about fifteen dollars. They, too, were freighted across the ice of the lake. Between one hundred and fifty and two hundred of these boats passed Stewart that spring in 1907. The click-clack of the oars in the rowlocks could be heard day and night. At whatever time we looked out a number could be seen floating by. The Yukon was still drawing the world with her golden lure.

Close behind them came the steamer *La France*. Her smoke

as she rounded a bend several miles above Stewart was the most welcome sight for months. Her whistle called out the joyous message that spring had at last arrived.

On her return from the run to Dawson she brought mail. Amongst mine I noticed a copy of the Dawson paper and was shocked to read the account of the death of Mrs. Franklin Steeves, the woman with whom I had such a happy visit the previous summer. I could hardly believe it possible; she had seemed to embody strength and vitality.

Almost immediately business increased for us, owing to new mining activity in the area that year. Some of the large dredging companies on the Pacific coast began to buy up ground in the Yukon. This caused a lot of stampeding and the lower part of the Henderson was among the first creeks to be restaked. One group of claims was financed by two schoolteachers in Dawson and was known as the Schoolteacher Group.

The agent for the schoolteachers, Asa Thurston Heydon, soon came to Stewart to look after their interests. He was a tall, spare man who hailed from the Hawaiian Islands, his grandmother having gone there as a missionary. He had a most peculiar personality, typical of the languorous superstition of the South. Mysticism and occultism fascinated him and there were times when his predictions were almost weird in their accuracy. I never knew whether or not he was qualified to practice medicine or surgery, but he knew a lot about both and was generally referred to as Doctor Heydon. He brought equipment and men to work on the claims and began operations on a much larger scale than had been previously carried on in that locality. When school closed, one of the teachers, Miss MacNeil, appeared in person. She exhibited a vast amount of self-assurance and for a while it seemed as though we ordinary people were to be shown a thing or two. Well, modesty is a commendable trait, so we quietly pursued our usual way.

During the summer we were further improved by the proselytisers on board the missionary launch, *Helen Gould*. They had a projector and several sets of slides and were most eager to entertain us. In return we tried to be as hospitable as circumstances permitted. The expedition was financed by the philanthropist for whom the launch was named and I have no doubt she felt a great deal of satisfaction in the good work being done. At least, a peep into the logbook when the launch made her second trip the following year gave me quite an insight into the lawless kind of people we were to whom they were ministering. It must have done her heart good!

That summer I took on still another duty. We lost the fellowship of the Mounties by the closing altogether of the detachment at Stewart and the work of the Post Office was turned over to me. One by one the activities of Stewart seemed to be falling into our hands.

Restaking of claims continued throughout the country and it began to be a genuine stampede. The Schoolteacher Group failed to live up to expectations and towards autumn Miss MacNeil ceased operations and returned to Dawson. She certainly was not the one to smile when everything goes dead wrong, but proved a very poor loser. Some bills she had guaranteed were collected with difficulty. Only Doctor Heydon and one or two other men remained on Henderson Creek.

Like the old sourdough he was, Bowen Smith could stand it only so long before joining the stampede. Since selling the store to us he had lived in a cabin a short distance away but now he decided to stake claims at Blackhills. Waldron took him and his outfit over to the claim. One autumn day a steamer made a landing while I was wandering in the grove behind the store. Hearing her whistle I hurried home to see three people on the store platform. The man and woman were watching the departing boat but the girl was on tiptoe, peering through the window of the store.

"I'm going crazy to get in!" I heard her say. "They've changed it a lot but it still looks familiar."

I tried to appear as though it were quite the usual thing to come home and find people peeping in my window and invited them inside. As soon as we entered the young woman turned to me.

"Have you got the key to papa's cabin?" she asked.

I had never seen any member of the group before and no attempt had been made at introductions. I was the custodian of no keys, neither had I the faintest idea who papa was. So I was rather at a loss. But just then Mr. Aish came in and he was able to throw some light on the situation.

The elderly lady was Mrs. Bowen Smith, the two younger

people were her daughter, Mrs. Hancock, and Mr. Hancock. It seemed that as a girl Mrs. Hancock had spent a winter with her father and on her arrival was eager to see the old place again. They had come expecting to join Mr. Smith at Stewart and go to the Blackhills with him. When they learned that he had already gone they made themselves comfortable in his cabin until he could be reached. Blackhills had been stampeded only recently and there were no accommodations there for ladies, so it was finally decided that Mr. Hancock would join Mr. Smith to take up mining and that Mrs. Hancock would remain at Stewart with her mother until a suitable cabin could be built. Mrs. Smith was a gentle, kindly, old lady, but altogether unsuited to the rigorous life of the North. Still it was good to have them as next-door neighbors and friends. Young Mrs. Hancock became our particular friend and she, Aish, Waldron, and I often made a merry quartet during the evenings of the following winter. We were a happy, carefree group in those days before a shadow had darkened any of our lives. Stewart was becoming, for me, more friendly with every passing month.

Waldron made his fall trip to Dawson earlier than usual in 1907 and when he returned he had been appointed as Agent to the Mining Recorder and also Crown Timber Agent, to act in place of the police. This was still another branch to the business and meant more work, but I had no part in that. Under an arrangement with Mr. Aish, Waldron would take applications for claims or timber permits when out with his team and Aish would do the remainder of the work after his office hours. They received a percentage of all money taken in and this often brought them quite a little revenue.

We had scarcely finished storing the winter outfit when slush ice began to run. It increased steadily and by the last week of October the Yukon was running bank-full of heavy ice. The Stewart River had already closed. All crossing to and from the telegraph office had been discontinued and messages were delivered through a megaphone.

One day, while Waldron was away, I went to get some wood for the fire. I heard shouting from upriver and was startled to see two small boats coming down in the ice. They were some distance apart and in the nearer one I could see a man, two women and a little girl. The man was laboring desperately to work his boat through the ice to the slack water at the mouth of the Stewart. I gave a sigh of relief when he had accomplished this. I knew they were safe.

The other boat was some distance behind the first and nearer to the opposite shore. It had been frozen to a large floe and was completely at the mercy of the current. There were two men in it and they had fastened some article of clothing to an oar which they kept waving to attract attention while they shouted for help. My heart seemed to stand still. I knew no boat could come to them from our side of the river and all Mr. Aish had was a small canoe—a mere cockleshell and not fit, I thought, to venture into such heavy ice. But there was no one in sight on either shore and I had the terrible feeling of being obliged to stand helpless while those men were carried to certain death. It would be only a short time before the boat was crushed by the ice.

Suddenly Mr. Aish appeared on the bank. He had been cutting wood for the cabin when he heard the shouting and realized that someone was in trouble. Without an instant's hestitation he ran to the canoe and launched it into a small space of open water some distance behind the boat with its frantic occupants. Then the struggle began. It was no easy task to work the frail craft among those heavy floes, any one of which could have crushed it like an eggshell. It required both a cool head and a strong and steady arm. Slowly he fought his way, now completely surrounded by ice, now taking advantage of a slight opening to work his way nearer the helpless men, while the current carried all of them swiftly downstream. I stood rooted to the spot, shivering with horror. Every moment I expected to see both boats crushed and their occupants disappear into the icy water.

At last an opening appeared directly behind the boat. Then, with a final sweep of his paddle, Aish drove the canoe to the very edge of the floe. They were now about three miles below Stewart and I ran for the field glasses. I could scarcely hold them and my teeth rattled like castanets. I saw Aish remove the loose flooring, made of slats, from the bottom of the canoe and lay it, with his paddles on the ice floe. The men added their oars and over the bridge thus formed they walked from the boat and took seats in the canoe. When all were safely on board Aish picked up the oars, flooring and paddles and pushed off, abandoning the other boat entirely. Just then they disappeared around a bend in the river and I returned to the house sick with nervousness. How could that canoe carry three men to safety through such a run of ice!

Some time after darkness had set in I gasped with relief when a light appeared in the window of the telegrapher's cabin. Someone had returned alive.

That night the ice jammed and the next day Aish made his way across to Stewart for remedies. One of the men had frozen several toes and the other one several fingers. We learned that they had succeeded in reaching shore seven miles below Stewart and had made their way back on foot along the shore in the dark. They traveled over shore ice, along the gravel beaches, and at times scrambled through thick brush. The frozen members soon healed but both men realized they had a miraculous escape. They knew, too, what Aish had dared for their sake. So do the men of the North stand ready at all times to risk life and limb in the service of their fellows.

After the river closed, our routine work went on. Each month showed an increase in the volume of business handled. The people of Thistle Creek, twenty-five miles above Stewart on the Yukon, were granted a monthly mail service and at their request Waldron was given the contract to carry it. By this arrangement the miners could transact any business in connection with their claims when he made his mail trips, saving them the necessity of making a trip to Stewart or elsewhere for the purpose. Twice during that winter I made the trip with him, a pleasant break from the steady work in the store.

We were also invited to Thistle Creek to spend Christmas but an aching molar interfered and instead Waldron took me to Dr. Heydon to have the offender removed. I did not particularly enjoy that drive with the prospect of what awaited me at the end of it and my fears were well founded. The tooth was stubborn and I returned next day with a very sore jaw and a number of black and blue spots adorning my countenance. A drive of twenty-five miles that took two days, when the thermometer registered forty degrees below zero, to have a tooth drawn!—that was adding insult to injury.

In February a traveler passing through Stewart told us of the death on Clear Creek, a tributary of the Stewart, of Big Alec MacDonald. He had dropped while cutting wood at his cabin door. I remembered, then, answering the store bell one day months before and finding a rather burly man standing beside the counter. He wore a pair of ordinary overalls and a black sateen shirt. I noticed his slender, graceful hands immediately, but what made a lasting impression on me was the cadence of his voice. No mother ever hushed her babe to sleep in gentler tones. He made some purchases, inquired about the steamers, and then left the store. It was my only meeting with Big Alec MacDonald, the Klondike King.

At one time he did not know the extent of his own wealth. Pack trains could be seen making regular trips from his claims to the banks, each animal laden with gold dust. By common report, all that remained of his wealth at the time of his sudden death in obscure surroundings was a few thousand dollars. But unlike many celebrities, the Klondike King did not squander his possessions. A kind heart and an open hand, with an every-ready will to invest in mining ventures which often proved worthless, left a general sorrow at his passing. There were many who had felt his kindness and none who were not proud that they had known him.

Another winter was passing even more quickly than the other. Freighting to the creek had been finished. Word came from Blackhills that the cabin was ready and Mrs. Hancock and her mother expected to move over as soon as the weather was fine enough for Mrs. Smith to make the trip. And then . . .

One cold night in March when the fires had been banked and we were preparing for bed the store bell rang, telling of the opening of the door into the store. (Doors were never locked in that "lawless" country.) A customer or visitor was unusual at that time of night and I hurried in. A man covered with frost and snow, bearing every evidence of having just come in from a long, hard trip, stood by the stove. I failed to recognize him at first but when he threw back the hood of his parka, "Mr. Hancock!" I cried. "What is the matter?" He looked like a man thoroughly spent.

"I want you to get Hattie," he answered. "Mr. Smith died last night and I came ahead to break the news. I was told to come to you first."

Surely I had not heard correctly! Mr. Smith dead—when his wife and daughter waited daily for a message to go to him? It was impossible! But it was only too true. After their long journey of six thousand miles to be with him, and the winter spent within a day's travel of where he was, the Messenger had come before either of them had seen him.

When I prepared supper for the traveler, Waldron went to Mrs. Hancock with a message that I wanted her and on the way from the cabin he broke the news. When she had recovered, in a measure, from the shock, I went with her to her mother.

Two days later one son, who had joined his father at Blackhills, and a couple of friends arrived with the body. Mr. Smith's last wish had been to have his body taken to Stewart for burial. Neither dogs nor horses were available, so they had drawn it the entire thirty miles over the rough mountain trails by hand. The cabin where Mrs. Smith and Mrs. Hancock lived was small and when the time came for the funeral the citizens of the entire community gathered in the vacant police barracks to pay their last respects to the kindly old gentleman who had lived among them for so many years. There was no clergyman in that isolated district, so Mr. Aish read the burial service and one or two hymns were attempted. I say attempted, advisedly. There were no singers in that group but in the heart of each one was a full appreciation of the pathos of the circumstances. I am doubtful if any funeral hymn, rendered by trained choir and accompanied by the rich tones of an organ, was ever wafted to the Throne of Grace one whit more sincerely than those quavering notes.

When the services were ended the homemade casket, neatly covered with black cloth, was drawn by hand to the little plot on the Police Reserve devoted to those who rest from their labors. As I watched the little cortege making its way between the giant spruce, with the clear afternoon sunshine filtering through to fall on the hand-sled with its quiet burden, I realized that this silent land had many lessons to teach me still.

Shortly afterwards Mrs. Hancock and her mother moved to Blackhills and I saw Mrs. Smith only once again.

The breakup came that spring, 1908, on the same date as the year before and once more the ice ran out very smoothly and quietly.

Early in June we had some excitement when Mr. Aish came to tell us a murder had been committed one hundred miles upriver and five miles below Selkirk. Two young cheechakos named Bergman and Anderson, together with an old-timer name Elfors, were on their way to Dawson in a small boat after spending the night in a tent on the riverbank. Elfors and Bergman went into the woods, presumably to look for a bear. In a short time Elfors returned alone, carrying a rifle, with the story that they had killed a bear. Bergman was skinning it, and Anderson's help was needed to bring in the carcass. Without waiting to put on his shoes, Anderson started. They had gone only a short distance when a bullet sang past his ear. Realizing instantly that Bergman must have met with foul play, he turned and grappled with Elfors. After a sharp tussle he got possession of the rifle and then ran the entire five miles to Selkirk where he arrived with his feet terribly lacerated.

Mr. Aish gave us the description of the murderer and his outfit and asked that everybody be alerted to report him, if seen. Everyone became an amateur detective and wondered how you dealt with a murderer. Lookouts were posted at different points along the river and a few days later the boat was seen passing Stewart. The police were notified and Elfors was captured a few miles below that point. He was taken to Dawson, tried, and executed within three months of the commission of the crime. Justice was meted out summarily in that region.

In the summer of 1908 we had old friends as closer neighbors when the telegraph office was transferred from the opposite side of the river to Stewart. This proved to be a great convenience to the public as it became possible to send or receive messages regardless of the condition of the river. And we were glad of the added companionship.

With all the mining going on, a subsidiary industry was also thriving. It was necessary to use steam for thawing the ground ahead of the huge dredges that were being installed. Wood was used for fuel and Mr. Frank Neill, who had large contracts to supply it, put several crews of men to work near Stewart. This, as well as the activity in staking, brought additional business to the store and with the mail and my housework I felt that my time and strength were being taxed to the utmost. But Waldron was working equally hard, so I tried to conceal how weary I often felt.

Then he returned one afternoon and found me with chills and a fever. As soon as he and the horses had eaten, he asked Mrs. Shand to stay with me and he went for Dr. Heydon. She stayed applying hot compresses until I became somewhat easier about three in the morning, and then went home to get some rest. Like myself, she had a lot to do. At dawn I heard the horses' feet on the gravel and a moment later Waldron came into my room. He looked so haggard after his thirty-six hours without rest!

The doctor made his examination. "A severe case of inflamation of the kidneys, with complications. You must have absolute quiet." Then followed three weeks during which I knew little and cared less of what went on around me. After that, Dr. Heydon consented to my going to Dawson to see Dr. Alfred Thompson. He had done wonders for me, but the facilities at hand were limited and under more favorable conditions I improved very quickly. My strength had not fully returned when I got back to Stewart and had to take up the work again, but I was fortunate in being able to get help from a Mrs. MacDonald. Although a half-breed, she was white in the moral meaning of the term and I have known many pale-faces who might have learned much from her in the matter of principle. She always seemed pleased to help me and I often enlisted her services.

When my strength had been completely restored I decided to go to Dawson for a minor operation that Dr. Thompson had advised, but said nothing to Waldron of the real purpose of the trip. The doctor had assured me that, though it should be done without delay, it really was nothing serious. I could have it done and return home in a few days. I had learned that whenever I was not feeling quite fit, it worried Waldron, so I had the operation without his knowledge. I was doing nicely when, for some unaccountable reason, I took a relapse and for several days I was in a rather serious condition. Just while I was feeling the worst, Waldron was suddenly called to Dawson on business—and my duplicity was revealed! I received quite a lecture on my folly, but perhaps not half as much as I deserved.

Again I returned home decidedly below par, but the fall's stock had been stored while I was away. There were not so many miners on Henderson Creek as formerly, consequently there was less freighting to be done and Waldron spent more time at home. This left him free to attend to the store work and, relieved of this, I regained my strength rapidly.

I missed Mrs. Hancock's jolly companionship that winter. Mrs. Shand lived within the distance of a city block from me but neither of us had much time for visiting. Weeks would often elapse without our seeing each other. She was much older than I, had come into the Yukon in 1897, and so had a wealth of experiences to relate. Being a native of Scotland she had at all times, and especially when excited, a delightful Celtic accent and on those rare occasions when I had time to visit her I thoroughly enjoyed her droll humor.

The question of that new building had been casually mentioned several times during the months that had gone, but one evening when we were alone Waldron brought the matter up in a definite manner.

"Let's come to a decision," he urged. "The freighting is about over for the winter. I have no other work for the team and, while cruising on the islands between here and the mainland a short time ago, I found a splendid group of logs. They are just what I need for the purpose, but it will be necessary to haul them in winter. I couldn't get them across the sloughs in summer. Now, what do you think?"

Like an Irishman, I answered his question by asking another. "What is your opinion?" I wanted to know. "We took stock and had a balance a short while ago. You know what our profits are for the time spent here. A building will cost a lot, in both money and labor. Do you think the business justifies it?"

"I've more confidence in the business than ever," he replied. "I've studied the situation pretty thoroughly. At present, we have no other prospects and business here is improving. We are handling twice as much stock as we did at first. There is talk of dredges being installed in the upper Stewart country and, if that is done, this will be a fine location. I think we can make ourselves comfortable and in a few years acquire a nice little nestegg. There's only one objection."

"What's that?" I asked.

"The isolation for you. I know it must be very lonely and hard for you, especially when I'm away. Several times I've wished I hadn't brought you here."

We agreed, however, that everything seemed to be for the best as we were and I agreed to make the best of it. It was decided that the new building would go ahead.

After I had gone to bed that night I lay for a long time, thinking. I studied the matter more closely than I had ever done before. I knew that if he went ahead with the building we would remain in the country indefinitely. Waldron had done his best in every way. He had taken advantage of every opportunity that presented itself to provide me with change or recreation. But a stubborn fact remained—the past three years had not been ones of contentment. Every day had been lived in protest, unvoiced perhaps, but none the less real.

There was a phase of the life for me of which, I think, Waldron was altogether unaware. Many and various were the things I had come to know, among them being that a woman in that country, and more especially one dealing with the public, is on trial every day she lives. I do not mean to criticize the men. I think the fact is a result of existing conditions. It seems hardly more than natural that, where the percentage of women is so small, men's desire for the company of the other sex often overbalances their better judgement. A woman must stand ready at all times to check any untoward attitude that may develop and it often requires a great deal of tact and finesse to so handle a situation that the desired result is attained while appearing unaware of that situation. Of course there are, too, the unscrupulous, and those who have an overweening ego which prevents their distinguishing between polite courtesy and familiarity.

I had always prided myself on my ability to read human nature. With all its idiosyncrasies, it had been almost an open book to me and here I found it stood in good stead. I had been able to separate the chaff from the wheat, but even this was sometimes productive of undesirable consequences. The chaff could not understand why the wheat appeared to occupy a different status from that which they held. To a certain extent I paid a price for my discrimination.

I was on the horns of a dilemma. For me, the life and surroundings were far from congenial. But—though I could persuade Waldron to abandon the idea of building, to sell and go outside—what then? In that case, he would be the discontented one and would that make me any the happier? Long I wrestled with the problem and in the dawn of the early morning I had reached my decision. I would accept conditions unreservedly and be his helpmate in spirit and in truth.

I think that one of the hardest battles of my life was fought— and I hope, won—that night.

Building Hopes

During the evenings of that fall of 1908, when there were no orders to fill, there was much discussion of the plans for the new building. I had never been one to do things by halves and now that I made up my mind to grow up with the country I was all enthusiasm. Mr. Aish often joined in the talk and planning. Although younger than either Waldron or I he had a more quiet, staid character and his attitude was that of an older brother. Many of his suggestions were gratefully accepted.

The main building was to have a frontage of sixty-five feet and a depth of forty-five feet. It would comprise the store and post office, storeroom and living quarters under one roof, with warehouse, stable, and other outbuildings adjoining. Of necessity, they would all be of logs. The water in front of the present site was shallow except during the early summer, when the melting snow in the mountains caused a heavy run. So Waldron decided to build about a quarter of a mile downstream where the steamers landed, and set to work to clear the site for the building.

We had been invited again to Thistle Creek for Christmas and, as the weather was mild, we closed the store and accepted the invitation. Waldron took the mail along and in order to allow him to attend to some business for the miners we stayed an extra day.

Shortly after the New Year, Waldron came in one day ready for the woods.

"Get your warm clothes on!" he told me. "I'm going to start work on the logs for the new building and I want you to help me cut down the first tree."

So I harnessed Hunter and Hero, my two pals since my days on Sixty Pup, and we rode out to the woods. When we had felled several trees, the man who was to help him asked what kind of a lumberjack I would make.

"I've sawn timber with those who didn't do nearly so well," Waldron answered. He was nothing, if not diplomatic.

Then, feeling that I had laid the corner-stone, I left them to continue the work and returned to the house with the dogs. I had broken them to harness myself and they worked very well for me, as a rule. But my discipline must have been at fault, because they had a habit of stopping in the trail and, as though suddenly seized with a new idea that delighted them, they would turn and jump on the sled to lick my face and swarm all over me. I appreciated their affection, but would be obliged to get out of the sled, disentangle the harness, and start them off again.

All during the winter, Waldron was logging during every hour he could spare from the regular work. But in spite of all he could do the middle of April came, the frozen hauling track was breaking up, and still some of the most important pieces were in the woods. Then his helper quit.

"I don't know what to do," he announced one evening. "There's still almost a day's hauling to be done. There's not a man available, and if the sun is as strong tomorrow as it was today the trail will be completely gone by noon. If those logs are left in the woods the building will be delayed another year."

"Could I help?" I asked.

He gave me an amused smile. (I weighed only one hundred and five!) "I'm afraid not. I really don't think you could do much at loading logs. But," he went on, "there's very little darkness now, so I'll take a few hours rest, feed the horses at midnight, and by the time they have eaten there'll be enough light to see to work. I'll do all I can while the snow lasts. It's just possible I may finish."

In the morning, when he came in after harnessing the horses, I had my outdoor clothes on.

"Where are you going?" he asked.

"To the woods with you," I answered.

"But—you can't do anything with those logs!"

"Perhaps not. But I can go along for company, can't I?" was my retort.

"You certainly can! I'll be delighted to have you! 'Company lightens the load and shortens the road.'" And he made a seat for me on the bunk beside him.

As we left the cabin the whole sky was suffused with the golden rays of dawn and a mighty hush was over all. Even the birds were still wrapped in slumber. I have never forgotten the stillness and glory of that particular morning. It was not unusual for me to ride a few miles with Waldron when he went with his load and walk back home, but this morning seemed different. Every detail of it returns to me most vividly. In my enthusiasm I was eager to have the building finished so we could feel settled and "at home."

When we reached the woods he found that I could place or hold a skid, could step the horses forward or back as necessary, and I surprised him by what I could do with a peavey. While he was away to the landing I shoveled snow on the bare patches in the trail which were rapidly increasing in size and number under the hot sun. About eight o'clock we stopped long enough for coffee and a sandwich and to feed the horses, then went to work again. At eleven the last log was rolled from the sled to join the others in the pile. As he picked up the lines he turned to me and his face was all smiles.

"Hurrah! We did it!" he shouted, "If anyone ever deserved a home, you do! You helped cut the first log and to haul the last one. I couldn't have finished without you!"

Yes. That was my greatest moment.

The breakup that year was very spectacular. The ice in the Stewart and that in the Yukon above us ran at the same time. This was unusual as the ice in the Stewart usually runs down and jams at the mouth about a week before that in the Yukon has begun to move. A jam formed diagonally across the Yukon from a point about half a mile below the village on the Stewart side to a high bluff about the same distance above on the opposite shore. Everything below held solid for several hours. When the heavy ice from above came crowding against this wall it was like a battle between two giant forces. The huge cakes, carried along on what must have been a ten-mile current, would come leaping, tearing and rushing, to hurl themselves against the great mass which rose to a height of over one hundred feet. Others crowding behind would force them up, up, up, grinding them to fragments as they went, till they came tumbling back in a cascade of glistening ice crystals.

The water rose rapidly and we hurried to get stock and house furnishings placed high enough to escape the water in case of a flood. This done, we went to the roof of the cabin to watch the marvelous spectacle. When the water was within an inch of coming into the buildings the jam broke. In a very short time all that could be seen was a mass of ice, black and dirty from its journey down the river, floating by. We were more fortunate than some of the people living along the river. In several places the water came into the buildings. One man and his wife were obliged to spend the night in their canoe among the trees.

When the usual spring work—housing new goods, freighting summer outfits to the creeks, planting the garden—had been finished, Waldron started the actual building. He hired an expert and assistant for the more particular work and he spent all his own spare time at it as well. It was much larger than the ordinary log building and the plan of it prevented the work from going ahead quickly. When the autumn of 1909 came, the walls and roof of the main building were in place and a runway cut through the high bank to the steamer landing. It would be impossible to have it ready to recieve the fall outfit, so he suspended work until the early spring. This would have the benefit of allowing the logs to settle thoroughly in place during the winter, before any openings were cut for doors or windows.

I had always delighted in sleigh-riding and that fall Waldron got a cutter and a set of light harness, with bells, for the team. He always kept his horses in the pink of condition and I was delighted the first time we went out and he gave me the reins. How happily we talked of the future!

The time seemed to go on wings. Christmas was again drawing near. Mr. and Mrs. Shand gave a Christmas dinner and social evening to which the people of the whole community were invited. About ten at night we sat down to dinner: turkey, vegetables, plum pudding, pie, ice cream, cake, tea and coffee. This was followed by the usual sociability until midnight, after which came several hours of dancing. The crowd was not large but everyone seemed to enjoy themselves. In the early morning hours, with a full moon shedding its steely brightness over the great white silence, Waldron and I walked home feeling that, after all, life together in the Yukon was good indeed. Looking into the future, our lives appeared as cloudless as the sky above us. I was so glad that I had been able to renounce all else and accept this land for whatever it held for me.

Foreboding

During the winter, Waldron's right foot began to trouble him. There was neither pain, soreness nor stiffness, but he seemed to have lost all power of the ankle. This was no doubt reponsible for what he had called his clumsiness when on several occasions he had tripped and fallen, unable to recover his balance. No suspicion of anything of a serious nature occurred to either of us. He applied different kinds of liniment, bathed and massaged it regularly, and continued his work as usual.

In March, 1910, when the weather and trail were both good, we decided it was time to return some of the hospitality we had from time to time enjoyed and we gave a party. The guests came from all the surrounding creeks, as well as points up and down both the Stewart and the Yukon rivers for a distance of forty miles. They came singly and in groups, with horses, dogs and "by hand," laughing and joking, all happy to put aside the more serious problems of life and foregather for a short interval of recreation. For two evenings and a day there was fun aplenty. Then came the morning of separation. The laughing group gathered in the store and encircled Waldron and me, while they sang "For they are jolly good fellows!" This was followed by "Auld Lang Syne."

Then the circle broke and each one made his or her way to the waiting rigs. It was the last gathering of its kind that Waldron and I attended together.

His foot failed to improve under the home treatment and when Dr. Heydon came to Stewart some time in April on business, Waldron consulted him about it. He examined it, then wrote a prescription for liniment. I had watched his face closely while he made the examination and a little later when Waldron had gone to wait on a customer, I questioned the doctor.

"What did you find?" I asked.

"It looks to me like a case of absorption," was the answer.

I had never heard the word used in a medical sense so I asked what it meant. His answer left me stunned. Every word burned itself into my brain. How could anyone, especially one connected with the medical profession, be so brutal?

"It means," he told me quite coolly, "that the patient dies by inches. They waste away gradually until there is practically nothing left but the skeleton. The disease is very rare and I can't see how Smythe could have contracted it, but that is my diagnosis and I'll lay a wager I'm right!"

Just then I heard Waldron's step and turned aside to hide the horror I felt must be written on my face. "This cannot be true!" I thought and then with relief remembered that Heydon was not a regular physician and was probably mistaken in his opinion.

"What did the doctor say?" Waldron asked, after he had gone.

I lied and was glad to do it. "He thinks you are working too hard and need a rest."

"I haven't been feeling as well as usual for the last few weeks," he admitted and my heart sank. "But now that the cold weather is over, I'll be glad to take a rest."

At the end of another month there was still no improvement and he decided to go to Dawson and consult Dr. Thompson. He rode to Blackhills to meet the stage and there turned the horse loose. The faithful animal returned alone, a distance of thirty miles over the mountains.

I rose on the morning of May twelfth, 1910, to find the river running open. The ice had moved during the night and all that remained were a few cakes piled along the shore. I was relieved, for with Waldron away I had dreaded a flood. He returned from Dawson on the first boat. Dr. Thompson had prescribed medicine and advised the use of electricity, with instructions to return in a month and report progress. When the month was up Waldron suggested that we both go to Dawson. At first I demurred—there was so much to be done. But he urged the point and finally I yielded. I like now to remember that I did so.

After making his second examination, the doctor asked for a consultation and when this was over he sent for me.

"I want to talk with you about Waldron's condition," he said when I went to his office. "I have suggested that he go to Vancouver or Victoria to consult some of the doctors there, but he says that would be out of the question. Is that the case?"

I thought of what that would mean. If he left, I would be obliged to shoulder the full load, to carry on with the building and also see that the business did not suffer. Could I do it? I had always had a good working knowledge of the business, but to assume full responsibility, even for a short time, was another matter.

"Will you be quite frank, Doctor, and explain Waldron's true condition?" I asked. "Is it serious?"

His eyes were kind and his voice gentle as he answered. "Yes, Mrs. Smythe. His condition is serious. Very serious."

The walls of the office seemed to be closing in on me. I wanted to throw out my hands to ward off something. He could not be talking of Waldron, who had never been ill in his life. There must be some mistake. I tried to steady my voice when I spoke again.

"My diagnosis—and my colleague agrees with me perfectly— is that the trouble is in his spine, but it is with the hope that we may be mistaken that I am advising him to go outside."

"You can do nothing for him?" My own voice seemed to roar in my ears as I asked the question.

"Nothing more than I have tried." His voice held genuine regret. He was more than our family doctor, he was Waldron's friend. "I know that you will be brave," he went on, and I wondered if he thought I needed just that spur. "You must not allow him to realize his condition, but urge him to do as I suggest."

"Is there any hope?" I persisted.

"If he takes my advice, yes."

"Then he must go!"

But even as I spoke I had no idea how it could be managed.

Travel to and from the Yukon is expensive, to say nothing of expert medical advice. While the business had steadily improved, it had been small when we started and the profits had been reinvested in it. Also, labor and materials for the building had made inroads upon our capital. But he *must* have this chance. I left the office with my brain reeling, my world in ruins.

Waldron knew nothing of my visit to the doctor, so I did not return to the hotel until my self-control had been in a measure restored. "Where have you been?" he asked, when I did appear.

"Gossiping here and there about town," I answered flippantly.

When we had gone to our room he told me what the doctor had advised and I discussed the matter with him as though the idea was perfectly new to me. It required considerable argument, but he at last agreed to follow the doctor's advice. This point being settled he gradually became more reconciled.

We remained in Dawson for a week and attended several places of amusement, among them a party at Gold Bottom, twenty-five miles from Dawson. It was our last pleasuring together and I still wonder how I went through with it, knowing as I did the darkness that hovered so near us.

When we returned to Stewart, Waldron immediately set about making arrangements to leave. This done he again went to Dawson to attend to some final details and on July sixteenth I received a telegram saying he would take passage for Whitehorse on the steamer *Whitehorse*, leaving Dawson that night. She called at Stewart about one o'clock the next day and I was at the landing. How wistfully Waldron looked at me and then at the unfinished building! But not for worlds would I allow him to see just how I felt.

"We'll do wonders while you're away," I assured him, "so hurry up and get well. That's your job for the present."

The gangplank was pulled in, the steamer headed into the stream, and as he stood waving from the deck I walked up the runway at the very spot where I had landed as a bride less than five short years before. I looked at the litter and confusion of the unfinished building—the building that was to have been our home and of which we had talked and planned so much.

Did it not symbolize the wreck of all our hopes?

On My Own

W hen I could no longer distinguish Waldron's figure in the group on the steamer's deck and even a waving handkerchief had become a blur, I returned to the empty house. As the door closed behind me and shut out other eyes, I threw myself on the couch in the little kitchen that had so often echoed to our merriment and gave way to tears.

I cannot say how long I lay there, but I was still sobbing when the door quietly opened and Mr. Aish, with the freedom of a close friend, entered without knocking. I can still see his look as I sprang up and tried to hide the evidence of my weakness. After talking for a while of impersonal things he rose to leave and remarked quite casually, "I just dropped in to say that while Smythe is away you are to regard me as entirely at your service. We talked it over and I promised him that it would be so. And by the way, he asked me to give you this."

He handed me an official-looking envelope and when he had gone I found it contained papers transferring everything we owned to my name. I thought my heart would break. They seemed an acknowledgment of what we had tried to prevent his knowing. I realized fully, too, that the burden of carrying on was definitely mine, although it was long before I would admit, even to myself, that his case was hopeless.

Waldron had arranged a weekly schedule to the creek and had hired one George Monson, popularly known as Mickie, to work for me. He was a capable man and as he had started work some time before Waldron left he was fairly well initiated. There was no point in waiting and there was certainly plenty of work waiting to be done. So we set to work at once.

The living quarters were finished except the interior walls. In the country, in lieu of plaster, cotton was tacked over the walls and the paper pasted to it. I busied myself at this whenever I could find the time, while Mickie worked at the doors, windows and floor of the store. Mr. Aish also spent his evenings at the more particular parts of the work.

When the store and living rooms were ready, I moved in. My feelings on leaving the old place were mixed. Few homes could be more humble but it had been rich in those little things that go to make a real home, things that money cannot buy and without which even a palace is merely a habitation. As the last article of furniture was carried out and I closed the door, I felt that all my bright hopes were being shut away and I went forth into a new world in which the burden promised to be more than I could bear. At first I was a trifle nervous over being alone in the new home. It was surrounded by woods and the nearest neighbour was Mickie, still at the old place. I missed the nearness of Mrs. Shand, the new store being a quarter-mile downriver, but was glad to be that much farther from the saloon. I had never been in such close contact with one before and the experience had at times been anything but pleasant. Besides I had work enough to make me forget my timidity. We had built on virgin ground and I dug, raked and burned till far into the night.

The steamer *Princess May*, on which Waldron sailed from Skagway for Vancouver, was wrecked in Lynn Canal. She left her course in a fog and ran on a saddle of rock at two in the morning. The passengers were landed on the bleak coast near Juneau and taken to that town the next day by small boat. Of all this I knew nothing until later. The papers containing the news disappeared mysteriously and were delivered after a letter had come from Waldron telling of his safe arrival. A stammering Mickie admitted he had taken them on the orders of Mr. Aish.

Within a few days I had a demonstration of what a curse a saloon can be in a community. Mickie had many fine qualities. He was honest and conscientious in his work. No unexpected bit of extra work was any trouble to him and his Irish wit lightened many a task. But it seemed he liked a social glass and one morning he went to do some work with the team and when he failed to appear all day Mr. Aish asked for an hour's leave from the office and went in search. He found the horses tangled in some stumps, but Mickie was conspicuous by his absence.

During the next week the entire male population of the island, with the exception of Mr. Aish and the principal of the Dawson High School who chanced to be there waiting for a steamer to take him up the Stewart River, went on a jamboree. Why they should wait till Waldron had gone to display their prowess I cannot say, but I am doubtful if one of that number could have told you his name while the spree lasted. One of them, I remember, was an egotistical nonentity named Graham, whose chief ambition was to become a man of influence and tell others to do thus and so. At least, he had once confided this much to me in an unrequested burst of confidence. One hot afternoon I was coming from the old place and saw this ambitious son of Adam laying on the gravel beach, having apparently rolled down the bank from the pathway. He had acquired a goodly collection of mud, dirt and filth on his way and about his up-turned bloated face the flies were buzzing in hundreds. I wondered how any being created in the image of the Father could so affront Him. Turning away, I decided that if he ever became a man of any influence that influence would be alcoholic!

Except for what I could do myself and with Mr. Aish's help, the work remained at a stand-still until the supply of liquor became exhausted. When overtaken with this calamity the revelers could do no better than return to work and a very nerve-shaken and crestfallen Mickie appeared. I was reluctant to take him back but there was no one else who would prove any improvement. Surely his conscience must have troubled him, for while he remained with us I never had any further difficulty on that score.

After the short letter from Vancouver announcing his arrival no word came from Waldron and this worried me. Many a night the sun sank and rose again without my eyes having closed. Still, I was able to get an extra man occasionally to help Mickie and there had in reality been much accomplished in spite of the time lost during the jamboree. The store and warehouse were ready for the fall outfit and the most necessary of the outbuildings were well under way.

In September Mrs. Lester, who had come in from Vancouver when I did, spent a week with me. During her visit we had a very severe electrical storm, rather an unusual occurrence in the Yukon. I have always enjoyed such a storm, something within me seems to react to the fury of them. I love to watch the swift, sinister lightning while the deep roll of the thunder always thrills me, and a Yukon thunderstorm makes up for its rarity in power and beauty. But the effect on Mrs. Lester was directly the opposite and her timidity prevented me from enjoying a display such as I shall never see again.

The mountains along the Yukon directly facing Stewart are covered with evergreen and hardwood in what is the most beautiful blending of the two that I know. In autumn, when the leaves are tinted by frost, the brilliant colors set off by the somber green of the heavy spruce makes a picture to delight an artist or nature-lover. On that night the autumn leaves were at their best. In the swift, vivid flashes of lightning the picture, as seen from my doorway, was breathtaking. In the foreground the mighty Yukon was turned to molten silver; beyond it rose the mountainside with its marvelous blanket of coloring, the whole surmounted by a billowing mass of inky clouds.

But I was not allowed to revel in the beauty. At the first roll of thunder Mrs. Lester fled to the bedroom, leaped into bed and drew the covering over her head. She insisted on pulling down the shades and fastening a thick blanket over the window! At each peal of thunder she gave a piercing shriek and huddled further into the bedclothes. When I had done all that was possible to render the room soundproof, I went out to enjoy the storm, but when she missed me from the room she became almost hysterical and I was obliged to return and remain with her in durance vile.

The fall outfit arrived some time later and I felt very much pleased when it was all snugly stored in the new quarters. Then, one evening in early October, I received a telegram from Waldron saying he would arrive home the next morning on the steamer *Dawson*. I had received only the one letter from him while he was absent and knew nothing of his progress. The boat arrived very early, but I was up to meet it. Keenly I watched him as he landed. He had gained in flesh and seemed more like his old chipper self. He was full of enthusiasm, insisted on visiting and inspecting everything immediately, and was delighted with what had been done. But—I noticed he carried a cane. His trip had been a disappointment in many ways. Dr. Jones of Victoria, to whom Dr. Thompson had particularly referred him, was on a trip to Europe. He had consulted several other prominent medical men but they could not, or would not, give him a definite report on his condition. Instead, one and all had prescribed some harmless drug, assured him that he would be all right in time, and pocketed their fee. As the season of navigation on the Yukon was drawing to a close and he was anxious about affairs at home, he had decided not to wait for Dr. Jones to return, in spite of remonstrances from his relatives.

"How is your foot?" I asked, when I had finally got him alone.

"There doesn't seem to be much change in that," he answered. "And for some time I've thought the other one was becoming affected."

I turned sick at heart. Were Dr. Heydon and Dr. Thompson right after all? But no, it could not be! He sat there laughing and talking and he looked as bright and animated as he had ever been. It was unthinkable that he could be smitten with anything so deadly that science was baffled; he who had never known illness.

"How is your general condition?" I wanted to know.

He laughed at this. "I feel as well as I ever felt in my life," he declared. "If it wasn't for the trouble in walking I could do a day's work with the best of them!"

Then he went on to tell of his trip. Several sisters whom he had not seen for years were living in Vancouver and had means and leisure to show him every kindness. Vancouver was booming at the time, his brother-in-law, Sandford Crowe, was an alderman, and they all vied in doing everything possible for him. He never tired of talking about the places, people and sights he had seen and enjoyed. I have always been glad that he took the trip while still able to take so much out of life.

"It would have been perfect with you," he told me, "but I felt almost guilty while you were slaving at home. We must take the trip together some time."

"Certainly," I agreed. "When our ship comes in, we'll take a good long one." Then I asked him why he had not written.

He looked at me in astonishment. "What do you mean?"

"I mean that I had only one letter, written just after you reached Vancouver."

"And you knew nothing of the wreck?"

"Only what the papers told me."

He was sympathetic and puzzled. "But I wrote every week and sent postcards, too!" he averred.

Later, the mystery was solved by the arrival of the whole lot from Stewart, British Columbia, where they had gone by mistake.

Shortly after his return there were some changes in the telegraph department. Mr. Aish was ordered to Selkirk, but as he had mining interests in Barker Creek which he planned to attend to personally in the spring, he resigned from the service in preference to going to Selkirk. He intended to go directly to Barker, but a few days later Mickie left for Coffee Creek and Waldron persuaded Mr. Aish to spend the winter with us. This was an excellent arrangement from our point of view. Between them they would do the team work and run the store, which left me with only my housework to do. I was practically a lady of leisure, but it was too good to last. We had often been urged to furnish roadhouse accommodations to customers coming from a distance. Hitherto we had not done so, but early in the winter circumstances arose that made it necessary and so yet another branch was added to the business.

The winter passed much as others had done. Waldron did most of the work in the store and made several trips to the creek with freight. But in February he began to fail again, more rapidly this time. In March, after much argument, he was persuaded to make another attempt to consult Dr. Jones who had now returned from Europe. I insisted that, this time, he spare neither time, effort nor expense. And when in remonstrance he had asked, "How can we afford it?" I had answered, "If you can get help, the money will come from . . . somewhere."

Mr. Aish took him to Dawson with the team and he went on the stage from there to Whitehorse. They left on March seventeenth, 1911, and when the team and cutter had driven away with him I again turned to our empty house. How eloquently present the absent can be! Everything spoke his name and asked the question, "How will he come back?" But for the time being I was alone with all the work to do again, so I could not afford to allow my feelings full control.

The operator who succeeded Mr. Aish was a burly descendant of some son of the Emerald Isle, Jack O'Regan by name. In many ways he proved himself a rough diamond, possibly with slight emphasis on the rough. The day after Waldron left Stewart I had a visit from O'Regan. I had not slept the previous night and I had just lain down that afternoon to rest when the bell rang. I found O'Regan in the store and knew instantly that he "had something on his chest," to use his own words. Thumbs in suspenders, he paced the length of the store in a nervous manner, if anyone weighing two hundred and thirty-four pounds could be accused of exhibiting nervousness! Then he wheeled and shot these words at me, "Mrs. Smythe. I don't know anything about your cirumstances. They're none of my business an' I'm given you no chance to tell me so. But I've something to say an' I'm going to say it. See?"

"I'm willing to listen to whatever is proper for me to hear," I told him. I was determined to remain non-committal.

"Well," he went on, his head on one side and looking at me over his glasses, "I do know you are left alone here. Mr. Smythe is laid aside, perhaps for good—who knows? I've sisters of my own and I'm talking to you like I hope Mr. Smythe would talk to them if things were opposite. I have a few thousand saved up and I think you know pretty well what my salary is. If you need any of it—or all of it—it's yours for the asking."

He paused and I waited, with a lump in my throat, for him to finish.

"That's all!" he added lamely. "And now, tell me to mind my own damn business!"

He gave me an embarrassed little laugh and—did I see a tear glisten behind the gold rims of his glasses? Perhaps I only imagined it, but I am not ashamed to say the tears were very near my own eyes and my voice was husky as I tried to answer steadily.

"Thank you! At present there is no occasion to take advantage of your kindness, but should the need arise I will remember what you have said."

"Then," he snapped, "let it go as it looks!"

The next minute he was gone.

After Mr. Aish returned from Dawson he worked almost night and day to get the spring work finished before leaving for Barker. He was anxious to be there when the spring opened up so, instead of waiting until the steamers ran, he would pole his way up in a canoe. The ice ran very quietly during the afternoon of May nineteenth and on a fine sunny morning a couple of days later, when he considered the shore clear of ice, Mr. Aish started. As I watched him carry the things he was to take with him to the canoe, I felt as though I were being abandoned utterly. He was a quiet man of few words, but his hand trembled slightly as he said in his smooth firm voice, "Good luck! Keep up your courage! You know where to find me, if I'm needed."

Then he stepped into the canoe, pushed off, and set his pole for the day's work. I stood on the bank for a long time, watching the rhythmic swaying of his tall figure as he worked his way upstream. I can still close my eyes and see the flash of the sunlight on the wet pole.

Now, as never before, I was on my own.

Indian Trader

By the first boat, I was expecting the arrival of Mrs. Oker to help me. We had met her husband and herself at several parties on the creeks and, on his death, she had gone outside. But no real sourdough is content anywhere else and Mrs. Oker longed for the Yukon. She failed to arrive when I expected her, but I was indeed glad to see her step off a steamer about the middle of June.

She was slender, dark-eyed, with black hair, straight as a rush, and radiating energy and animation. The time spent outside had actually improved her appearance as she looked several years younger. I am doubtful if she ever ceased to grieve for Mr. Oker but she had become accustomed to being without him. There was much to be told of what had happened since we had met and in a short time I found myself laughing as I had not done for months. The era of short skirts, low necks, and short sleeves was just beginning to dawn but had not yet reached the Yukon. Coming from outside, Mrs. Oker had some dresses of the latest style and, donning one of these, she went to visit Mrs. Shand. The old lady eyed the innovation in disapproving silence awhile until finally her thirst for information got the better of her.

"Is that the latest?" she asked, pointing to the abbreviated garment.

"Yes," Mrs. Oker answered. "How do you like it?"

"O-o-h!" came the answer, in a delightful Scottish drawl. "I thought that ye had on your bathing suit!"

Mrs. Oker told me of the incident later, amid peals of laughter. "Perhaps that will hold you for a while!" I teased her.

Business at Stewart still came ahead by leaps and bounds that summer. Mr. Neill increased his woodcutting operations and this meant the employment of more men. In addition to his activities there were a number of individual camps located in the vicinity of the village and it all had the effect of stimulating business in both store and roadhouse. Although she had no previous experience, Mrs. Oker proved an ideal hostess. She went to great pains to make people feel comfortably at home and under our combined efforts things developed very satisfactorily. We rarely talked of the shadow that hung over me, but I knew that from the depths of her own experience she thoroughly sympathized with me. She and her guitar helped to chase away many a bad attack of the mullygrubs.

Word came from Waldron that the verdict of the great Dr. Jones was definitely discouraging; that branch of science could to nothing for him. But shortly after this I had a letter from his sister saying that he had consented to going east to take osteopathic treatment from his brother in Haverhill, Massachusetts. The next mail brought me a letter from Waldron, written just before leaving Vancouver. So by the time this letter reached me he was already in Massachusetts. How far away he seemed and how much could happen before I could reach him! But these were corroding thoughts and I fought them resolutely.

During the early summer some of the Indians from Selkirk came to Stewart to work and I found there was something more for me to learn. I had never had any experience in dealing with Indians and I was not long in realizing that I was never intended, by either ability or inclination, to be an Indian trader. In many respects I found them much like children and dealing with them required a great deal of patience. They were a shiftless lot with no appreciation of time or the importance of getting a thing done. At times they would come to the store and, after standing around jabbering half the afternoon, go away without having asked for a thing. In the meantime something of importance to me was lying undone. At other times they would have an orgy of buying until every cent they had on them was spent, usually for things that were utterly useless to them. Possessed of the curiosity of magpies, if allowed to do so they would swarm all over the place and one day when a squaw had gone to the kitchen for a drink she spied a toothbrush.

"What him?" she asked. They have only one gender. Then, when its use had been explained she wanted to buy it immediately. "You sellum?"

Being refused, she returned to the store and after more jabbering with her companions the whole stock of toothbrushes was purchased and they departed, quite happy. I often wondered what became of those toothbrushes. Indian teeth worth brushing were none too plentiful.

Another afternoon the squaws came to the shop en masse. I had turned to take something from the shelves and heard a strange gutteral noise from one of them, followed by a sound of scurrying, and then the door opened. When I turned around, a young Indian stood in the middle of the floor, but the squaws had disappeared. He bought some trifle, then went out. But, where were the squaws?

I went to the kitchen, where I found two of them huddled in a corner with stark terror written on their faces. A visit to the Post Office located another, a couple more were found in the storeroom, but there were still two to be accounted for. I looked into my bedroom which, for convenience in handling mail from the steamers at night, opened off the store but I failed to find them there. Again I made the rounds without success until I looked under my bed. There I found two of the most terrified creatures I ever saw!

"Come out of there at once!" I ordered and they crawled forth, clutching their bundles in their arms, to join the babbling group in the store. "What matter you?" I asked, reverting to their own dialect in order to be understood more readily.

With staring eyes and open mouths they all stammered at once: "B-b-billy B-b-bim, he-he come!"

"Well, what matter him?" I demanded.

"Him bad Injun! Him bad, bad! You no fright him?"

"No," I told them. "I no fright Billy Bim."

Again the whites of their eyes appeared. They seemed very much surprised that I was not. He must, however, have in truth been a bad Indian for some days later he and another Indian named Bobby came to the store together. They were both about half drunk and Bobby was careful to keep between Billy and me until he had a chance to assure me that he was there to protect me. "You no fright him. Me here. I no let him hurt. You all same Mission Man's girl!" This was a very high compliment in their eyes as a Mission Man's girl—either wife or daughter—was almost sacred. But I fear poor Bobby's protection was more intentional than real, he being so drunk that he was obliged to hold to the counter to steady himself.

This and other incidents taught me that while I had no liking for dealing with them, from their point of view I was not altogether a failure. Several of the more thrifty formed the habit of leaving their money with me for safe keeping and one of the squaws, much to Mrs. Oker's amusement, taught her little papoose to call me Auntie Smythe. What a dear little thing it was, too—when its face was clean!—with its round copper-colored countenance, straight black hair and beady eyes. I always felt a desire to preserve it in alcohol, just as it was.

I also found that they, too, had their human side and was quite touched when one of the squaws tried to express her sympathy for me.

"Your man sick. Maybe him die. Me sorry. All same Albert (her husband). Him sick, me hurt here," laying her hand on her heart.

After all, we were sisters under the skin.

Towards midsummer a letter came from Waldron at Haverhill. He had gone with his brother to consult specialists in Boston, Lynn, Haverhill and other towns throughout Massachusetts, but in each case the verdict repeated what we had already been told. However, his brother was still optimistic about osteopathy and Waldron was taking treatment from him. About a month later another letter told me his brother was to be married and would move to Bremerton in Washington State to live, so Waldron was returning to Vancouver to continue the osteopathic treatment there. He seemed to be influenced chiefly by his relatives so I forebore making any suggestions. My job seemed to be to keep the home fires burning and have money forthcoming for expenses which were by no means light. I did feel, though, that there was time, money and effort wasted to no purpose. But later, when I learned that his mother was in Haverhill at the time, this feeling changed to one of thankfulness that he had made the trip. It was the last time they met.

One day in mid-July I was surprised to find Mr. Aish in the store. His health had broken down suddenly and he was going outside for treatment. He remained with us until some business matters were arranged and put his time to good purpose in going over the books and accounts for me and bringing them up to date. Besides, it was a great comfort to be able to talk things over with him. I had never realized what a tower of strength he had been, nor how much I had relied on his counsel. While he was at Barker Creek I always felt that he was within call. And now he, too, was going.

When the morning of his departure had come and the steamer was ready to cast off, he held out his hand in farewell and I almost made an exhibition of myself by breaking down completely. What a morsel that would have been for some of the chaff standing around! With that fine perception that never failed him, he flashed me a look of warning and his manner was cooly casual, but the clasp of his hand spoke volumes! I could not trust myself to watch the boat get under way, but instead found something to do at the rear of the store.

As summer wore away and the fall—and an election—drew near, business in both store and roadhouse was rushing. There were days when I could not afford the time to walk anywhere. I ran! We rose early and I worked late. Midnight often found me filling orders, packing goods or making up a mail sack. But I was thankful for the business as the money was sorely needed. And when at night I dropped into bed thoroughly exhausted, sleep came to the relief of my tired brain and body.

O'Regan brought me a telegram one afternoon and I knew instantly there was more to follow from him. Also that he would tell it when and as it suited him. So I waited. Presently he struck his favorite attitude—feet wide apart, thumbs in suspenders, looking over his glasses—and asked in his staccato speech, "Mrs. Smythe, do you know the latest news?"

I looked at him in surpise. As a rule, news was scarce in our little village.

"Well," he went on, "I've just learned that the firm you've been buying goods from is closing down on you and everything you have is to be seized."

I knew this was his way and idea of doing me a good turn and was not resentful of what in another would have been rank presumption.

"I'm sorry that the wiseacres can find no better form of entertainment than discussing my affairs," I told him. "Why not try another card game instead and see whom they can fleece? Or are the lambs pretty well shorn? You might suggest that they possess their souls in patience. Time usually tells those things."

And he knew that he had been answered, in my way. Knowing him as I did there was no doubt in my mind that the conversation would be repeated verbatim to the right people.

Yet I was fully aware, too, there was some real fire behind the smoke. The reputation of Stewart as a business stand had become noised abroad and I began to hear rumors that I was to have opposition from one Rupe, who had been trading with the Indians in one of the more remote districts. The story was that he and Mr. Shand were going into partnership on a large scale, carrying everything from a needle to an anchor and including, of course, a large assortment of choice wines and liquors. In a small community almost any topic for conversation will suffice and this one did yeoman service.

I never quite understood just why, situated as I was, I should be considered legitimate prey, but there were times when one could hear the snap of slavering jaws. Scarcely a day went by that some kindly gossip-monger did not drop in to remind me of what danger the business was in. I confess that I myself had grave misgivings. There would be two perfectly healthy men, aided by the big drawing card hooch, to reckon with, while I was alone fending for an invalid husband. I could only do my utmost and trust for the rest.

In July Rupe and his half-breed daughter, Maggie, arrived. She was a bright, elfish, little thing of five or six and with her dark skin and unkempt appearance looked more like a little animal than a child. But after a trip to Dawson, where she was fitted out with the best of everything, she was hardly recognizable. Who says the clothes do not make the man! Soon after Rupe's arrival a great quantity of building material appeared and several men were put to work on the new store. There was great activity. Saws and hammers could be heard from early morning till late at night, while the partners strutted about, hands in pockets, superintending the work. This time, things were being done with some class. Mr. Rupe had made money with his Indian trading and did not mind people knowing he was ready to spend some of it. Looking back, our efforts seemed very puny and insignificant! Even before their building was completed a large stock of goods arrived from Vancouver. Our own outfit came about the same time and while I was engaged in the housing of it we had a visit from little Maggie. With childish curiosity she asked to be shown over the place and Mrs. Oker, very fond of children, took charge of her. The store was the last place visited and when she had eyed it all very thoroughly, she remarked, "You have a nice place here, but soon it ain't goin' to be a store."

"Is that so!" said Mrs. Oker. "Why not, dear?"

"Because my papa says he's going to do all the business and you'll have to get out."

Yes. Out of the mouths of babes there cometh other things than wisdom at times!

I was very glad when the goods were finally stored. The men I had to engage were unskilled at the work and I personally examined every article. I am doubtful if I was more tired at any time in my life than I was when the last item was checked off. A few mornings later I had a visit from Mr. Rupe himself. He was past middle age, had several very prominent gold teeth, and his skin on hands and face was roughened and tanned by weather and camp fires. He was quite corpulent and usually walked with his hands in his pockets, which helped considerably to display a massive gold chain and seal stretched across his waistcoat. His whole manner as he entered the store and stared at the people whom I was serving was one of pompousness. After scrutinizing everything within, he went out and made an appraising survey of the premises outside.

When the customers were leaving and I stood at the door chatting with them in the easy friendliness of the North, he returned from his tour of inspection. He approached me with quite a swaggering gait, giving his coat-tails an extra flip as he walked, and assumed a patronizing air.

"I suppose you don't want to sell?" he asked.

"I think not," I answered, meeting his stare with an impersonal look and trying to keep my voice steady. "At least, not just yet."

The fellow's manner was insolent in the extreme and I must confess that all the cattishness in me came seething to the surface. For a moment I wanted to forget all effort at being a lady and to spit and scratch—literally. I would . . . yes, I would! . . . have enjoyed spitting in his grinning face! But by supreme effort I controlled myself and my voice was as smooth as velvet.

"Well," he continued, "I just came down to tell you that if you're ready to get rid of the place, I'd buy it. Of course I don't need it, but if you want to quit I'll take it off your hands."

"You are very kind and I thank you." I told him, still managing to be unctuous. "Everything depends on Waldron's condition. If he recovers, of course we wouldn't think of making any change. If not—well, that is a question for the future."

Did he get the rebuke? I doubt it. But his manner was a trifle less self-assured as he went on.

"Well, if you get ready to quit, let me know."

"Thanks!" I answered, and this time my voice expressed all the contempt I felt.

When he had gone, I made my way to the kitchen where Mrs. Oker was busy. My hands were clenched until the nails bit into the flesh and my breath hissed through my nostrils. Her sharp eye caught the storm signals at once.

"What has happened to stir you up so?" she demanded.

The sound of her voice broke the tension and brought me back to earth. I laughed, but even to myself the sound was strident.

"And men talk about the huskies attacking each other when down! Bah!"

As the days went by a great bond of goodwill and affection developed between Mrs. Oker and myself. The fact that we were both alone seemed to draw us together and we would have fought for each other tooth and nail. There was a great similarity in our dispositions, but she lacked a fiery viciousness with which I had constantly to contend. Her cooler temperament often came to my rescue. Too, the strain of what I was enduring was beginning to tell and I think that she was once the means of saving me from manslaughter.

The saloon was behind it this time again, for with the increased activity around Stewart it was doing a land-office business. I concede to every man (or woman) the right to indulge in intoxication to his heart's content. Also, I claim the right of refusing to be annoyed by one in that condition. Waldron was perfectly in accord with me in this and our attitude was well known. Some voluntary advisers had informed me that it would be impossible to run a roadhouse unless we sold liquor.

"In that case," I answered, "there will be no roadhouse. There will be no drunkenness or social drinking in or about these premises. Nor will I tolerate the company of anyone under the influence of liquor."

One afternoon a fellow who had been drinking came to the store, made some purchases and went away, but soon returned. This time he did not ask for anything, simply stood around jabbering. I had work to do in the stockroom, so told him I was busy and if he wanted nothing more I would leave him and continue my work. He became impudent.

"I know," he growled, "I'm not wanted here. When I've spent my money I'm supposed to get out."

"I never encourage loitering," I agreed, "especially by those who are drunk."

"I'm not drunk!" he snarled.

"We'll not argue that point. If you've got what you wanted, I'll thank you to leave."

He went out muttering to himself and I returned to the stockroom. After a time I went to the kitchen and found him annoying Mrs. Oker by insisting on trying to sing to her. I had had a hard day thus far, I was tired, and his persistence frayed my nerves.

"Why are you here?" I demanded. "Didn't I tell you you're not wanted when you're drunk?"

"I'll come here when I like, drunk or sober," he retorted truculently.

Mrs. Oker looked frightened and I was not overconfident myself, but I determined to remain master of the situation if possible.

"I want you to go about your business," I told him again.

"I won't! And I'll show you I'll do as I like!"

He made a step in Mrs. Oker's direction and I never knew just what happened next; whether he went to take hold of her and stumbled or whether in his drunkenness he merely staggered. But he lurched against her and the next moment was sprawled on the floor. In a flash my temper was out of control. If I must protect myself and her from this kind of thing, I would do it—thoroughly! With one leap I reached the broomhandle and wielded it with all my might, regardless of where the blows fell. I heard one landing on his head and was coming again (for the moment I was demented) when Mrs. Oker caught my arm.

"Stop, Mrs. Smythe!" she screamed. "You might kill him!"

"I wouldn't care if I did!" I barked. And at the time I meant it.

"But, think what it would mean!" she cried.

I threw open the door. "Get up and get out!" I ordered. "And be thankful you're alive to do so!"

He staggered to his feet and just then a customer on his way to the store came to learn what the trouble was. No explanation was necessary. The scene spoke for itself. "Get out of here," he told the culprit and took him by the collar.

Mrs. Oker was much concerned. "Your temper will get you into trouble some day." she warned me.

"Well, I don't expect to have any more trouble from him at least." I answered grimly. And I never did.

That was not the only time I came to grips over the liquor question. Near the end of the season a boat landed one evening with mail and freight and while the latter was being unloaded a number of passengers came to the store for cigarettes. The majority of the residents had come for their mail, so there was quite a crowd gathered in the building. Mrs. Oker was serving in the store and I had just finished sorting the mail, when the door opened and the two leading saloon touts entered. They were both pretty drunk and one carried a well-finished bottle of whisky. He invited the first man he met to have a drink and the effect on the crowd was like an electric shock. My attitude was known, of course, to all and instantly every eye was focused on me while in every face there flared an interrogation point. What would I do?

I realized at once that this was a deliberate affront, a test. I was on trial before the whole community and if this attempt at defiance was successful my life henceforth would be a misery. The room was tense as everyone waited. Then I walked over to the drunken lout.

"Please put that bottle out of sight," I asked quietly.

He ignored me and offered another fellow a drink, which was refused. I spoke again, a little more sharply.

"Drinking is against the rules of this place. Put that bottle out of sight."

He laughed sneeringly and offered the bottle to his partner, who took a drink.

"Are you two crazy?" asked one of the men sitting near.

I turned to him. "Thank you, Mr. Graham, but I think it will be better for me to handle this myself." And to the other, "Are you going to put that bottle out of sight, or are you not?"

I had no idea how the matter would end, but was determined to come off victorious somehow. The fellow gave me a defiant look and placed the bottle on the counter, then turned to me with a leer.

"I'll put it up, but not out of sight!"

This was my chance and I took it. I seized the bottle, opened the door, and hurled it as far as I could—and was much gratified to hear it smash to fragments on the beach.

"Now you follow the bottle!"

Then the accomplice became ugly. "If you throw the bottle out, you may as well throw me out, too," he said impudently.

Either one could have broken me like a bit of matchwood. But the drop of fighting blood that has come to me through the generations from the family of General Wolfe was up in arms.

"If you give me any lip, I'll do that!" I snapped savagely.

By this time my action was having its effect. As the bottle left my hand the ringleader had dropped into a chair, pale to the lips. He now rose, perfectly sober.

"That's enough, Joe!" he cried. "Mrs. Smythe is perfectly right. I shouldn't have done what I did." Then, to me, "I'm sorry. I was drunk, but that is no excuse and I frankly apologize before all hands here."

Together the two left the building. Not a word was spoken by any of the others and in a twinkle the store was empty.

Later, Mrs. Oker teased me about it. "Do you realize," she asked, "that the bottle was almost as big as you are?"

For myself, I thought that I had surely traveled a long way since that morning a few years before when I had landed here a timid girl. It would take more than the howl of a huskie now to faze me!

The Truth at Last

As the fall of 1911 drew near and the close of navigation was at hand, I felt very lonely. I dreaded the approach of winter with Waldron so far away. So much could happen in a short time and during those long, cold months ahead travel would be difficult. I had never yet had to see a winter through alone.

I, myself, made the usual business trip to Dawson in the latter part of September and renewed my friendship with Miss Geer. I had met this young friend at Shand's Christmas Party in 1909 when she was working on Barker Creek. Since then she had become the accountant for a large firm in Dawson and I had seen her there on several visits. Now I was just in time to see her before she left for a visit to her old home in the State of Washington. I noticed the attention paid her by Albert Pinska, one of the dry goods merchants. My liking for her grew hourly and I hated to say good-bye, but she assured me with a sly smile that she would be back before navigation opened, so I was not surprised to see Mr. Pinska's name on the passenger list on one of the first outgoing stages, nor when—sometime in the winter—he brought her back a bride.

After my return from Dawson, O'Regan came in one morning accompanied by a young man whom he introduced as Mr. DeWitt, the new operator at Coffee Creek. Then he added, with a laugh, "A cheechako, Mrs. Smythe, and green at that!" But the other only smiled—wistfully, I thought. They offered a striking contrast. O'Regan was corpulent, florid, baldheaded, and garrulous. Mr. DeWitt was small and retiring; had heavy, wavy, black hair, blue eyes and dark lashes, and his face was pale to the point of being colorless. I invited them back to dinner at six and they accepted. The result was a very pleasant evening, with other neighbors coming in as well, and when the music and fun were over the stranger admitted it was the happiest hour he had spent for some time.

When the fall outfitting began a certain Harvey Smith applied for the job of driving the team. I knew him to be a good worker, particularly with horses, but in other ways I was not impressed in his favor. He had the common failing, drink, but there was no one else available just then and he was put to work. I soon found that in point of breeding and manners he was very different to Mickie. I could never feel the same confidence in him and I knew that he sensed and resented my distrust. On the other hand Mrs. Oker and he got along quite well and so things ran smoothly for a while.

The last mail by steamer brought word that instead of remaining in Vancouver, Waldron had gone to Bremerton to resume osteopathic treatment from his brother. It was a far from encouraging letter and, watching the boat make her way upstream, I found myself wondering what fate held for me before I would see her on the river again the following season.

When the river closed we welcomed some old friends back to Stewart, among them Mr. and Mrs. Hancock and our old comrade, Mickie. As the holiday season approached we learned that Mr. and Mrs. Shand would give a dinner and social evening on Christmas Day, so we issued no invitations for that date but arranged a short program for the following evening. It always interested me to know the faraway corners of the earth from which the lure of gold had drawn them all to the Yukon, and as I came to learn the story of many of the people I met the feeling of wonder continually increased. This program was more or less casually arranged from among those who were, for the time being, present in Stewart and yet it represented a worldwide talent. Here it is, with the birthplaces of those participating:

Music:
    Mrs. Oker, Montana, U.S.A. (guitar)
    Ed Holmberg, Sweden (violin)

Stump Speech:
    Samuel Fry, Philadelphia, U.S.A.

Sword Dance & Highland Fling:
    Jack Gilroy, Australia

Song:
    Mrs. Waldron Smythe, New Brunswick, Canada

Reading:
    William Middleton, Aberdeen, Scotland

Club Swinging:
    Fred Kennedy, Prince Edward Island, Canada

Male Quartet:
    Ed Lindbeck, Finland (Tenor)
    Carl Smith, Washington, U.S.A. (Baritone)
    Andrew Norman, Sweden (Bass)
    W. Hancock, New Brunswick, Canada (Bass)

Reading:
    J. Lawrence, Montreal, Canada

Song:
    Fred Bastin, New Zealand

Song:
    J. Verhelst, Belgium

Monologue:
    Mark Antony's Address to the Romans

The last item on the program was the surprise of the evening. It was given by a man in overalls which were far from new and being a newcomer his name was not on the list. Wishing to make him feel at home, I asked him to contribute something. After apologizing for being unprepared he offered to give us this bit of Shakespeare and began. For the next few minutes we sat spellbound. He had scarcely completed the first sentence before we realized that here was no buffoonery, but art. As the oration proceeded he lived the character he portrayed, his voice rang with power, his gestures were superb, and he finished in a hushed silence. One never knew (and in this instance we never did know) to whom one was speaking in that isolated community.

The drama of our lives at Stewart was not always on the Shakespearean level, however. On at least one occasion, romance called at the store. On this particular evening Mrs. Oker and I were enjoying the rare treat of a quiet bit of needlework, when we had a visit from O'Regan. Instead of using the store door, he presented himself this time at the front entrance to the house, thus signifying to all that he had come to visit and not to purchase. He was more carefully groomed than usual and had partaken of some Dutch courage. He refused the chair offered him and pranced around for some time before he was able to assume his favorite attitude directly in front of me.

"Mrs. Smythe!" said he, with his thumbs nearly bursting his suspenders. "I've come down this evening to declare myself!"

I looked up in surprise and met his glance over his gold rims. There was something on his chest this time, with a vengeance!

"Yes," he went on, "I'm going to tell you just where I stand. I don't want you to think I'm trying to double-cross you, or anything like that. I'm perfectly open and aboveboard. In a question of this kind, I'm true blue. Anything I say, I'll stick to!"

Still I waited, wondering much. "Well," I suggested at last, "why not say it first and stick to it afterwards? I'm waiting."

"It's just this: I've made myself plain to you, but I don't know what she'll say. She may listen to me and she may not."

Now I began to suspect how the wind was blowing, but said nothing and Mrs. Oker went on with her needlework as though oblivious of the conversation. Finally, he burst out, "Yes, I'm here to declare myself. In short, I'm here to ask Mrs. Oker to marry me. I've a steady job and can take care of her. I know she isn't much on looks, but then I'm no beauty myself! So I'm here to offer myself, if she'll accept me."

What a bombshell! Had whirling dervishes appeared before me I should not have been more surprised. I gasped, then stole a look at Mrs. Oker. I saw her stiffen in her chair, her ears turned crimson, and then she rose. She gave me a look that said with perfect clarity, "You laugh and I'll brain you!" Then she swept from the room.

The deserted lover looked quite crestfallen for a moment, but his ardor was hard to dampen. "She didn't give me a chance to finish!" he complained.

By a great effort I maintained my gravity. "You had better let the matter drop now," I advised. "If you care to mention it again, do so directly to Mrs. Oker." I was by no means sure I could stand another shock like this one!

He gave me a keen look and then snapped: "I want something from the store."

We went in and he bought a large box of chocolates and handed it to me.

"Give this to Mrs. Oker, with my love. Tell her to put it under her pillow and dream of me."

What a dream he was! When I presented the gift and the message, I was peremptorily ordered out of the room. So I retreated hastily to the kitchen, where at last I could laugh in safety.

In many ways I had found Harvey Smith's work satisfactory and, while he had visited the saloon regularly, he had kept within moderation until well on in the winter. Then he appeared one morning much the worse for a free-for-all the night before. He had cuts about his face and was smeared with blood in a most disgusting way. Harry Nesbitt (brother of the notorious Evelyn Nesbitt Thaw) was with him.

Smith began in his best bull-in-a-shop manner. "There was a row at the saloon last night, Mrs. Smythe, and all hands turned on me."

Looking at him I felt both anger and aversion. "I'm glad to hear it," I informed him. "Had you gone to bed at a decent hour instead of going to the saloon, you wouldn't have been mixed up in any brawl. Now take yourself off and never show up here again in such a condition!"

"He mustn't go until I've dressed his cuts!" Mrs. Oker cried. But I was firm. "He's not fit for you to touch! He can go for treatment where he got his mauling. I am not going to be harassed by the overflow from a saloon!"

Nesbitt then offered to look after Smith if I gave him the materials, so I allowed him to take what he wanted from the store. Mrs. Oker was ashen.

"How can you be so hard-hearted!" she protested.

"Call it that, if you please. But if we begin to take care of cases like that, we'll be well occupied. And I don't propose that either of us will stoop to that!"

Soon afterwards, when the freighting to the creek had been finished, Smith decided to quit and to work for Mr. Neill. I was not sorry to see him leave.

About midwinter we had a visit from one of the traveling clergy and the vacant Police Barracks was fitted up for the purpose. There were quite a few who wished to attend such a service and we asked Mickie to encourage as many of the boys as possible to attend. He must have done his best, for when we arrived we found the place filled and everyone on his good behavior. The service was about half over when the door opened and a late arrival entered. My heart sank. It was too evident that he had visited the bar recently. Nothing could have excelled his jauntiness as he closed the door and greeted the minister with a cheery, "Good evening!" Then he started on his way to a seat and I held my breath, waiting to see what would happen next.

I had not long to wait. The floor sloped gently away from the door and it had lately been given a heavy coat of wax for dancing. He was wearing moccasins, rendered hard and slippery by the frost. Only a couple of steps had been taken when suddenly both feet shot from under him and he sailed along for about a yard on his back, feet elevated. Then he rose, nothing daunted. He merely regarded the minister with a look of surprise and exclaimed, "That G— d— floor is slippery!"

However, the service did continue and at the close of the sermon a generous collection was taken. The last hymn was sung, the minister raised his hand for the benediction, and we bowed our heads. Then, as the first words were uttered, an awful groan sounded just outside the door. The minister paused with hand uplifted and the congregation raised their heads. The groans continued. The minister lowered his hand and looked inquiringly at a couple of men in the front row who rose and slipped quietly out.

Presently one returned, with blanched face, and I heard the words, "Jack has taken carbolic acid!" In a moment pandemonium reigned. The people sprang to their feet. Chairs were pushed back. The minister started for the door but was stopped by one of the men. Then Mickie came to where Mrs. Oker and I were standing.

"I think you women had better go home," he advised, "This is a job for us men to handle."

So we left by the rear door. As we went I heard various emetics being recommended and, above all else, Mrs. Hancock's voice crying excitedly, "Be sure to tell them to hold his nose!"

Later, Mickie told us just what had happened. It seemed that Jack, a callow youth addicted to dime novels, had arrived in Stewart the previous afternoon from upriver. He had visited the bar too often for his own good and conceived the idea of breaking up the service in a truly Wild West fashion. He obtained some disinfectant containing a small percentage of carbolic acid and smeared it on his lips and clothing, pretending to have taken poison. So they made him pay for his practical joke in the Wild West fashion he seemed to like. He was compelled to swallow mustard and water, salt and water, warm milk, olive oil and the whites of eggs. Then he was rolled over a barrel until he confessed. Next morning the men suggested that the trail leading out of town was in good condition. They also hinted that some of the women were capable of wielding a blacksnake, while there were men who might enjoy sponsoring a flogging. So the misguided youth decided that discretion was the better part of valor. He left town that day and Stewart knew him no more.

Early in March something of a triumph came to me. Mr. Rupe suggested that I buy *him* out. His business venture had been anything but satisfactory and he was anxious to quit. After due consideration I decided against accepting his offer, so he disposed of part of his stock to Mr. Neill, shipped the rest to Dawson, and the store was closed. Soon after this he came to board with us and as I grew to know him better I found him to be a very generous and kindly nature. No doubt the circumstances had been misrepresented to him and he had been prejudiced against me.

I had now been alone for a whole year. Word came regularly from Waldron in Bremerton, but nothing definite regarding his condition. He was "feeling about the same" or "not quite so well today." So I waited, not daring to press for a specific report. One evening in early April I went for a short walk and found myself considering what I should do in the event of hearing that Waldron was much worse. Perhaps I was subconsciously expecting just that message. In any case, I was somewhat startled when, on my return, O'Regan handed me a familiar green envelope. "A telegram, Mrs. Smythe. Please sign."

Was it the dreaded message? But it proved to be only an order for goods for a party coming upriver, so I breathed freely again.

Yet as a matter of fact the blow was simply delayed. Our next mail brought two letters. One was from Waldron and contained information that could no longer be withheld from me. The disease had progressed until he was now practically a helpless invalid, no longer able to wait on himself. His brother wished some other arrangement made for his care since a rising young doctor could not give him the necessary time, and his wife's social duties prevented her from carrying out the agreement made when Waldron went to them. The latter piece of information surprised me since his care, up to a certain date, had been paid for in advance.

Waldron's sister, Mrs. Sanford Crowe, who lived in Vancouver, wrote the other letter and assured me that they would do all they could for him until I could make whatever arrangements I thought best; also, that in addition to osteopathy he had tried many other forms of healing, including hot sulphur baths, chiropractice, Christian Science and in fact everything that could be suggested. All had been without avail and we must now accept the inevitable.

Again, through the long hours of the night, I wrestled with a problem that seemed too large for me to cope with alone. What course could I take? On the other hand, this was the only home we had. If I brought him back, could I carry on and give him the care necessary in his condition? Human nature has it limitations. Even though my strength could stand the test how would he, in his helplessness, react to conditions such as I had been contending with for more than a year? Also, how long would I have Mrs. Oker's help and cooperation? Of late I had noticed a growing interest between her and Ed Lindbeck. Then, on the other hand, if I decided against bringing him back, the home must be sold and where would we go next? To take him to a new place among strangers and try to provide for both him and myself was unthinkable. Furthermore, I hated the thought of turning the home, crude and humble though it was, over to strangers. How eagerly we had planned and worked to rear it on virgin ground together! It was ours! Every nail, every mark of the axe or hammer was dear to me. I could not bear the thought of others in it.

As these and other questions crowded thick and fast upon me, I grew rebellious against the fate that had served us so cruelly. Were we not as deserving of our lives together as any others? But all this tumult of thought benefited me not a whit and morning found the matter still unsettled. Before the day was over I had decided that, if possible at all, I would go to Waldron and leave the final decision until after I had talked to him.

In order to do this there was much to arrange and very little time in which to do it, as I was afraid to delay the trip until the boats would run in dread of what might happen. In winter when the trails were good it was possible to reach the stage-line at any one of three different points, but at this season of the year the snow was gone, which left only one possible route, Pelly Crossing. This would mean one hundred and ten miles by dog team over the ice of the Yukon to Selkirk and then five miles up the Pelly to the stage-line. Even that route would not be possible much longer.

Mrs. Oker agreed to assume full charge and I hired a young Swede, Ed Holmberg, to remain with her while I was away. He had no previous experience, but he was quick to learn, industrious, and sober and I felt I was fortunate to get him. There still remained the means of travel to be provided. The place boasted only two dog teams. One belonged to Walter Street, an old Hudson Bay factor and famous dog-musher and now bartender at the saloon. The other belonged to Harvey Smith, who had worked for me the previous winter. I decided to try Street first.

The trip was certain to be a hard one. For years there had been none but local travel on the river in winter and very little of that. In some places there was no trail at all for a number of miles. Between Thistle Creek and Selkirk, over a hundred miles, there was no roadhouse or regular stopping place, neither were there any women living on the route, so I would be obliged to depend on the kindness and hospitality of the trappers and woodcutters located along the river. A chance musher had brought me a letter from Dawson DeWitt, the operator at Coffee Creek, who had heard I intended making the journey and offered accommodation while I was there. Thus the second night on the trail was already provided for; beyond that I must trust to luck.

Street was unable to give a definite reply until he asked Mr. Shand for leave of absence. The next day he informed me he was very sorry, but business at the bar required his presence and it would be impossible to get away.

"Why not get Harvey Smith?" he asked. "He has a good team."

I knew it was the only alternative, but—make the long trip with him?

"I don't want to go with him!" I blurted, gulping down the lump in my throat. Was I going to break down and blubber like a weakling?

To my surprise Street's manner became almost fatherly. "Listen to me, Mrs. Smythe," he urged. "I know that Smith, like a lot of us, is rough in his ways but he's a good fellow at heart. And he wants to take you. I've been talking to him and if you go with him you'll be all right."

I turned away sick at heart and when I reached home Smith was in the store. He came right to the point.

"I hear you want someone to take you to Selkirk," he began, "and I'm here to offer my services. I can start any day."

Still I hesitated, while his keen eyes searched my face. He sensed my reluctance and he met it bravely.

"I know you don't trust me and it's my own fault. When I worked here I wasn't what I should have been, especially under the circumstances. But I'm not altogether uncivilized and, if you say so, I'll get you there if it can be done!"

And so, after some further discussion, the matter was finally settled. I could find no other driver.

The few remaining details were soon arranged and Mrs. Oker was given some last instructions. My suitcase was packed. The sled was made ready for an early start and I went to bed, but not to sleep. During the hours of the night, I made that trip over and over again. One hundred and twenty miles over rotten ice by dog team, twice the distance by stage over wild country and across rivers no longer safe for man or beast, another hundred miles by train, and a four or five days' voyage by steamer. How long would it take and what would I find at its end?

Neither silence nor the stars blinking at me through the window answered the question. At grey dawn I rose to face the reality.

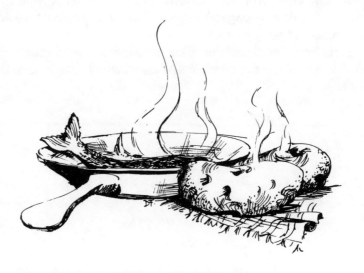

Rotten Ice

April eighteenth, 1912, dawned clear and bright at Stewart in the Yukon. Mrs. Oker prepared a particularly tempting breakfast, but I was too nervous to feel that I could ever eat or sleep again and it took me but a short time to be ready for the journey. Then the robes were arranged in the sled. My suitcase and the sack of dog feed were lashed in place. The dogs were hitched, Mrs. Oker and young Holmberg wished me luck, and with my heart in my mouth and a mist before my eyes I took my seat in the robes. The dogs, eager for the trail, strained at the tugs. Smith gave the handlebars a jerk to loosen the runners. He shouted, "Mush!" The dogs sprang at their collars and as the watchers waved we dashed down the bank and out on the ice of the river. We were away and the long trail lay before us.

I am a lover of the outdoors and as we sped along in the early morning light all nature was so peaceful that I wondered why the human heart should be in such a turmoil. The sun was just coming over the horizon and not a breath of wind was stirring. The sound of bells and the pat-pat-pat of the dogs' feet mingling with the zing of the steel-shod runners on the trail were a music all their own.

To Thistle Creek would be today's journey. By making an easy stage the first day the dogs would be gradually broken to what was to follow. In having an early start we had the benefit of the night's frost and arrived at Thistle about noon, before the trail had become softened by the sun.

We stayed at the roadhouse overnight, but drove down to the river again with the first rays of the rising sun. I had been to Thistle Creek many times with Waldron in the happy days gone by and knew the river thus far like a book, but beyond here all was new and strange to me.

About five miles from Thistle we met a musher. He carried the long pole that has proved a boon to many who take the risk of traveling on ice not known to be safe as, in case of breaking through, it is of great assistance in scrambling to safety. His carrying this told us at once that we might expect trouble ahead, so we asked him about the trail.

"There's a bad place a few miles ahead of you," he told us. "I got by safely and I think you'll be in time to cross while the frost holds, but you'd better hurry. And be careful—it's very bad! Take this pole. I'm going to Thistle and won't need it any more."

"Is there no way to get around the bad place?" I asked.

"Possibly, by crossing the river. It'll add eight miles to your journey. But I think you'll make it, if you hurry."

We thanked him and took his advice. I had no idea how good a judge of ice Smith was, but my various trips over it had not been in vain and I had learned to judge it fairly well by its color. We passed several places that I considered far from safe and I was just beginning to hope that one of them was the place referred to when there suddenly appeared ahead of us what I at once knew to be the danger-spot. On each side of the trail there was a yawning hole in which the boiling action of the current could be seen. Or it might be more correct to say there was a stretch of open water about one hundred and fifty feet in width and about twice the length of the team and sled, across which the old trail—packed hard and still frozen—hung like a narrow bridge.

Smith stopped the team and we both went ahead to investigate. It looked awesome. Although it was not in the main channel it took but a glance to tell that the water was both deep and swift. Even as we looked we would see the ice at the lower edge of the hole being eaten away by the current!

"What do you think is the best thing to do?" asked Smith as we looked at the trail.

I thought of the eight-mile detour and the probability of finding conditions just as bad, if not worse, elsewhere.

"I think we had better bring the team as near to the edge of the hole as safety will permit. Then you take the pole and cross alone. I'll take the handlebars and when you reach solid ice, call the dogs. I'll drive them at the same time and we'll try to make it on the run. In that way our weight will be equally distributed and we may get across before it has time to give way."

He grinned. "Just my own idea, but I didn't like to suggest it!"

He brought the dogs up, looked carefully to see that none of the harness was fouled, gave each one a pat on the head and then successfully made his way across the narrow bridge of ice. I was thankful to see him reach the other side in safety and wondered what my own luck would be.

I had adopted a short skirt and knickers for trail work so, throwing off my long outer coat, I took the handlebars. "Say when you're ready," Smith called and when I had again made sure that all the tugs were free I gave the signal. "Come, Busk! Come, Paddy! Come, Pardner!" he called and simultaneously I shouted, "Mush, Busk! Mush, Paddy! Mush, Pardner!"

In the next few flashing moments I again had cause to be thankful for my fleetness! The huskies leaped at their collars and with tails arched over their backs, yelping at every bound, tore across the narrow span like the wind. I clung desparately to the handlebars and raced behind the sled. About midway across the bridge I heard the ice crunch, felt it bend and give under our weight. But we made it and I took my seat in the sled, trembling in every nerve.

"Well, that's behind us!" I remarked to cover my nervousness as we got under way again.

"I'm not sorry," muttered Smith.

Several times during the day I turned sick as I felt the ice bending under me on that swift passage and Smith himself admitted that a cold sweat broke out on him when he saw it sag. Every instant he expected to see it give way and plunge us into the boiling current.

We reached Coffee Creek about three in the afternoon and the operator, Dawson DeWitt, met us at the bank. After showing me into the cabin and bidding me make myself at home, he went with Smith to stable the dogs. I learned that his lineman had been to Ballarat, some miles above Coffee, on the previous day so I asked about the trail ahead of us. His report was not very encouraging.

"I found open water in a number of places," he told us, "and you will likely have to detour pretty often to get around them."

Again we were early to bed. The cabin was a snug affair of three rooms and our host very kindly gave me his bed, which was in the office, and he and Smith occupied a couple of cots in the other rooms. He had gone to considerable pains to provide for our comfort, among other things replenishing the mattress for me with fragrant meadow hay. But his motive was far superior to his method. The hay had been stuffed in by armfuls and I was no sooner up on a hill than I was down again in a hollow! However, I slept fairly well, although several times during the night I wakened in terror, thinking I was falling into the icy waters of the river. Cowards die many times before their deaths, you know.

There was no frost that night and the next morning, shortly before day-break, we started with a warm breeze from the south in our faces and scattered raindrops falling. When I was in the sled, DeWitt brought out his fur-lined coat. "Some mornings will be chilly and this will be more protection that your own. Leave it at Whitehorse till you return, or express it from there." Then he handed me a letter. "You can open this letter. It contains a list of one or two errands I would be glad to have you do in Vancouver, if you have time."

A warm handclasp, the familiar command to the dogs, and we were away. The next two days were to prove one of those experiences one never forgets. The river is quite narrow at Coffee Creek, but a few miles above it widens out suddenly and before us lay a great expanse of dark, dirty, treacherous-looking ice over which we must pass. How small and insignificant the dog team and we two atoms of humanity looked on its broad surface. How quickly we could have dropped through the ice, leaving nothing but another gaping hole amid the Northern silence!

About one o'clock we came to a woodcutter's cabin. He was not at home but we took the sourdough's privilege of the trail and made tea and had our lunch, then continued our nerve-racking journey. Once, when we were traveling close to the shore and behind a bluff that curved sharply ahead, I called to Smith that I could hear the sound of open water.

"I think you're mistaken," he answered. "You likely hear the wind in the trees."

"Nevertheless, we'll stop and investigate," I insisted.

He stopped the dogs and went ahead—to find open water beyond the bluff, with at least a fifteen-mile current and a wide fissure extending a couple of hundred yards diagonally into the river! We were obliged to cross almost to the opposite bank and work our way beyond the fissure. This added several miles to the trip and delayed us a good deal, but that was a small consideration compared to what would have happened had I not heard the sound of the water in time.

As one danger-spot after another was passed, I clutched the sides of the sled and clenched my teeth. Several times I wondered where and how we would pass the night. But at four o'clock and about thirty miles from Coffee Creek we came to the cabin of Mr. Blanchard, another woodcutter. The dogs, Smith, and myself were about all in, so we did not demur when Mr. Blanchard urged us to stay for the night. He bustled around and true to the spirit of the North soon had the best the place afforded in the way of food set before us. When we had disposed of this and were somewhat rested, he turned to me.

"I am going out to do some work and Smith is coming with me. If you want to rest, just take the corner bunk. the blankets were aired today and you'll find them quite fresh."

When they had gone I followed his suggestion and in my utter exhaustion I was soon dead to the world. The sun was quite low when I heard voices and, going to the door, I met the men coming in. Mr. Blanchard carried a dish of fresh grayling ready for the pan. This, I suppose was the work that he had had to do. The fish taken from the glacier-fed streams of the North are superior to those caught in other localities and a pan of grayling, caught in the spring when the winter diet has begun to pall, is something to tempt an epicure. I had not expected another meal that evening and when I saw preparations being made for one I offered to assist. But my services were waved aside so I decided upon a walk along the riverbank to exercise my muscles after the strain of the day. How good it was to feel the solid earth under my feet! I fancied the river had a sinister look, as though it had been cheated of its prey. I opened the letter from Dawson DeWitt and found, not only the list of errands, but a blank cheque and a note asking that in any "unforeseen contingency" I fill it up to the amount of his credit with the bank and use it as needed. "I do this," the note told me, "as I should like a favor done for my mother, were she alive and in your position." Surely, if the world held men of undesirable character it also held those of noble impulse.

Returning to the cabin, I was greeted by the smell of fried grayling and baked potatoes and instantly felt famished. I suddenly realized that so far on the trip I had really eaten very little, so I was prepared to do full justice to the meal and I did. Mr. Blanchard had no cause to complain. When the chores were finished we sat outside in the long Yukon twilight and talked of many things. I learned that our host had known Waldron for some years and was overjoyed to be able to help in our time of need.

While talking, my mind had been busy with the question of accommodation for the night. Although quite roomy, the cabin was a one-room affair and I could not see just how we were to manage. However, my being there was due to circumstance and not to my own choosing, so I decided to accept conditions as I found them and be thankful that I was not obliged to spend the night on the riverbank beside an open campfire. But I was soon to have demonstrated to me the fact that among the lessons the North teaches is a fine consideration for ladies. The atmosphere of crudity occasionally described in magazine articles is usually evolved in the fertile brain of some wandering would-be satirist or sensation-monger. Life at best in any pioneer country is fraught with hardship and unpleasantness, but were it not for those courageous souls who brave such a life, there would not later be the cushy jobs in towns and cities held by many a smug critic who would flounder and sink in the mire of his own weakness if thrown on his own resources.

When we rose and returned to the cabin, I brought in my own robes and arranged them in the bunk assigned to me. Then Smith called for hammer and nails and with a couple of pairs of blankets and some safety-pins (which I furnished) a snug little room was soon fashioned and placed at my disposal. I was given a candle and a basin of water ready for the morning and I retired feeling that I had accommodations fit for a princess.

Next day we were astir at dawn, only to find an overcast sky and the south wind still blowing. For a couple of miles the going was excellent. The snow had melted from the ice, which was clear and firm, the dogs trotted along as though enjoying the run.

But trouble soon began. When we reached the place where the ice had jammed in the autumn we found it piled into great mountains. In places it looked as though nature had thrown up a breastwork against some advancing foe and over and through this we made our way with never the sign of a trail to guide us. To make matters worse the snowfall had been much heavier here than in other places. This had been partially melted by the hot sun, and slush and water lay in puddles everywhere. Up one side of an ice hummock and down the other; around or over great cakes several feet high, piled on top of each other or standing on edge; skirting miniature lakes or floundering through them; the poor dogs struggled hour after hour. Then the clouds cleared away and the sun came out to add its heat to the suffocating wind, while the glare reflected from the snow and water was blinding. We had not traveled far under these conditions before the dogs and harness were dripping, and in his efforts to keep the sled on an even keel, Smith was soaked to the armpits. Several times I suggested getting out to walk but each time the suggestion was definitely waved aside.

"If the dogs can't pull the sled with you in it, they can't pull it empty," I was told. "You'd only be drenched for nothing!"

During that day I learned to know and appreciate the sagacity and endurance of the malemute dog. It was thrilling to watch the work of Busk, the leader. Carefully he picked his way among the rough and broken ice cakes, seeming to know by instinct where the best footing was to be found. Often he would stop, and unable to come to a decision himself, would look back to his master for the word of command. If this was not forthcoming, he gave a sharp little yelp of inquiry, as if to say, "Can't you tell me what to do?" Then, on the order being given, he took up his task and would gee, haw, or mush as directed. In the meantime Pardner, the wheel dog, struggled to control the nose of the sled and prevent it from running into a small crevasse or under a cake. He would scan every rough spot, then turn to look at the sled, and labor to avoid the danger. Sometimes he gauged the distance by a matter of inches. The two swing dogs had only to exert their strength in pulling the load. The whole group was a beautiful example of perfect teamwork.

We knew that somewhere near the mouth of the Selwyn there lived another woodcutter, Finlay Beaton, and about noon we saw the smoke from his chimney quite a distance ahead on the opposite side of the river. So it was still some time before we reached the cabin, having taken since before sunrise to travel thirteen miles. We must have presented a woeful spectacle as we climbed the bank. With all his efforts Smith had not succeeded in keeping the sled out of the water. Some of my clothing and parts of the robes were wet, Smith was soaked, and the dogs and harness were, of course, drenched. As soon as we reached the top of the bank the poor animals threw themselves down and lay with lolling tongues and heaving sides.

I had met Mr. Beaton several times and as he came from the cabin to greet us he looked with amazement at first one, then the other.

"Where in the world are you people going!" he exclaimed.

"Mrs. Smythe is on her way to Pelly to take the stage for Whitehorse," Smith answered and I caught the look that passed between them.

"Well, come in! Come in!" he urged. "I thought all travel on the river had stopped some time ago. It must be pretty bad in places. I'll put the kettle on first—you'll be needing a cup of tea—then get you some dry clothes, Harvey." He smiled when he looked at me. "Sorry I have nothing in line to offer you, Mrs. Smythe. You'll not be going any farther today?"

"Not if we can impose on you for the night," I answered.

"I'll be glad to have you, if you can put up with a bachelor's quarters. You see, I'm not used to having company, especially ladies, so you'll have to take things as you find them!"

So we did just as he asked and with dry clothes and a good meal, life became a lot brighter for all of us. I offered to clear the table but my help was refused again: in regard to work I was certainly getting off easily on this trip. Later, when Smith went out to help Mr. Beaton shoe his horse, I spread my robe on the bunk and was glad of the chance to rest. I must have slept for some time when the sound of my own name roused me. Then I heard Smith say, "Yes, I guess Smythe is pretty bad."

"Poor little thing!" the other sympathized, his voice revealing his feelings. "She has a hard trip ahead of her and she looks so frail, too!"

"She'll have no picnic, whichever way it goes," Smith agreed. Then they both fell silent.

The next time I awoke I smelled something very appetizing and came out to find a steaming supper waiting. Freshly cooked potatoes and fried grouse! People were not going to allow me to go hungry at any rate. The birds were delicious and we rose from the table ready to face the world!

Once more we were early to bed, hoping that in the morning we would find a frozen trail. This time our hopes were realized and at dawn we rose to find the ice an inch thick on a pail of water outside the door.

"You'll have no trouble between here and Selkirk," Mr. Beaton assured us. "After last night's frost everything will be frozen solid and you can easily follow the winter trail."

He was right, of course. In contrast to the treacherous rotten ice and rough, slushy going of the last two days we had a smooth and solid trail and the dogs trotted along at a steady pace. Our only drawback was that the sharp ice lacerated the pads of Pardner's feet and Smith had to stop and put on his moccasins. These are little round bags with a flat bottom, made of tanned moose or caribou and drawn over the dog's feet and tied around the ankles.

About ten in the morning we saw the buildings of Selkirk shining in the distance and I could scarcely believe we had come thirty miles in so short a time. Soon the fiendish bedlam of the Indian dogs reached our ears. They had sighted ours and I was afraid the half-starved creatures might tear them to pieces. We both walked up the bank ahead of the team to where a group of Indians and squaws were standing and among them I recognized some of my old acquaintances, including Alice who had taught her papoose to call me Auntie Smythe. A few guttural sounds from the Indians and their howling dogs slunk away. Then the squaws crowded around the sled, seemingly delighted to see me and much to the amusement of Smith.

"How you? Long time no seeum! Where you come? Where you go?" they cried. When I explained, "My man sick. I go him. Choo-choo!" they nodded in understanding.

Alice had disappeared but soon returned with an old Indian she introduced as "My papa, Chief Jackson." As I looked at him I recalled all I had read of the dignity of the Indian chief. Clear-eyed and straight as a rush he stood, staff in hand, while Alice performed the introductions, then he bowed, mumbled something in the native tongue, turned, and stalked back to his cabin. I never knew whether he approved of me or not, but am inclined to think it not very likely.

We now discovered that there was a big potlatch (the Indian equivalent of a party, and sometimes lasting for days or at least until the food and presents became exhausted) and they had at first taken us for some of the visiting Indians. Many and pressing were the invitations I received to join in the feasting and celebration.

"You come? Hi-yu grub! Hi-yu potlatch!" they urged.

But when I told them, "My man hi-yu sick. Me go quick!" they shook their heads and grunted sympathy. Remembering that their favorite potlatch menu included an unborn caribou calf stewed whole with tail, head, and entrails still attached, I was not sorry to have a good excuse for refusing. But I could have wished there was less truth in what I told them.

The telegraph office had no word for me from home but I asked the operator about the ice of the Pelly.

"Shaeffer, who runs the roadhouse at the Crossing, was down yesterday," he told us. "He reported open water in some places. I'd advise you to stay here till evening; then you'll get the benefit of the night's frost."

We did as he advised. Before leaving we got in touch with the roadhouse at Pelly Crossing by telephone and Shaeffer carefully instructed Smith as to the condition of the ice. Pardner's feet had become so sore that Smith left him at Selkirk in the care of Alice, who lent us one of her dogs to complete the team. After sunset we started on the last lap of that part of the journey; five miles up the Pelly to the Crossing. I was thinking how glad I should be when it was over and then remembered that Smith still had the return trip ahead of him over a trail growing worse every day.

We traveled about half the distance without incident. The dogs were trotting along briskly, Smith riding on the rear of the sled and adding his best effort at song to the music of the sleigh-bells, when suddenly—not fifty feet away and directly in our path—I saw a large stretch of open water. I knew instantly that it was not overflow as I could see the action of the current as it seethed in whirlpools, shimmering in the after glow.

"Whoa!" I shouted without waiting for any preliminaries, and the dogs stopped.

"What's the trouble?" Smith demanded.

"Open water ahead!"

"Can't be," he argued. "We are still on Shaeffer's trail."

"No, we left that a while ago," I told him.

"Then this must be the old trail, so we're still all right."

"I don't care what trail it is!" I maintained. "There's open water ahead!"

He retraced his way, to find that I was right. We had left the safe trail some distance behind.

"A close shave!" he admitted, veering to the right and my teeth chattered when I got a clearer view of the gaping hole.

From that moment I never ceased my careful watch of the trail ahead, nor relaxed a muscle till we pulled up to the Pelly Crossing roadhouse at eleven at night. We had made it again. Thus far—safe.

I Go Outside

We had known Mrs. Shaeffer in happier times and she was genuinely grieved to learn of Waldron's condition. There would be no stage for three days, so I was obliged to possess my soul in patience. Smith waited only a day to rest the dogs, then started back to Stewart. Mrs. Shaeffer did her best to make my stay with her comfortable and in reality I was glad of the rest before beginning the stage trip to Whitehorse. At that time of year it would be rough and tiresome as the snow was gone and wheels were being used. On the third afternoon, the stage, with its six weary horses, arrived and the river was crossed in safety much to the relief of all. It was an open four-wheeled carriage, the driver's seat being well up in front in the style of a tally-ho. The driver in this instance was a brawny Dutchman and the first question he asked, as he entered the room adjoining that where I was sitting, came booming through the open door.

"Any passengers?" he demanded.

"Yes," Mrs. Shaeffer answered. "One—a woman."

I knew by her voice that she expected an explosion and she was not disppointed.

"Well, I'll be damned!" he shouted, "What does any woman want to go traipsin' around the country for at this time of year? Don't people know we've enough trouble on our hands with six horses, the mail and the stage without taking care of any fool woman! Who is she, anyway?"

"Mrs. Smythe, from Stewart."

"Oh!" His voice held a world of relief. "That's different. I know her and she's a real old sourdough!"

It is very doubtful if I ever received a more sincere compliment. There was only one other passenger, a Mountie bound for Whitehorse, and when the stage was leaving at five the next morning, the driver asked me where I wanted to ride.

"I've never ridden in one of these stages before," I confessed, "so put me where I'll be the least trouble."

He gave me an odd look and hesitated a moment, then ventured with a grin.

"I guess you'll not be much trouble anywhere and if you're not nervous you'll find the seat beside me on the box the best place. But if you are nervous, you'd better get in the body of the rig."

"What is there to be nervous about?" I enquired. I wanted to know the worst before I started.

"Nothing, really," he answered. "But some parts of the trail are steep and rough. They look worse from the high seat in front, but that's where you'll get the best view."

"Then I'll ride there," I decided and he helped me up. When he had gone around the rig, Mrs. Shaeffer whispered, "Don't be nervous. He's the best driver on the route and he'll take good care of you. His bark is worse than his bite!"

The horses were brought out, fresh and mettlesome; the leaders rearing on their hind legs. When the driver was in his seat, reins in hand, the hostler jumped clear and we sped away, the heavy stage lurching and swaying from side to side. There was only a weekly service at this time of the year and the horses, idle for that length of time, were in fine fettle and even the lumbering stage seemed no hindrance to them. They raced over the rough and broken ground and I clung to my seat, heart in mouth, but a few miles sufficed to show that it was truly an expert who held the lines. He had the splendid animals under perfect control every moment and gradually I relaxed.

Late in the forenoon we came to the awesome Minto Bluffs.

"There are a few miles ahead where it might be better for you to walk," the driver suggested to me.

"Why so?"

"The trail skirts the bluff and it looks bad to a timid person. Most of the women and some of the men prefer to walk."

I remembered his reference to taking care of any fool woman and answered rather shortly, "I prefer to ride!"

"Good!" he exclaimed, "but don't look over the side too much. You might get dizzy."

In the hour following, I realized that fools do rush in where angels fear to tread, although angels might be all right around the bluffs. They could fly! In some places the trail had been hewn and blasted from a face of solid rock. It was little wider than the stage and as we rounded shoulders of mountains I wondered what would happen were we to meet a team coming in the opposite direction. On the left my eyes met the frowning face of the mountain, hung with great masses of rock which had, apparently, nothing to hold them in place. They appeared to be waiting until we were just below, when they would fall and crush us. I saw several great boulders already lying in the trail, proving that it did happen. On the right I saw nothing but a rocky, broken mountainside falling away in a sheer drop to the river, still wrapped in its winter ice, a white ribbon far below. As the horses swung around the bends with only the smallest margin between the wheels and the precipice, I grew dizzy and repented on my rashness.

"Frightened?" the driver enquired once and, prevaricator that I was, I answered—cheerily, I hoped, "Oh, no!"

At last the trail gradually descended to the level and at noon we reached Minto on the Yukon River. Here we picked up another lady passenger who was bound for Montague, a post further along the line. The day was beautifully fine and all afternoon we drove up hill and down dale over a road from which the stage raised a thick cloud of dust.

The sun was low when Yukon Crossing, where the stage-line crosses the river, was reached. The village was on the opposite side of the river—quite wide at that point—so the driver decided not to attempt the crossing with the stage. Horses and vehicle were left, the mail and express were taken over by hand-sled, and we walked. The telegraph operator and the stable-man had come to meet us, so we two ladies were sent on in their care. We were told to keep close behind them and step in their tracks as much as possible. Each carried the usual long pole for testing the ice and it was a wise precaution. Once when the operator, who acted as my bodyguard, brought his long pole down it went right through the ice. Had one of us stepped on that spot . . .

I was rather tired after the long hard ride of approximately fifty miles but after removing some of the dust of travel and having a good supper, I was quite prepared to join the friendly group around the fire.

We were up and away with fresh horses and another stage early on a second, fine, though chilly, morning. For the next twenty-five miles to Carmacks the trail runs parallel with the river and we could still see the white ribbon on our left. There was a bar at Carmacks and when I took my seat beside the driver after dinner I was alarmed to catch the smell of liquor from him. A sharp look also revealed an added glint in his eye. God help us, I thought, if the lines of those six fiery horses become tangled by a brain befuddled with alcohol. A few miles from the post he suggested that he demonstrate his expert horsemanship for my benefit, claiming that he could pick a fly off the ear of the near leader with the whip. I assured him that I had no doubt of his ability but was too much of a coward to have him prove it.

"Of course, I wouldn't like to frighten you," he soothed, "but I could do things with that whip!"

I felt sure that he spoke the truth, but the effect of the stuff soon began to wear away and I breathed normally once more.

At Carmacks the trail left the river and we traveled inland, reaching Montague (where the other lady passenger left us) that night.

The next two days were uneventful and had it not been for the nature of my mission I should have enjoyed them thoroughly. The road ran through rough country where the air was fragrant with the opening buds of spring. In the distance to the right we saw the mountains of the beautiful Kluane country, rising in their majesty into the fleecy clouds above. There was a mysterious other-worldly charm to this vision of beauty always abiding on our horizon, offering the secret refuge of the spirit which the soul in trouble is ever desiring. I longed to leave the familiar way and lose myself in the vastness of their towering strength. Above the call of the Yukon, the Kluane uplands have a voice of their own.

On the evening of the fourth day we came to the Takeena River and were again faced with the question, "Will it hold?" To protect the ice from the hot sun the trail had been covered with brush and trees, some of the latter quite sizeable. As at Yukon Crossing, the village was on the opposite bank. The driver asked through a megaphone about the ice but could get no definite assurance. After some consideration he decided to attempt the crossing with the rig and left the passengers the choice of remaining in it or getting across on foot. The two male passengers decided without any hesitation to walk, then the driver turned to me.

"If you stay with the rig, you'll be entirely responsible for your own safety," he warned. "If anything happens, I'll have all I can attend to and perhaps more!"

I looked at the brush. It would be a hard struggle on foot and the ice on either side was badly rotted by the sun.

"In for a dollar, in for a dime!" I decided recklessly. "If the horses go through I'll make the rest under my own steam."

So we started. As we left the bank the expressions on the two men's faces said quite plainly, "There's one born every minute!" And I was convinced of it myself as the horses floundered along. The stage rocked and swayed and lurched, sometimes almost upsetting altogether. I clutched the seat rail with both hands and hung on for dear life, wondering if we should ever reach the other bank. It looked now about a hundred miles away! Several times, as the stage careened, I left the seat entirely and only my grip on the rail prevented my being hurled into space—to fall amongst the brush or under the plunging horses.

But step by step they fought their way and reached the other side. As we left the brush behind the driver gave some attention to me for the first time. "Are you there?" he called.

"Present!" I snapped.

He laughed. "You'll do!" he declared and from a group of men on the bank I heard the exclamation, "Damned if there isn't a woman on board!"

Then I watched the others making their toilsome way across and have never decided which of us had the hardest time. This was the last stop before reaching Whitehorse. The last real danger-spot had been left behind and I went to bed with a thankful heart.

Mrs. Shaeffer's prediction had been fulfilled: the driver had indeed taken good care of me. At several roadhouses I had heard his order to "see that the little woman is well looked after; she's had a hard trip." So when we reached Whitehorse the next day I felt almost as though I were parting from an old friend. But in spite of his care of me I could not resist the temptation to let him know that I had overheard his opinion of any fool woman who went traipsin' around the country at this time of the year. He laughed rather sheepishly when I told him and admitted, "I know better now."

The trip had tired me but after dinner and a hot bath (what a luxury a bath-tub was after that journey!) I went to my room and slept soundly for hours. When I awakened I went to the telegraph office, hoping for a message from home, but as at Pelly Crossing only disappointment awaited me.

The train left for Skagway at nine the next morning and as I took my seat I felt transferred to a strange land. Even the whistle of the engine seemed like an echo from the past and as the train labored up the grade to The Summit my thoughts traveled backward. Many things had happened since, full of hope, we had made that trip together. How well I remembered seeing my first Mountie, standing in the snowstorm, his huskie at this heels.

In Skagway I stayed for two days at the Golden North Hotel, waiting for a steamer southward. While I was there, the hostess brought me the papers containing the detailed account of the sinking of the *Titanic*, news of which had reached us by wire just before I left Stewart. By a coincidence it was the *Princess May*, the same vessel that had been wrecked in Lynn Canal in 1910 with Waldron on board, on which I took passage. She had been salvaged and reconditioned and was apparently as good as new. The dismal weather continued during my stay and we went on board one evening with the barometer lower than at any previous sailing. So with the wreck of the *May* herself and other disasters along that coast before me, I sought my stateroom with a mind far from at rest.

The night proved that the barometer had not lied. When only a few hours out a hurricane of rain struck. The waves rose to mountain height and in them the vessel rolled and pitched and tossed with terrific violence. I had a stateroom forward, and off the observation room on the upper deck, and here I got the full benefit of the motion of the ship. As she rolled one way I was, to use an Irishism, lying in a standing position. The next minute, as she wallowed in the opposite direction, I clung to the bedclothes to keep fom falling—I was not sure whether it would be up or down! With every dip of the boat I could hear the waves dashing against the stateroom window. Hour after hour this continued and I lay in terror, expecting every moment to hear a crash as she struck a rock. It was a long, long night. Toward morning the storm eased a bit and a few battered fragments of passengers assembled at breakfast, where the captain informed us that it was "the dirtiest night I was ever out in." We believed him.

Sunday came while we were still en route. It was four weeks after the sinking of the *Titanic* and the Rt. Rev. I.O. Stringer, Bishop of Yukon, who was a passenger, held a service in the saloon as a memorial to those who had perished. A collection was taken for those who had been widowed or orphaned. It should have been generous for we had just had our own taste of what the sea could do if it liked.

At Prince Rupert I went ashore to send a wire to Mrs. Crowe, telling her when to expect me in Vancouver. Prince Rupert was then in the making and the whole scene was one of confusion and bustle. Literally hewn from the rock, the town consisted of a conglomeration of unfinished and finished buildings, with huge piles of material ready for the erection of others. Amongst this litter ran the broken spaces later to be streets and running parallel to them were rickety wooden sidewalks, in some places supported by wooden trestles several feet from the ground. On all sides I could hear sawing, hammering, and the occasional detonation of dynamite.

One afternoon the city of Vancouver appeared in the distance. As the *Princess May* slowly beat her way toward the dock, I stood at the rail idly watching the milling crowds. I felt afraid, aloof. After the quiet and the peace of the North how could I fit in with the vital, pulsing life of the growing West? Vancouver was now as foreign a shore to me as Stewart had been to the bride of nearly seven years before.

Coming Home

After staying a couple of days with Waldron's sister Jennie (not Mrs. Crowe, whom I was shocked to hear had died just two weeks previously) I left for Victoria. Jennie came with me and we arrived in British Columbia's beautiful capital city about noon. An electric car took us out to the hospital which stood on a hill, surrounded by shade trees alive with songbirds. The lawn was dotted with flowerbeds and patients were being wheeled among them, enjoying the sunshine. Leaving me seated on a bench, Jennie went to learn if one of them might be Waldron.

I was glad to sit down. I trembled like a leaf and there was a roaring in my ears. It seemed impossible that we were looking for Waldron, always so full of the joy of life, in this refuge for the sick and suffering. Jennie soon returned. Waldron was not feeling well and had not cared to be taken out. Then she left me again to prepare him for my arrival. She was gone a long time and her expression when she came back told me, in a measure, of the change I should find in him.

When we came to the door of the ward where he lay, she whispered, "The bed in the corner. The one reading the paper."

Then she left me. I took a few steps toward him, he lowered the paper, and my heart stood still. That pale, thin face with the burning eyes! That emaciated frame could not be Waldron! As I came slowly nearer and knew it was indeed he, I wanted to cry out again at the fate that had befallen us. To live out our own lives, to leave the world a little brighter in our corner for our having lived in it—we wanted nothing more! And now . . . this!

When we had both recovered our self-control, we talked. I found that Mr. Aish was working at Esquimalt, five miles away, and had visited Waldron several times. This was cheering news for I knew what those visits would mean to him. I told him of my trip and gave him as much of the Stewart news as I thought would not pain or worry him. I had always strictly kept from him anything of a disturbing nature, but in a pause in the conversation he gave me a piercing look and asked abruptly, "How is Rupe getting along?"

Surprised, I countered, "What do you know about Rupe?"

And he answered, with another sharp look, "Oh, I got more news from Stewart than you gave me."

Apparently my caution had gone for naught.

Jennie returned to Vancouver the next day. The same evening I telephoned to Mr. Aish from the hotel and he took the next car into town. His health had improved and he had much to tell of his movements, including a trip to his old home in England. It was a great comfort to be able to talk to him unreservedly of all I had gone through.

In the days that followed I tried a number of times to learn from Waldron what his wishes were in shaping our future course, but always I met with a noncommittal answer.

"You must do what you think best," he insisted. "The burden is now yours and you must assume it in your own way."

Finally, I appealed to Mr. Aish. "Smythe never told me in so many words what his wishes were, but I'm quite satisfied that he would prefer returning north to finish the journey," was his opinion.

A few days later I made another attempt with Waldron and received the same answer as before, so I announced that I should start preparations at once for returning north. Instantly his face lighted up and he was all smiles as he cried, "Yes, it will be nice to get home!"

From then I set my plans definitely on going north and when navigation on the Yukon had been reported open I was almost ready. The famous Dr. Jones granted me an interview, for I wanted to learn what phase the final stages of the disease would take. Other doctors had told me I was crazy to attempt caring for him and they had somewhat shaken my courage. When I entered the office his keen but kindly eyes lost no detail of my appearance and I am sure that my qualifications—mental, physical, and financial—were instantly and correctly tabulated. I put the matter simply and directly.

"Dr. Jones, I should like to get your opinion in regard to taking Mr. Smythe home to the North."

He continued to study me while he asked several questions. "You understand, I presume, that he will gradually grow worse until he becomes quite helpless? Do you think you can care for him in that condition? Can you provide what he needs and make him comfortable?"

There was a look of wonder in his face and that of the nurse when I said, "I think so." Perhaps they both thought that I was undertaking more than I realized. But only too well did I realize it.

"Is it his own wish?" was the next question.

"I believe so."

"Then take him, by all means! It is all that can be done for him."

He asked a few questions about my own health and I rose to leave; the time of a famous doctor is valuable. There was a great sympathy in his manner as, at parting, he took my hand in both of his.

The door closed and I walked down the corridor. "Keep up your courage! Keep up your courage!" My footsteps beat it out as I walked. God alone knew how hard I had been trying to keep it up—for years now!

When the evening of the departure arrived, Mr. Aish left the office early and came to the hospital to be of what assistance he could and I was glad that he did so, since Waldron was in a fretful mood. Although I had ordered the ambulance to come early it failed to arrive until half an hour past the time set. He claimed the nurses had been clumsy in dressing him and some of the personal belongings which he had brought to the hospital could not be found. This all tended to irritate him and Mr. Aish remarked sadly,

"I'm afraid you're going to have a handful!"

He rode with us to the dock where the steamer lay and when Waldron's wheelchair had been taken on board he carried him to it. Here again confusion greeted us. I had taken reservations on the *Princess Sophia*, scheduled to make her maiden voyage on that date, but at a late hour some alterations were made and we were to travel to Vancouver on the *Princess Adelaide* and transfer there to the *Sophia*. When I took Waldron to the stateroom I found it already occupied and neither purser nor head steward would be on board for hours. There was nothing to do but wait in the saloon until they came and the necessary readjustment could be made. Why such things never occur except when one is bearing unusual burdens has puzzled wiser heads than mine.

After making Waldron as comfortable as possible, Mr. Aish left. I went with him to the dock and there, with a warm handclasp and a further admonition to be of good cheer, he passed from our lives. The time dragged tediously. Waldron grew more fretful at every moment and it was with a thankful heart that I saw preparations for sailing get under way. Immediately on the purser's arrival our stateroom was arranged and I got Waldron tucked into bed. Then I went for a turn on deck to steady my nerves before turning in. Yes, I could see that I was going to have a handful.

We docked at Vancouver during the night, and in the morning, as soon as we had breakfasted, we transferred to the *Princess Sophia*, lying alongside. She was a beautiful craft, palatial compared to the *Princess May*. In the evening Jennie came to stay with Waldron, while Mr. Crowe, his family, and I went to the cemetery where Mrs. Crowe lay and I left a spray bearing Waldron's name on her resting place. Then Mr. Crowe insisted that we all go to the theater. "I want Emma's last evening with us to hold something pleasant for her to remember," he declared.

On my return to the steamer I found that many tokens of love and kindness had been sent to the stateroom. The boat was to sail at midnight and the relatives had come for a last word. We all tried to maintain a cheerful front, but when the moment of parting arrived it was with heavy hearts that we said good-bye. No hint of the fact had been given, but all knew that he and they would meet no more on earth. Before leaving, Mr. Crowe drew me aside and took my hands in his.

"I'm so glad you came out, Emma," he said in his deep voice. "I did think of insisting that Waldron come to us for the time left to him. We have a big house and Annie would have wished it. Now I realize he will be better with you in his own home. I want to say this: If ever the time comes when he needs anything which you cannot give him, let me know. Will you remember that?"

I tried to thank him, but failed, and he went on, "I know you want to care for him—I'd feel terrible if you did not—and my mind is at rest. But don't forget what I've said. Good luck. God bless you!"

His tall dignified figure went slowly down the gangplank.

During the run north the weather was warm, Waldron's nervous restlessness continued, and he required almost constant attention. On the second evening, during a short respite and suffering from a violent headache, I sought the coolness of the promenade deck. The captain, whom I recognized as having been a passenger of the *Princess May* when I came down from Skagway earlier in the season, was standing at the rail. Under the impression that he had met me previously in China and having seen me come on board with Waldron, he entered into conversation. He kindly enquired as to the service we were getting and assured me that anything on the boat was for our convenience.

"Ask for anything you need," he told me. "If you don't get it, let me know, and I shall see that you do."

But I had no cause for complaint. Every possible kindness was rendered to us throughout the trip. When I sent for the barber to shave Waldron and tendered payment, he shook his head.

"No, no!" he cried. "Surely I can do that much for one in his condition. How do I know I won't need the same myself sometime?"

These little kindnesses comforted and even inspired me more than those concerned could ever know.

We arrived in Skagway at evening. The train from Whitehorse would leave in the morning, so I asked permission to remain on board overnight and thus save the trouble of transferring uptown to a hotel. This was readily granted. Early the next morning I wakened to the dismal sound of heavy rain beating against our window and my heart sank as I thought of having Waldron transferred in that downpour. I rose immediately; the train would leave at nine and with my own preparations, Waldron to care for, and packing to do I should need all the time there was. I was but partially dressed when there was a rap at the stateroom door. The captain had come to tell me I need not hurry; he had learned that the train was to be run to the wharf and he was standing by to see that all our needs were met.

When I stepped from the stateroom, three stalwart lads stood at our service and Waldron, his chair, and our baggage were quickly transferred to the dock. The captain himself walked with us to the waiting train and held the umbrella to protect Waldron from the rain. When I tried to thank him he, too, bade me keep my courage and wished me luck.

On the train as on the steamer everything possible was done for us. When the stop for refreshments was made at Bennett and I hurried into the restaurant, I found that the conductor had already ordered our dinner and a waiter stood with the tray ready to take it to the car. Thus we were both able to have dinner. When I thanked the conductor, he explained, "I promised Captain Locke to see that you were taken care of and landed safely on the boat at Whitehorse."

At that town we found the steamer *Casca,* with Captain Bloomquist in command, ready to sail at midnight and when we got on board it seemed like being at home. The captain stood on the deck as Waldron was carried up and when I followed with cushions and steamer rug his round jovial face showed shocked amazement. He stopped me at once.

"That wasn't Mr. Smythe I saw carried on board, was it?" Being told that it was, he was all sympathy and repeated the words of Captain Locke. "Ask for whatever you want. If you don't get it, let me know."

This trip gave us even less need for complaint, for by now we were in our own North again.

At Yukon Crossing we reached the area which had been swept by a forest fire during my absence and from there to Stewart little could be seen but charred and blackened desolation. Yet it was but a picture of what lay in both our hearts.

The weather continued warm and as Waldron grew tired he became even more nervous and fretful, so I gave a sigh of thankfulness when, about midnight on the tenth day, I saw the buildings of Stewart appear in the distance. I had hoped that the lateness of the hour would prevent the usual crowd from gathering to see the steamer land, but was much disappointed to see the bank lined with people. Poor Waldron's face quivered pitiably as he was carried into the house.

It was a sad homecoming for both of us.

Yukon Crossing

In order to provide for Waldron's care and comfort, now that he was home again, several alterations were necessary and for several days I was kept busy attending to these. He wanted to sleep outdoors, so a comfortable table with a log foundation and a floor was prepared, his bed was moved out, and as long as the weather permitted he was carried to and from it. Also a special seat was prepared for the canoe and whenever he cared to do so he was taken for an outing on the river.

When all that was possible for his comfort had been provided I applied myself to the task of picking up the broken threads of the business. Mrs. Oker and Holmberg had both been faithful to their trust and I doubt if I could have done better in any way. I learned that on the return trip from Pelly Crossing, Smith had broken through repeatedly and several times he had had a narrow escape from losing his life, not to mention the dogs.

I also learned why I had been unable to get any message by telegraph during my journey. Shortly after I left, O'Regan had, to use a colloquial expression, "fallen off the water-wagon." He had renewed his old association with John Barleycorn to the extent of neglecting his office duties entirely. After repeated remonstrances and warnings from his superiors he had finally been dismissed. He was now in Dawson and the operator from Ogilvie was substituting, pending the appointment of a successor.

The country for miles around had been swept by the fire and Stewart Island alone remained untouched. This was no doubt due to the width of the sloughs surrounding it. At one time the inhabitants had their belongings packed and stood ready to vacate had the wind altered.

Shortly after our own arrival the shipment of goods which I had ordered while in Vancouver followed us and the housing and storing of them was added to other things. Under the strain of his enforced inactivity and his helplessness Waldron's irritability increased. On some days he was rather cheerful and took a great interest in what was being done. He would have his chair wheeled to the spot of activity and his comments and suggestions were usually very helpful. But at other times nothing suited him and I was often in despair. Everything possible under the existing conditions was done for him, but to one of his active energetic nature it must have been torture to sit passive while the things in which he was interested and which he would have enjoyed doing himself were done, or half-done, by others. I think if I could have devoted myself exclusively to him he might have found the time less dreary, but the business required my very best efforts and he was obliged to spend much of the time alone.

About midsummer he suggested that I ask my sister Ruby (Mrs. Morris, living in Maine) to come to us for the winter, which I did. In the shortest possible time we received an answer saying she was just convalescing from a severe illness, but as soon as the doctor would let her make the journey she would be with us. This was good news to me. She had always been a favorite with Waldron and while I felt rather guilty in asking her to come to conditions such as existed there, I hoped that her companionship would do us both good. And I salved my conscience with the knowledge that I was doing it for his sake, for he, on his part, looked eagerly forward to her arrival.

When you are bearing one heavy burden, others always seem to be piled upon you. Perhaps they are merely felt more keenly. In any case I found it increasingly difficult to shield Waldron from worries and annoyances. For one thing, there was no policeman regularly stationed at Stewart and the saloon was in the full tide of prosperity. In spite of my best efforts Waldron was occasionally troubled by its patrons. Financially, our business began to react to the effects of the fire. With the results of their winter's work destroyed many of our customers looked for an extension of time in meeting their bills—although most of them appeared to have money to spend freely at the saloon. I tried to keep this situation from Waldron, too, as much as I could.

With my efforts to stand between him and drunken men, trying to collect bills from those who claimed they had no money with which to pay, satisfying exacting customers in both store and roadhouse, as well as attending to all the minor details of the business, my strength and patience were taxed to the utmost and at times I exhibited anything but an angelic disposition. For myself, I prayed only for strength to carry on while he needed me. Beyond that I never allowed my thoughts to travel.

In August the superintendent of telegraphs from Whitehorse made a tour of inspection of the offices along the line. Dawson DeWitt made a personal application to be transferred from Coffee Creek to Stewart and the change was made immediately. I was glad of this arrangement. His quiet air of friendliness had always inspired me with confidence and his coming gave me an assured feeling that in case of need I would have someone to whom I could turn for help.

My loneliness had indeed been increased by a change in the attitude of Mrs. Oker. I never knew why, for to my knowledge I had always treated her the same. She was perhaps influenced by Ed Lindbeck, whose attentions were now quite marked. Whatever the reason, the old feeling of camaraderie was gone and it left an added need for friendship and support.

The saloon was always my chief thorn-in-the-flesh. Its fortunes were varied but usually triumphant. Following a report on conditions it was refused renewal of license. A paper, signed by the great majority in and near Stewart and by many who had never set foot there, was instrumental in overcoming this difficulty. After this triumph they threw caution to the winds and Stewart became a veritable hellhole. At any time of the day or night I was obliged to rise and refuse admittance to drunken, truculent Indians. Bloody noses, and cut and bruised faces, became the order of the day.

Finally, in desperation, I did for Waldron's sake what I had never done for my own, and appealed for protection. I wrote to the Commissioner and asked that, if it could or would not be done for decency's sake, then for God's sake and the sake of humanity, some arrangement be made whereby a helpless invalid might be spared such treatment. Otherwise, I was prepared to take the law into my own hands and if at any time some drunken brute who sought to annoy us met a bullet or a charge of buckshot, I should not hold myself responsible. So once more there was a policeman stationed at Stewart for the winter months.

Ruby arrived in September, to my great delight. She was very shocked to learn under what conditions I was struggling and marveled that I should continue so to struggle. She brought me a message from Father urging me to abandon the North and bring Waldron to the old home, where I should be given help in caring for him. But at this suggestion he shook his head.

Soon after Ruby's arrival Mrs. Oker announced that she intended making a trip to Dawson and might remain for a week or two for medical attention. "You will be returning to Stewart?" I suggested, but her answer was evasive and after assuring her there would always be a home for her with me should the need for it ever arise, I dropped the subject. She and Lindbeck left for Dawson the next morning in a small boat and she appeared quite broken up at leaving. Two days later I received a wire asking me to forward her belongings to Dawson and shortly afterward I heard that she and Lindbeck had been married. I saw her only once again.

Holmberg also left us to seek work in Dawson and in his place we now had Amos Noyd, "Big Amos." The sobriquet suited him. He weighed well over two hundred, with not an ounce of superfluous flesh on him, and his heart was as big, figuratively, as his body. He soon won Waldron's heart, to whom he was always gentleness and kindness itself. To watch that great brawny man lift and handle him with the tenderness of a mother for her child was more than touching. But he had the common failing of so many. When he took the inclination to have a "bust," nothing could stop him! So after a while I grew to regard it as a necessary evil and usually hired a substitute to fill his place until the jamboree was over. I did, however, make it plain that at such times he was expected to absent himself from the place and he usually respected my wishes.

When the subject of replacing Mrs. Oker was mentioned, Ruby would have none of it.

"Indeed, no!" she declared. "Your expenses have been, and still are, heavy enough. I think that between us we can handle the situation."

Although general conditions were very different from those to which she had been accustomed, she applied herself wholeheartedly to the task and soon she was working away like a veteran. She was fascinated, though awed, by the spirit of the country.

"It's glorious!" she cried. "But oh, so cruel! Take yourself, for instance. I find it hard to realize that anyone as fastidious as you once were could live this life!"

I began to wonder just what changes the country had wrought in me. Were they creditable or otherwise?

At Christmas we gave a dinner, to which about forty sat down. In his wheelchair Waldron took his place at the head of the table and, although unable to join in the conversation, he enjoyed the fun and merriment. And more than one remarked how well The Boss looked. I had not found the actual care of him as hard as I had feared. Almost instinctively I sensed the easiest way to handle him and I was much relieved when I found that I could carry him from the bed to his chair. From that particular angle his helplessness had worried me a lot. In the course of the work Amos was often absent from the house for hours and I often wondered what I could do in case of fire. So one day, when I had dressed him and Amos was not at hand, I insisted jokingly that he let me make the attempt and at last he yielded. I succeeded in getting him into my arms and was about halfway to the chair when Amos came in. It gave him quite a surprise.

"Well, well!" he exclaimed. "I've heard of a cat lugging a kitten, but that's a kitten lugging a cat!"

In the general laugh that followed I narrowly escaped dropping my burden. But after that, one source of worry was removed.

The matter of his shaving also gave me a hard struggle. While Holmberg was with us he did it but when he had gone Waldron refused to allow anyone except me to attempt it. I had always stood in wholesome awe of that tricky weapon, but Waldron insisted. The result of my first attempt was decidedly ludicrous. Each time the razor started to cut the beard I imagined the skin was coming too and eased my pressure on it. His face looked as though the beard had been dubbed off with an adze! When I gave him a mirror to see the effect he laughed until I feared he might strangle. "You will do better next time," he assured me and to please him I persevered, although for a long time each attempt left me bathed in perspiration. Eventually I grew quite expert in manipulating the razor and the day came when, with a sad heart, I was thankful for it.

The days shortened and lengthened again. The winter passed and spring was once more close at hand. Ruby waited as eagerly as I had done for the breakup. "I'd like to see that ice piled mountains high!" she declared. But, although her wish was gratified before she left the country, she failed to realize it that spring. The ice moved out very quietly one night and in the morning all that remained were a few cakes distributed along the shore.

She was also anxious to visit the mining area on Henderson Creek. So while the clean-up was in progress we had Amos act as her bodyguard and she paid the creek a visit. She, too, made the trip on horseback and being a good horsewoman she thoroughly enjoyed the ride that had been to me a terrible ordeal. But she had an advantage in that the horse she rode was neither as big nor as clumsy as Old Dobbin. They saw several bears as well as a couple of moose, but they were all quite a distance away so she had no opportunity to use the rifle she so proudly carried. The miners were very kind and went to great pains to explain the work. Several presented her with a nugget as a souvenir and she returned perfectly thrilled with it all.

"I think I could grow to like the country," she told me and then repeated her first impression. "But it's cruel! Cruel!"

During the summer months we heard rumors of a rich placer strike in the Chisana country, across the International Boundary in Alaska and about three hundred miles southwest of Dawson City. By September the rumors were confirmed and a lively stampede started from Dawson and vicinity. As the favorite route was up the Yukon River to the mouth of the White, then up the White River and its tributaries to the Boundary, we soon found ourselves, figuratively speaking, in the line of march. Every boat that stopped on her way upriver carried stampeders and no matter how carefully they had outfitted in Dawson it would be found at the last moment that some item had been overlooked. Stewart being the last supply point on the route it became a case of, "Get it at Smythe's." An even heavier stampede was predicted when winter would set in and we were advised to lay in as much stock as possible. With this in mind I went to Dawson City earlier than usual and invested every available dollar in merchandise.

Dr. Thompson was soon to leave for Ottawa to attend Parliament, in which he represented the Yukon Territory, and had placed a stranger in charge of his practice, so I thought it wise to visit this doctor and discuss Waldron's case with him. I had been seated in the waiting room only a short time when Dr. Thompson came in. He seemed surprised and asked, "Where did you come from?"

"From Stewart, this morning," I answered, wondering.

"That's strange. I was just explaining Waldron's case to Dr. Chipman and was quite surprised to find you here!"

"That's why I came," I explained, "I thought it best to talk the matter over with him while I was in town."

"I'm glad you did. Come in and meet Dr. Chipman."

Going into the office I found myself facing two men, very similar in type and yet dissimilar, too. They were both large men, but while Dr. Thompson radiated geniality and goodwill the other might have been picked as a pugilist had I seen him in a crowd. The set of his jaw and the firm line of his mouth spoke of a nature that would brook no nonsense. It was his eyes that belied all the sterner characteristics. When we had been introduced and he had withdrawn his eyes from me, I had the same feeling as with Dr. Jones, that my qualifications had been noted and mentally asssessed. More than that, he seemed the embodiment of sympathy and understanding and I felt that I had a friend on whose support I might rely when the hour of my need should come.

I left Dawson City on the steamer *Dawson* on October thirteenth, her last trip for the season. It was a memorable journey. We left the wharf with a falling temperature and heavy slush ice running. The thermometer dropped steadily until at ten o'clock it had reached sixteen below zero. As a consequence the slush in the river thickened rapidly, parts of the boat became encrusted with ice formed by the escaping steam and the spray from the paddle wheel and several times it became necessary to tie up while men chopped the ice from the wheel. I slept none that night. The crunching made by the huge ice floes as they struck the bow and went grinding along the hull struck terror to my heart. I expected them to cut right through the side and shortly after landing me at Stewart that is exactly what happened and she was beached for repairs.

When navigation closed, the winter stampede set in in earnest. A mushroom town sprang up at the mouth of the White River. Day and night dog teams, horses and men on foot came and went. All had the same story to tell: the richest strike since the Klondike! And some, at least, had gold to show as proof. It was my first experience of a legitimate stampede and I confess it was thrilling to listen to the talk in the store or around the tea table, as one after another produced their findings and explained how and where they had been discovered. Travel was so heavy that scarcely a night passed when we were not obliged to turn people away for lack of accommodation, so Waldron suggested having another story added to the building. Neither Ruby nor I favored the idea; I realized what disorganization it would entail. But he pressed me to have it done, urging that it would be an advantage in case of flood.

"But the oldest residents claim that Stewart has never been flooded," I argued.

"Conditions this season are just right to cause one," he warned. "I'd like to see it done."

So I yielded and the work was started. Then Big Amos joined the stampeders, a few days later the other men followed his example, and we were left wihout any help. Next a cold snap set in and in the general confusion it became almost impossible to keep the building warm enough for a human to live in with the temperature at sixty-five below. Finally one of the miners on Henderson Creek who had not been infected with the stampede virus was willing to go to work, so eventually things were reduced to at least a semblance of order.

As Christmas again drew near I advised those who might be interested that this year we would omit the usual Christmas dinner to our patrons and spend the day quietly by ourselves. Already I feared it might be Waldron's last Christmas with us, since his condition was rapidly growing worse. He was now quite helpless and required as much care as a child. But in spite of that fact he seemed possessed of driving interest: as one who, with the prospect of a long journey before him, must needs see that many things are done before he leaves. Each day he became more exacting. It was only under protest that he allowed anyone except myself to minister to him. He insisted on knowing all that went on, to the last detail. It was now that I missed Amos's help. Gradually Ruby had assumed more and more responsibility and she was doing the lion's share of the work. It would have been impossible for me to have gone through that terrible winter without her. The strain was taking heavy toil of my strength, but each morning as I rose I prayed for strength for the cares of the day. I must get through today. Tomorrow would come itself.

So the weeks went by and March came in. The strike in the Chisana had not developed according to expectations after all. Rich pay had been found only in a small area and though there had been much prospecting done nothing further had been located. Now the disappointed stampeders were returning singly and in groups. Always the first question from the travellers was, "How is Mr. Smythe?"

And then one day he refused his dinner. Asked the reason, he merely shook his head. But there was a strange look in his eyes, as of one who sees things afar off.

"Have you no appetite?" I enquired.

Another shake of the head, his eyes filled, I saw his chin quiver, and suddenly a cold hand seemed to clutch my heart.

I had been carefully prepared by both Dr. Jones and Dr. Thompson, who understood my isolation, as to what form the final stage of the disease was liable to take. "If he develops a difficulty in breathing and complains of pains in the lungs, be prepared for the worst," they had cautioned me. "When the diaphragm becomes affected and the lungs are no longer able to function, the end cannot be long delayed. It will strongly resemble an attack of pneumonia."

So the following morning, when he did complain of sharp pains in his chest and his breathing became labored, I realized that I was face to face with the most severe trial that life would ever hold for me. Full well I knew that no power on earth could aid my dear one, but as a drowning man will clutch at straws I wired a full description of the symptoms to the doctor and asked that if possible he would forward medicine by the first stage.

In a matter of minutes I received his reply, "Forwarding medicine as requested. Outlook grave. Be prepared for the worst."

When I read that message I felt that a black curtain, through which no ray of light would ever shine, had fallen before my eyes. How I longed for the comforting nearness of a doctor, a nurse, or someone with skill and training to support me through the ordeal. But I had none to look to. Ruby was kind and loyal, but she lacked training and her experience with sickness was less than my own. It remained for me to meet the supreme test of my life, to all intents and purposes, alone.

There followed two weeks of agony for us both. As he battled in the cold and darkness—he would have no light and the window must be opened wide even in the sub-zero weather—I felt and could almost hear the Grim Footsteps coming ever nearer. In the beginning of the second week Big Amos returned from the stampede. He had plans made to start work for Mr. Neill, but on learning of Waldron's condition he immediately cancelled them. "That little woman may need me. I'm staying here in case she does," he announced. I was glad that he was with us. In his suffering Waldron seemed to prefer that someone should hold him in their arms and when, numb and chilled, I could no longer support him and called, no matter at what hour of the day or night, Amos was on hand to relieve me.

Three days before the end, speech failed Waldron completely and, used as I was to interpreting his every wish even when it was intelligible to no one else, this time I was helpless. Repeatedly his eyes sought mine with yearning entreaty and blindly I groped, "Is it . . .?" But to every query came the ever sadder and more despairing shake of his head. When I realized that he must leave me with his last word unspoken, I felt that my Gethsemane had indeed been reached!

During the early hours of March nineteenth I held him in my arms. At half-past four, knowing that the sands of life were fast running out, I called Amos and Ruby.

Even then the Crossing was long and tedious. Just after twelve he signified a desire to be replaced among the pillows and we laid him there. Slowly and wearily the tired eyes kept seeking, seeking . . .

"His sight is failing. He wants you!" Ruby whispered.

I bent my face to his. "I'm here, dear," I called.

A faint light of recogniition—so fleeting as to be scarcely

seen—broke for a moment over his face. A tired sigh . . . and all was over.

The River had at last been crossed.

A Long Farewell

Waldron was gone but as yet I did not realize it. I felt no added responsibility or loneliness. There was a numbness of the spirit matching the physical numbness of the cold.

Ruby was weeping bitterly and Amos's eyes were by no means dry. But no tears came to my relief. An iron band about my head grew tighter every moment. I longed to scream and could not.

At last Amos led me from the room and then returned to Ruby. Together they would care for Waldron.

Before long Amos and Ruby both came to me. Amos looked very upset. "Do you think you could shave Waldron?" he asked. "If not, and you want me to do it, I'll try. But I've never shaved anyone but myself and I'd feel terrible if I cut him."

A great cry rose within me, "No! You can not do that!"

"Try to do it, dear," Ruby begged. "I know how hard it will be, but you have never failed him yet. Don't do so now. There is no one else and he will not need much more."

I knew there was no escape. Only I had done it before. I must do it now.

We returned to the room. Amos prepared the equipment and

he and Ruby stood in silence beside me while I performed the hardest task that I pray God I may ever be called upon to undertake. Several times I thought I could not go on, but at a reassuring word from one of them I would again nerve myself to the task.

At last it was finished. I had left one tiny little scratch, the first that I had ever given him, but I knew he forgave me. My numbed fingers refused to relax and Amos gently released the razor from their grasp.

There was still much to be done, of course, and the rest of the day was mercifully filled with labor. Messages must be sent to his relatives and mine and to friends in Dawson City. Friends nearer at hand did not fail to be kind.

When Dawson DeWitt heard that I was alone, he came to me immediately. His manner, as usual, was quiet and direct.

"If there is anything I can do," he told me, "please remember that I am standing by."

Toward evening Frank Wilkins came to the store and his first question, as always, was, "How is Mr. Smythe?" He was an Irish lad and a prime favorite with Waldron. My voice failed me altogether when I tried to answer.

"He left us this afternoon," Ruby explained quietly and his face went white. It was some moments before he spoke and then his voice trembled.

"I'm sorry for your grief, Missus," he sympathized, "but it's better for ye both."

Yes, better. I knew that he was right. Many times during the last two weeks I had wondered in the morning how I could carry on for the day. And for Waldron . . . yes, far, far better. But, oh, the loneliness . . .

Knowing that the end could not be very far away my sisters had written urging me against laying Waldron away in that far-off frozen country. So preparations were begun for taking his body to Dawson City, there to be prepared for and wait his last journey out when the boats would run. Harvey Smith fashioned a neat casket, which Ruby carefully upholstered inside and painted black. This of course would be replaced in Dawson by one of special type. There was no trail for a horse on the river, so Amos would take the body via Henderson, Blackhills, and the stage road with our horse, Casey. I would go by dog team down the river with Angus Morrison, son of a friend from Coffee Creek.

I like to remember the kindness of all with whom I came in contact on that sad journey. At the various roadhouses where I lodged no detail that could add to my comfort was omitted. On the third day I reached Dawson City and was taken from the hotel to the home of friends. During all the duties I had to perform there I was never left alone. The North is cruel, as Ruby said, but it also knows when to be kind.

Later on the day of my coming, Amos also reached Dawson. The picture of that arrival is seared into my very soul. The trail had been soft, for the last few miles it had been entirely bare in many places, and both man and horse were weary. Amos was tanned by the hot spring sun until he resembled a creole and his clothing was bespattered with grime and slush. Casey, the horse, stood with heaving sides. He, too, was throughly bedraggled, his coat was wet with sweat and flecks of foam dropped from him. The crude double-ender sled also testified to the condition of the trail and, despite the best efforts of Amos, the long tarpaulin-wrapped bundle had become smeared.

Our hopes had reached a sorry ending.

Some days later a modest service was held in the little chapel connected with the undertaking parlour. They told me that the sun shone that day, but I failed to see it. To me everything was enveloped in a dull grayness, a fog. I remember nothing of the events of the day, except that I seemed to waken from a dream at the door of the chapel to find the place packed and many people standing on the sidewalk. I walked up the aisle between two friends, Miss Buckles and Mrs. Ellingsen, who each held a hand clasped firmly—and oh, so kindly—in theirs. The chapel was nicely decorated with potted plants, loaned by the Men's Club. The sermon was brief, but comforting. I heard Charley Riley, Miss Buckles's head clerk, sing "Then I Shall See Him Face To Face," then Mrs. Saucerman's clear sweet voice leading in "Rock of Ages" and "Nearer My God To Thee." Not till then had I ever understood the import of the line, "E'en though it be a cross . . ." Mrs. Saucerman was an old friend and she was first to come to me at the close of the service. Many people remained to express sympathy, among them ones whose very existence I had forgotten.

As I was taking a last look at the dear face, Mr. Steppe the undertaker, came near to ask if I had any further request and mentioned the tiny scratch.

Without thinking, I answered, "I could not help it. My hand trembled."

In a horrified whisper, he asked. "You didn't have to do *that,* did you?"

When I bowed my head, I heard him ejaculate, "My God!"

As Waldron lay, so calm and peaceful, I lived again the time we had spent together: the gay, happy days before the Klondike had called him; his long-looked-for return and our journey, so full of bright anticipation, to the land of gold; our hopeful struggle at Stewart; the agony of the last few years.

At last Mr. Steppe said, "Come, Mrs. Smythe." He gently raised me to my feet and with Miss Buckles and Mrs. Ellingsen I left the chapel.

A few days later I started back to Stewart.

And Now Alone

We anticipated an easy trip to Stewart, so the day was well advanced when I said good-bye and we headed up the river. I felt no urge to hurry! All need for that seemed blotted out. As the dogs plodded along in the warm spring sunshine the only desire I had was to lie back in the robes and rest. I was tired—tired—tired!

On the second evening, as the full moon rose to shed her steely white light over everything, I thrilled anew to the calm splendor of the Yukon night. Not a breath of wind stirred and the only sound that came to our ears was the music of the bells, mingled with the song of the runners and the patter of the dogs' feet.

As the moon climbed higher Angus's feelings asserted themselves. "Do you mind if I sing, Mrs. Smythe?" he asked. "I don't want you to think me inconsiderate of your feelings, but to be out on a night like this with a good dog team makes me want to make a noise."

I assented and, filled with the joy of living, he sang and whistled to his heart's content. Would I mind if he sang! God bless the exuberant spirit of youth! It did me good to know that there were still hearts with a song to sing.

The hours sped by and toward midnight the buildings at Stewart appeared in the distance, shining in the moonlight. At the sight of them the desolation to which I was returning struck me afresh. When we came to the trail leading from the river to the house I felt no desire to take the turning. Somewhere, anywhere, into the moonlight . . . but not to that empty house!

The place was wrapped in slumber and while Angus cared for the dogs I made my way in. Softly I entered and in the utter stillness I found myself listening for a voice that would never call again. I prepared lunch and when Angus had eaten he held my hand for a moment. "God comfort you this night!" he whispered, as he left me.

It was nearly morning when I crept, shivering, to the empty room and lay down upon the bed. Not to sleep—that was impossible. Slowly the clock in the adjoining room told off the minutes. Tick-tock, tick-tock. Every stroke was a hammer beating upon my brain. Never since then have I been able to endure the sound of a clock at night. One by one the minutes passed by. The moon's rays gave place to the light of dawn. The sounds of the awakening household filled the air and I rose to meet the future.

The ordeal had taken its heavy toil of my strength. Overwork, grief, loss of sleep and irregular meals had so affected my stomach that I began to fear that I had cancer. But this I carefully kept from Ruby, for she laid plans to take passage on the first boat upriver. It was only natural that she should be anxious to return to her own home, although my heart quailed at the thought of her going. She had come to us for only one winter and now nearly two years had gone by. She repeatedly urged me to abandon the North entirely and return with her to the East. But now, less than ever, could I bear the thought of leaving. It is true that through suffering our attachments are formed. This had been *our* home, this cabin. Every log had known the touch of Waldron's hand. How could I leave it now, without him?

There was no respite for us, although this time we were concerned with another's sorrow, not our own. A six-year-old lad at White River was very ill as a result of pneumonia (he had, in fact, an abscessed lung, as we learned later) and we were asked to nurse him. Following this, he had to be taken by some means over the treacherous ice to Dawson City to a doctor. We could not have refused had we wished to do so and one glimpse of the white, sweet little face would have made anyone love him. Not once did he complain, in spite of his suffering, but it meant care-filled hours and broken rest for us and then Ruby made the dangerous trip to Dawson and return. I was sick with worry, for I knew what the ice conditions were. When little Jack died after all our efforts I felt as though a child of my own had been taken.

Into the business I could put my heart with more willingness than into any other activity. I still felt that it was *ours,* somehow. For myself I would have done nothing, but the sense of partnership, with Waldron, was too deep to be so soon eradicated.

As the time for the breakup drew near I remembered Waldron's warning about a flood. Conditions were right. There had been some extremely cold weather before the snow had come and consequently the ice in the river was unusually thick. In various localities the snowfall in the hills had been reported as heavy, the warm weather was late in coming and was likely to bring the melting snow in a rush, and that, with the heavy ice might cause serious jams. Also, Big Amos confirmed Waldron's fears. "I saw flood-marks on trees on the flat here over three feet from the ground," he declared. "Stewart has been flooded before and it can happen again."

So, although the old-timers scoffed at the idea, the possibility of a flood became a favorite topic for conversation. I was more anxious than I cared to show. In anticipation of the Chisana stampede we had laid in a heavy stock the previous fall, and when the stampede failed to materialize as we expected, we were left with a large supply of goods on hand. Some of these were easily moved to safety, but it was impossible to do anything with the heavier lines. We simply took what precautions we could and waited. The water in the river rose steadily and anxiously we watched for the great mass of ice to move. What on earth could be holding it!

On May twelfth we rose early. About six, just as we were sitting down to breakfast, I heard a familiar "boom!" and going to the bank I could see the ice from the Stewart River forcing that in the Yukon steadily downstream. Above the Stewart the Yukon still held solid. The river was running bank-full of heavy ice around our island and I prayed that all below us would clear out before the ice above would give way. For a time all moved smoothly. Then there was a mighty jam and the ice stopped moving. Someone shouted excitedly, "She's jammed below!" Immediately the water started to rise. For a few minutes I kept my eyes glued to that rapidly rising waterline, then swept my gaze both up and down the river and started for the house.

"Come!" I called. "Stewart may never have been flooded before but there's a first time to everything. We're going to have one now!"

There was not much to be done in the warehouse, that had already been attended to. So while Amos and a couple of men went to the store, Angus Morrison, Ruby, and I worked at removing the household goods to the upper story. Ruby had the presence of mind to remember that we had not yet breakfasted and the coffee pot, platter of bacon and eggs, and plate of toast, as well as a generous supply of dry wood and kindling, were the first things she salvaged. "A bird in the hand is worth two in the bush!" she reminded us.

It was now that Waldron's judgment and foresight were vindicated. I have often wondered how we could have managed in that flood without the upper story. Although we worked with all our might the water gained swiftly on us. When it was above our ankles Ruby came to me. She had discarded her skirts for hiking breeches and carried a pair of boy's overalls from the store over her arm.

"You had better put these on," she advised. "They'll be a lot more appropriate for paddling around in this icy water."

I took her advice, but in the chaos that followed I failed to find my own clothes for three days!

When the water started to come over the bank, I thought of Casey and the cow tied in the stable and decided on giving them their liberty to shift for themselves. I sent Angus to turn them loose. Casey was already pawing and whinnying and as he came from the stable the first trickle of water ran past the door. He sniffed at it, threw back his head and neighed, and then galloped up the trail with the cow at his heels.

When the water was above our knees I insisted that Ruby abandon all further effort and we went upstairs. Soon after this the water started to drop—although the jam still held—and about nine-thirty the buildings were clear of it. Ruby, always practical, hastened to replenish the fire. The neglected breakfast was re-warmed and in our bedraggled condition the coffee, to quote the men, "went right to the spot." Then she and I started to clean up, but Amos returned from the river, where he had been studying the outlook, and advised us to wait.

"I'm afraid the worst is yet to come," he warned. "The water is rising again and if the upper Yukon ice comes down while the water is above the level of the bank there may be serious trouble. We've tied one boat in front, just below the upstairs window, and another just outside the window of the post office, so you can't be trapped. Angus will stay with you women and the rest of us will try to stretch some of those boom pieces across the front of the building to protect it from the ice. We want you to stay at the upper window and tell us how things are going."

One of the men turned to Ruby. "If things get rough here, you stay close to the Missus and don't be excited. Remember what she's been through!"

From my station at the window my outlook was bad enough. For miles in both directions the Yukon as well as the Stewart was choked by a heavy, compact body of ice. Suddenly the whole mass of ice began to move again. But instead of the water drop-ping it continued to rise until it was three and one-half feet deep in the buildings. In front, it was up to the men's armpits as they struggled in it to fashion a bulkhead against the ice. Solidly the pack moved down stream. Where was it all coming from? Then, far up the Yukon, I could see great cakes tumbling over each other and I realized that the ice of the upper river—with all that that might mean—was coming in our direction.

"The Yukon has broken loose!" I called to the men.

"There's nothing more we can do but wait and see what happens," one of them called back.

Forced by the weight of the ice behind it the current now set directly toward the house. I looked at one enormous cake and shivered with fear. It appeared to be at least a mile in length and almost as wide, but then—I was badly scared. Straight for the house it came and I knew that if it struck, the building would go down like a house of cards. The men were standing on the boom pieces holding the painter of the boat. They, too, had spotted the big cake. It drifted nearer to the house with every moment. The forward end of it came beyond the edge of the bank till it struck the bulkhead. We held our breath. Then its speed slackened, the drifting ice caught the portion that projected into the stream, and it broke in two. One part went floating downriver and the other grounded in front of us. By actual measurement it was forty-five feet wide, eight feet thick, and more than sixty feet long. Had the water surrounding the building been a foot deeper and thus given it greater momentum the house could not have withstood the impact.

The ice was now everywhere in motion and the depth of the water remained stationary, so we knew that the dangerpoint was past. When they were certain of this the men poled a boat up one of the back trails to learn what had become of Casey and the cow. They found them contentedly grazing on the only dry land in sight, a patch about twenty-five feet square on a hummock near the telegraph office.

When the men had gone, Ruby and I, our teeth chattering from cold and fright, made our way through a hatch out upon the corrugated iron roof to warm ourselves in the sun. Her wish had been fulfilled. She had seen the ice piled "mountains high!"

Hour after hour the run of ice continued and the height of water held. Then about six in the afternoon it began to drop, the ice thinned, and by eight o'clock the river was confined within its banks.

But what a state of chaos and destruction it left behind! The house and store had been pretty well cleared of their contents, so there the worst feature was the silt that lay in a thick carpet everywhere. The garden fences had been carried away bodily. Huge cakes of ice were piled around the buildings on all sides and what the flood had left of our year's supply of wood, already cut into stove-lengths, was scattered among these in every direction. In the feed room tons of hay, oats and other feeds were ruined. But the warehouse presented the most heartbreaking sight of all. As the water had risen many of the piles of case goods had toppled over and tea, coffee and other groceries were strewn loosely over the floor. Tiers of sacks of flour, cornmeal and rice were damaged to the height of the water. Sugar at the bottom of the tiers had melted away, allowing those above to settle until they in turn melted. The floor was covered with a thick syrup. When I first saw this, I wanted to turn my back on it all. It seemed that, this time, there was far too much for me to cope with. Even when we had recovered all the stock it was possible to rescue, the loss and damage ran into four figures.

And still there was more to follow. Order had been only partially restored when the first boat upriver, the independent steamer *Prospector* running without a spark-screen, set fire to the building. Fortunately there were a number of men at hand and it was soon extinguished, but not before considerable damage had been done, particularly to the stock. That evening, as I looked at the evidences of fire and flood, I wondered what I had done to deserve it all. It seemed that God's hand must be turned against me.

Ruby, of course, was still preparing to leave and when she again urged me to leave it all and return with her I considered the question very seriously. Finally, when I could come to no decision by considering the matter from the viewpoint of leaving Stewart, I tried to picture what my old life would hold for me now. This was a different matter and I soon decided that to attempt a come-back amid old scenes would require more courage and strength than I possessed—more than to stay. For once I decided to follow the line of least resistance. Stewart was home now. I would stay.

In July Ruby went to Dawson City and within a week was en route outside on the *Whitehorse*. To spend a few more hours with her I arranged with Dawson DeWitt to take a dory along and when the steamer arrived at Stewart we boarded her and went as far as Coffee Creek. Waldron's remains were also on the *Whitehorse*, beginning the last long journey to his home in Bathurst, New Brunswick, for final burial.

The veil between those who have "gone before" and those mortals still held captive in the flesh may well be thinner than we know. As the vessel approached, the whole atmosphere seemed charged with Waldron's presence. I found that it was no longer Ruby, the living, whose coming I awaited. It was Waldron. I felt the same expectancy that I had always known when he was returning after an absence. Had his spirit come to bid our home and me a last good-bye? Then, I suddenly realized what date it was. On July seventeenth, 1905, he had left Stewart for Bathurst to be married. On July seventeenth, 1910, he had left on his first trip in quest of health. Now this, his last leave-taking, was on July seventeenth, 1914.

We reached Coffee Creek in the late afternoon. I had brought some flowers and before leaving the boat I went below and laid them on my beloved's casket. I knew it was his, although there was another. The cold impersonal wording of the doctor's certificate attached to it told me so. And so did the chill at my own heart as I laid my poor offering at its only altar.

When at last the time came for us to leave the boat Ruby was inconsolable.

"It breaks my heart to leave you alone in this wild country!" she sobbed. "Why . . . oh, why! . . . will you not come with me? Please promise that if I am needed again you will send for me!"

With leaden heart and trembling voice I tried to reassure her. "Have I not proved I can take care of myself?" I asked her.

Still she would not be comforted, but wept as I kissed her good-bye. The dory was put off and Dawson offered his hand to steady me down the gangplank. The steamer backed into the stream, swung about, and headed for Whitehorse.

As long as she was discernable in the crowd on deck, I stood waving to Ruby. To its other burden I should never wave again.

Then I turned to face the empty days ahead.

The Road Back

My home stood silently waiting as I stepped ashore again at Stewart. Yes, mine—*my* store—*my* roadhouse—*my* business. It was no longer *ours*. In that moment I tasted unimagined bitterness in ownership.

My life was also my own. No one to work for now—no one to live for, to save for and to cherish. No one to care how I lived or if I lived at all or, instead, sought peace beneath the swift waters of the mighty Yukon. Waldron—Ruby—both were gone and I was left with my reminders and my memories.

I stood at the door and looked about me. I was in my own hands, utterly. It is an awful thing to stand alone. It is the deepest pit into which a human soul can fall. To climb up to normal living among my fellows was the task of the days to come. The heights could be reached only step by step and the turnings of the way were marked by the kindness of friends.

Dawson DeWitt I found one of the truest. Now that I was alone he asked for the privilege of brotherhood.

"I have no desire to put you in an equivocal position," he told me, "but will you let me do the things I would for my sisters and may I look for the kindnesses from you I should expect from them? You should have someone near to whom you can turn in case of need."

I thought of my utter loneliness and of what the steamer ploughing upriver carried. Finally, I said, "I can see no reason at present why it should not be so."

It was a wise decision, as time was soon to prove. As if the sudden inaction of my own life were but a mirror of the world around me, conditions at Stewart became almost stagnant. Both stampede and returning stampeders had entirely ceased, mining on Henderson Creek was at a standstill, and the woodcutting industry had also moved to a new locality. Had not Dawson arranged to take his meals at the roadhouse, although still sleeping at the telegraph office, the next two weeks would have been unendurable. His coming into meals saved me from being altogether alone.

The days followed each other, totalling into months without my knowing or caring how they passed. The outbreak of war in August caused a flurry of excitement, naturally. The entire force of Mounties volunteered, but the Government refused to accept any from the Yukon. They were needed there.

By this time I was too ill myself, and knew it now, to take either interest or action. I was trying to hold on till October so as to combine medical treatment with the annual business trip, but the effort proved a failure. One day in early September I was feeling worse than usual and had just gone to my room to rest when a gang from Scroggy Creek arrived. It was supper, bed and breakfast for sixteen men. I had no help and I was sick but I needed the money, so I set to work. Somehow I managed the meal and was just clearing the table when an Irish chap named Wilkins (he who had been Waldron's friend) arrived. Six more wanted the same service!

Again I tried it and again I fed the lions, but as I was clearing the table this time everything became dim and I staggered to a chair.

Just then Wilkins returned to the dining room. "Missus! You're sick!" he cried.

"Just a bit tired," I claimed.

"Tired, is it! You're not fit to be on your feet!" he declared in his Irish brogue. "I was noticin' ye at supper and I thought ye were goin' to faint, so I did. Just sit yourself down there. Here, Ross!"

he called to one of his men. "We dirtied these dishes an' by cracky we kin wash 'em!"

I tried to object but it was useless.

"Not one word out of your head!" he ordered. "Don't I know a sick person when I see one? It's in bed you should have been the week and more!"

Even when the dishes were done he was not satisfied. Kindling must be placed ready and all possible preparations made for breakfast.

It proved to be just as well. That night nature presented her bill, now long overdue. I went to bed and when morning came I was unable to rise. Under Wilkins's leadership breakfast was served, somehow. When everyone had gone Dawson DeWitt locked all doors against the public. For three days I lay in practically a stupor, my only nourishment an occasional glass of milk which he handed me. On the third day I struggled to my feet and wired to Dawson City for a housekeeper to come by the first steamer. After her arrival I took the first boat back for Dawson myself.

A surprise was in store for us on our arrival. Some of the passengers had been exposed to contagious disease and we were all placed in quarantine. Fortunately for me the health officer proved to be my doctor and he agreed to visit me professionally on the boat, even phoning my friend Miss Buckles to have her look after my urgent business. The next few days were the most restful of my life. It was a veritable godsend, considering my condition at the time. The passengers were congenial companions, being nearly all old sourdoughs, and as guests of the company we were treated royally. The steamer was taken to Sunnydale Slough, across the river from the city, and we were allowed to go ashore over there or to go boating in the ship's dories.

While we were there the first contingent of Yukoners left for overseas. This company was recruited and financed by the famous Colonel Joe Boyle, rescuer of Queen Marie of Romania and the Grand Duchess Marie of Russia. The steamer *Lightning* passed us on a bright moonlit night, flags flying, band playing, whistles blowing. Like a graceful white specter she sailed on into the night and few that she carried returned to their Northland again.

By the time the quarantine was lifted navigation had ended for the season and we were given just twenty-four hours before she left for winter quarters at Whitehorse. I made it, but when I got home things were in a shocking state of neglect and disorder. My housekeeper was neither capable nor willing, so I shipped her back to Dawson City in a small boat.

For the next few months business was dull and so was I. Being a semi-invalid, reduced to a diet that prevented my regaining strength, did not make for a sound or healthy outlook on life. I slept little and after tossing for hours I stood on the river bank in many a gray dawn, trying to estimate how far I should need to walk from shore before the Yukon would take charge of the situation. It would not have been far. The truth was that I had no desire to live, perhaps no reason to do so, and I tottered on the edge of a complete breakdown. The condition was aggravated by the calling of steamers bearing contingents for overseas. Nearly all came ashore to say good-bye, little thinking what they were doing for me. I had known these boys for years as they went up and down the river. I had chided their misdeeds, laughed at their fun, and sympathized with their sorrow. If my heart was not broken before, it suffered severely then.

The strain was becoming too much. Winter and spring were one long nightmare, so I went to Dawson City for a summer of medical care. There I was the guest of the Pinskas at their cabin in Sunnydale. It was a return to the scene of the restful days of our quarantine with the added blessing of the sisterly care of Olive Pinska. Their cabin was at the base of a thickly wooded hillside and within a stone's-throw of the beach. Across the water came the hum of the busy city, but no other cabins were nearby to break the peace of the quiet spot. It was the ideal place for rest and Al and Olive Pinska were the most considerate of friends, trying in every way to erase from my memory the trials I had borne. No words of mine can tell what they came to mean to me after those days of love and tenderness when I stood most in need of both. It was, I think, the turning of the tide.

During the summer I went to my doctor and demanded the whole truth.

"I feel as though I could not possibly go on any longer," I told him, "and if the end of the trail is in sight, I think I should know it. There are business matters to consider."

It turned out that, except for my lungs, every organ in my

body was affected. Nature's bill was a heavy one.

"If you give up work for a time and take systematic treatment, I can help you," he decided. "Not otherwise."

On my way to the drugstore I wondered if the game were really worth the candle. But the Pinskas put me to shame. They established me in a room of their town house and there I spent an indolent existence for the balance of the summer. A strict diet of milk eliminated even the bother of meals.

Every form of kindness was shown to me. Any recreation in which I could join was shared with me. Some privileges came my way, too. One of my choicest memories is of being invited to spend an afternoon at Government House. George Black was then Commissioner of the Yukon and it was a privilege to meet the gracious and distinguished Mrs. Black, later more widely known (and therefore more widely honored) than she was then.

The languid summer drew to a close. I was still far from well, but thanks to doctor and friends, mind and body had begun to heal. I returned to Stewart on the last boat of the 1915 season feeling at least a little more interested in taking up life where I had left off. Oddly enough I found things at Stewart just as peaceful as while I was idling away time in Dawson. It was like the calm after a storm. The population had so decreased that business was sporadic and yet I welcomed the condition. During all the autumn, winter and spring we passed our days in little things not worth the telling, but it is such things that make for peace. Our chief interest and topic was the war and we anxiously awaited the daily bulletins. I was still a semi-invalid and did little else that was patriotic other than knit for soldiers.

In July, 1916, I returned to Dawson City for a checkup on my progress. It was encouraging. Only a heart condition remained and it still does, the aftermath of my ordeal. I was with the Pinskas, of course, but could undertake more pleasuring now and , with Miss Buckles, we were often a happy group of an evening. We did patriotic work, too, for changes were becoming daily more apparent. George Black, having resigned as Commissioner, led another contingent overseas that summer.

Also, more personal to me, Big Amos Noyd went, he who had shared with us the last hours of Waldron's agony. I felt that I had lost my chief bodyguard, for on one occasion he had eyed a noisy group at the store and told me, "See here, Missus. If any fellows ever get fresh, let me know. I'll attend to them for you."

And, looking at him, I never doubted his ability!

Some time after my return to Stewart that summer history repeated itself. A group of talkative, boisterous travelers landed one evening. I had never had any trouble, but there is always a first time to everything. So when Dawson was leaving after supper I asked him to return and remain all night.

"I'm glad you asked me to do that," he said with evident relief. "I've never felt satisfied to have you alone here, so far from anyone, when strangers are liable to arrive at any hour. While Amos was here I didn't worry, but now it's different. So if you have a spare room I'll engage it permanently."

After that, I was not alone so much and as time went on I grew to appreciate his congenial companionship. Our tastes in most things were identical. During the summer whenever we were both free from duty, we roamed the countryside in search of flowers or berries. In the fall we hunted game birds. I had learned to use a gun and many a brace of ducks or grouse fell to my aim. When winter set in we tramped the hills on snowshoes.

On one of my favorite routes we arranged a cosy place to eat lunch. It was located on a sunny hillside below some tall spruce. Two windfalls, one a little above and behind the other, made a splendid seat. A little to one side of this there was an ideal spot for a camp fire and as we sat silent in the bright sunlight the birds sang in the trees behind. Several whiskey-jacks became so tame that they ate from our hands and we named the spot Whiskey-Jack Camp. At other times we harnessed the dogs and went spinning over snowy trails by moonlight or the softer glow of the northern lights.

One evening, when I had been alone about two years, we found ourselves considering the advisability of spending the remainder of our lives together. There was no impassioned declaration or heroics of any kind. Dawson made the suggestion in the same quiet way in which he had proposed many other things.

I drew his attention to the difference in our years and although he countered this objection I was not satisfied. What if I consented and later, under less isolated conditions, he should meet one more qualified to perfect and share his life? Besides, I felt that for me the romance of life had passed. Waldron had too completely filled my life to leave room for another. So we agreed to remain merely the staunch friends that we had always been. Our attitude caused no little concern among the various arbitrators-of-other-people's-affairs around us and no doubt makes duller reading here than the story of a love-life. But I respect the truth.

If I belonged to no one completely I was fast being assigned the position of doctor, lawyer and Indian Chief. They came to me at any hour for help.

"Don't be askeered, Missus, but would ye mind gettin' up to dress Gilroy's face for him?" It was Wilkins Irish voice at my window before dawn. "He was tyin' up his raft and the snubbin'-pin gave way and hit him a bad puck in the face, so it did!"

I found that he had not exaggerated the case at all. The taught rope had been a catapult and the snubbing-pin had given him a three-inch cut in his scalp. It surely was a "bad puck!" My nursing and first aid was being learned in a good but hard school.

Neither had my fight against John Barleycorn been in vain. Now it was only very rarely that anyone, even slightly under the influence of liquor, came to the place.

The crews of the various steamers plying the river, from stokers to captains, exhibited toward me a marked friendliness, apparent in many ways. They always contacted me when passing, no matter how rushed they or I might be. A steward ran in with the captain's compliments or an engineer dashed up to convey his own. Or a mate looked in to ask exactly where and how I wished my freight piled. Little things, but not done in a small way. It was the sourdough's way of saying, "You are one of us."

Once, when I tried to thank one of the mates for his thoughtfulness and mentioned their kindness, he looked at me in surprise and blurted in a delightful Scottish accent, "Ma guidness, Mrs. Smythe! There isna a man on the river but thinks he has tae look oot for ye!"

It was no wonder that I began to think that my mission in life might after all lie in this northern outpost. I began to feel of some use in the world, which was both a good sign of returning health and also a very pleasant feeling.

Sometimes I had to deal with more than "a puck in the face." They brought me a woodcutter named Thorne, who had been found in his cabin with badly frozen feet. I was alarmed when I saw

148

them. This called for more than antiseptic and adhesive tape. For a few days they improved and then their condition became stationary and I knew the frost had touched the bones. He had to go to the hospital and a part of each foot was amputated but the doctors told me I had been the means of saving the remainder of his feet and probably his life.

Another instance was too late for any such success. An old prospector, Paul Lester, was found dead on the trail. For days and nights of sixty-below zero weather two of his dogs had guarded his body, licking the face free of snow and frost as they waited for him to awake from sleep. A third dog was never found, only signs of a struggle and his tracks leading away across the river. Had he, in his cold and hunger, reverted to the wolf strain in him and been driven into the wilderness by his more loyal companions? They were so emaciated and weak that a separate dog team and sled went out to bring them in.

There was little we could do, but what we could was done. In the plot on the police reserve another Northerner found rest.

Captain Telford, the coroner, said in thanking me, "If ever I fall on the trail, Mrs. Smythe, I hope it will be near Stewart."

If this were true, then I was filling a niche in life and I was thankful.

It was in February of this winter in 1917 that I went on my first, one, and only stampede. A rich strike had been reported on Brewer Creek, about twenty miles up the Stewart River, and I had just finished a hard day's work when Wilkins and his partner arrived greatly excited.

"Missus," Wilkins announced, "Me and Bill are goin' on the stampede and we're takin' you along. See?"

"I don't think you are," I answered lightly, "I've never been on a stampede and I'm not going to start now!"

"If you've been all these years in the country without goin' on a stampede, it's high time you started!" Wilkins retorted. "Besides, the trail on the river is like the floor and Casey's just blue-mouldy for want of a little exercise. You've been cooped up here for weeks and the outing'll do you good. There's no moon, but there'll be bright northern lights. Come now, say yes!"

I cared nothing about the stampede, but the thought of an outing after having been "cooped up for weeks" appealed to me, so I said yes. We were ready about eight o'clock. It was quite dark and for some time we traveled by the light of a "bug," a candle fastened into a tin can which is open on only one side. About ten we came to a woodcutter's cabin on a hillside near the river and seeing a light in the window we decided to pay him a visit. The expected cup of hot tea did taste good and we all went on our way rejoicing. The sky was now brilliant with the vivid northern lights, so the bug was put away. As we traveled along in varying light the only sound to be heard was the crunch of Casey's shoes on the frozen trail and the clink of his harness as he trotted.

We had been told that we should have to go about three miles up the creek before getting a chance to stake a claim and that there was no trail for a horse. So Casey was fed, rugged, and securely tied to a tree on the bank. Then, taking our own lunch, we followed the footpath up the creek. Just as dawn was breaking we came to the cabin of the discoverer, and the only one on the creek which was inhabited—if one can use such a term in regard to it. Receiving no answer to our knock we concluded the owner was not at home and, according to the ethics of the trail, we entered. Of all the cabins I ever visited, as a "home" that cabin stood alone! It must have been built in early days. The greater part of the roof had fallen in and the debris lay scattered over the floor in all directions. Through the hole above, God's clear sky could plainly be seen. In one corner, under a portion of the roof still remaining, there was a bunk in which some blankets were carelessly tossed and in the opposite corner a small Yukon stove with dry wood and kindling placed ready. Near it stood a rough deal table on which were some unwashed dishes, fragments of a meal, cans of various cooking and household necessities, as well as pipes, tobacco, matches and ashes. Along the wall were ranged several sacks of flour, sugar and so on. With the axe which he had brought Wilkins cut wood from a dry tree, we kindled a fire to boil the kettle, and ate breakfast seated on empty boxes near the stove.

As it was now clear daylight we continued our way up the creek. Whoever estimated that three miles must have lost his pedometer—we walked eight if we walked a foot! It was a steep grade, the trail was heavy and my enthusiasm for stampeding was a minus quantity by the time we reached the last of the stakes. Wilkins prepared and placed my stakes, so all I had to do was to write my "claim" and sign my name. This done, he advised me to return to the cabin and wait for them there.

I can still envision that little scene, "staking my claim." It seemed to be, and indeed was, so far off the beaten track. Like every other spot which I visited in that country I should like to see it again.

I found the return journey, being down grade, much easier going. I had thrown off my skirt for greater ease in walking and was running along in my knickers, sweater and cap when I met two sourdoughs.

"How far do we have to go to stake?" they called without any preliminary greeting.

"About three miles," I directed, repeating the information we had received.

At the sound of my voice they looked at me, startled, and one of them began to stammer:

"Oh! Ah, we . . . ah . . . thought it was a boy. We . . . er . . . never expected to . . . ah . . . meet a woman alone up here!"

"Well, you're liable to meet me anywhere," I laughed and ran on, leaving them, I knew, consumed with curiosity.

By the time Wilkins and partner returned to the cabin the day was more than half gone. I had a kettle boiling and when we had eaten and they had time for a smoke and to rest a bit, we returned to the river where Casey was whinnying impatiently. He felt that he had been neglected long enough.

We reached Stewart just twenty-four hours after we had left it. This, added to the day's work we had done before setting out, made thirty-six hours of steady going. No lullabies were needed that night! I went to bed feeling that I could sleep the clock around.

We never realized anything from our claims, of course. The stampede was just another wild-cat, but the experience was worth the effort. I had not only been to the Yukon. I had been on a stampede and had staked my claim.

Perhaps the road back did have some new adventures for me, after all.

Hopeful Journey

T hings had been quiet and comparatively inactive for a long while. It was about time my nerves had another jolt. They did.

One warm day in August, 1917, I answered the store bell to find a Mountie waiting to see me. He looked a mere stripling, although a corporal, and he was obviously agitated. It developed that he had been ordered to Blackhills to bring down a sick man named Reynolds to hospital at Dawson. Coming down the Stewart he was startled to find the old man had quietly died in the canoe. Could I let them have a cabin in which to prepare the body for burial?

Yes, that was quite easily arranged. He went to the telegraph office when the body had been carried to the cabin, and I thought my duty done.

Some time later the corporal returned, more agitated than before. This time he had Dawson DeWitt for reinforcement. The Mountie was to catch the steamer *Whitehorse* going upriver to complete his patrol, but she was found to be due in an hour and you cannot prepare a body, make a coffin, dig a grave and conduct a funeral all in one hour, quite apart from the unseemly haste of such a proceeding. He wanted us to dispose of the body, if they made a coffin and got everything ready.

It was not a task that one would readily assume, but neither did I wish to refuse. My own hired man was away but should return by evening.

"Can we do it tonight after Billie returns?" I asked.

"I think so," the Corporal answered.

Then Dawson chimed in with the remark, "When the office closes, I'll do what I can."

So I agreed and the Corporal and his helper set to work. Hardly had the last nail been driven in the coffin when the *Whitehorse* landed and with sincere thanks the two men departed. But we had counted our chickens before they were hatched: Billie did not return as I had expected. No one else was obtainable and because of the warm weather burial must not be delayed. It was not a pleasant prospect, but there was no help for it. It was up to us to see the job through.

As soon as the office closed Dawson and I went to the little plot on the reserve. He demurred at my going, claiming that he could do the work himself, but I was insistent. I preferred action to remaining in close proximity to the cabin and its silent occupant, although I made no mention of this fact. Daylight had gone by the time our task was finished and another of those heavy thunderstorms was brewing. We knew that the burial could not be completed that night and neither of us had any desire for such a task by the light of a lantern, but the body must be placed in the coffin.

With a lighted lantern, we hurried to the cabin where it lay. Already several vivid flashes of lightning, followed by heavy thunder, told us that the centre of the storm was not far away and I trembled in every limb as I tried to nerve myself for the task ahead.

At the door of the cabin Dawson paused, lantern in hand.

"Are you at all nervous?" he asked.

I was determined to at least appear plucky and tried hard to prevent my teeth chattering, as I answered, "Oh, no! But . . . I'll be glad when it's done!"

Within the cabin all was complete darkness but by the dim light of the lantern I could see the body, which the men had prepared as best they could, lying on the table and the crude coffin leaning against the wall. Dawson placed the lantern on the table near the feet of the corpse and gave directions in a soft undertone, "We'll just lay the coffin on the floor beside the table, lower the body in it, then nail it up and leave it here until the morning. That should not take us long."

How I wished that we had refused to undertake the horrible task! Had it not been for the sheer cowardice of the act I should have screamed and run. When the coffin had been placed ready he went to the head of the body and motioned me to the feet.

"If you can steady them, I will lift the weight by the shoulders," he directed.

I stepped up to the ghastly thing and forced myself to stay there.

"Are you ready?" he asked, and I nodded.

Perhaps in my nervousness I struck the lantern—I cannot be sure. But scarcely had we lifted the burden clear of the table when the lantern fell to the floor with a crash and went out. At the same instant there was a blinding flash of lightning and a terrific clap of thunder. Then horrible darkness enveloped us.

In that breathless instant I thought all the demons from Hell were shrieking about my ears. I stood petrified; every drop of blood seemed swept from my body in that ghostly crash.

From the blackness Dawson's smooth voice came to me and even it held a slight tremor.

"I'm sorry, dear. Just lay the body back on the table while I relight the lantern."

Just lay the body back!! Had he no nerves at all?

Then I realized I was still holding the thing and I flung the feet on the table with no respect for the dead. Had I had any voice I should have screamed and had I been able to move I should have fled. I could not do either, so I stood immobile.

The lantern was relit and we did the job somehow.

For hours I fought off hysteria and finally yielded to a mild opiate and towards morning I slept. Next day we buried William Reynolds and I was sufficiently myself to lay flowers on the casket for a mother whose name we had never heard.

It was weeks before my jangled nerves recovered from the shock and when it became necessary in November to visit Dawson City on business I secretly welcomed the thought of the change. I had Casey take me to Blackhills and from there went on by stage.

These stage drivers were a jolly lot, much given to banter, and this one on my trip was no better than the others. At the Blackhills roadhouse I asked him what time he was going to leave the next morning. He told me and then added, "Are you a good sleeper?"

Rather surprised, I answered, "Nothing to boast about. Why?"

"Well," he continued, with a look he tried to make serious, "don't be nervous if you hear strange noises during the night. Some people say this place is haunted. I've often seen the bureau moving about the room on a moonlight night myself."

"You should have taken a milder drink before going to bed," I admonished him.

The next instant I remembered that a few years previously a triple tragedy had occurred at the house. The jealous drink-crazed proprietor of the place had shot and killed both his wife and the stable-man, then turned the gun on himself. The day after the shooting a stage with a load of passengers arrived and seeing no sign of life, the driver went to the stable where the hungry horses were stamping and whinnying for food. Much alarmed he hurried to the stable-man's cabin where he found the body in the bed, riddled with bullets. On searching the house he located the body of the murderer with a .40 U.S. rifle beside him, lying in a room downstairs and that of his wife in an upstairs room, seated at a table with an unfinished letter before her addressed to her daughter. The last words of it were, "He swears he'll kill me if . . ." Then the pen had trailed across the paper. Doubtless at that moment the fiend had arrived. The deed had been done from behind and two bullets had passed through the body and into the floor.

I dismissed the matter from my mind, chatted with the hostess for a short time, then went to my room. The floor was uncarpeted with here and there a rug thrown down and I was about to turn out my light when, in moving a large chair that stood before the table, I disclosed a couple of small holes in the floor with dark brown splotches scattered near them.

I looked hastily about me. There was the chair, the table, the bullet holes and the blood. Ugh! This was the room and it had never been repaired. I managed to overcome my desire to ask for another room and went resolutely to bed, but the clock had long since struck midnight before I slept. Once I awakened and in the shadows of the room better nerves than mine could imagine seeing a huddled form in the chair beside the table. I shut my eyes, clenched my teeth, and waited for the dawn.

Next morning I took my revenge on the stage driver by enlarging on my terrors of the night. He became very apologetic.

"I'm really sorry, Mrs. Smythe," he assured me, "but I had no idea you were a nervous person."

"In any case it was an assinine thing to do!" I informed him, which was quite the truth.

At Dawson, Mr. Pinska met the stage and it was like getting home again to see his smiling face welcoming me. My business was barely completed when the mercury began to drop and traveling was out of the question. It was one of the worst cold spells in the history of the Yukon. For thirty-three days the temperature averaged fifty-one and a decimal below zero. At this time of year there is a period of six weeks during which there is no sunshine in Dawson and this twilight, aided by a thick frost haze that hung like a mist over everything, gave to the little town an atmosphere of gloom.

Thus it came about that I spent Christmas, 1917, and New Year's 1918, with my friends the Pinskas and Miss Buckles. I am tempted to linger over the happy times we had, tempted to do so for more than one reason. Yet the tale of Christmas festivities and of New Year parties reads much the same in every land and clime. There is nothing new in a happy heart at such a season.

No, I am wrong. There is, sometimes; for it was new to me. That was the supreme meaning of those days and evenings together—I found happiness again after all the years of heartache and sorrow. When Al Pinska awakened us on Christmas morning, dressed as Santa Claus and bearing a huge sack of presents both possible and impossible, he reawakened the joy of living in my soul. And when, at the New Year's masquerade, postponed because we waited until the weather moderated, I danced into the early hours and never missed a dance, it was the first time I had done so, gaily, since many a long year.

The road into the valley had been bitter and none of my seeking. The journey back had seemed at first not worth the effort. But I was winning after all. I came home from the party sick and trembling with a weird foreboding, but I put it down to nerves and thanked God for these my friends. The road I traveled, so long a weary trail, was now a hopeful journey. Within a few days I returned to Stewart, determined once again to put my hand to the plough of business to some purpose.

Shipwreck

Back at Stewart I found that business was waiting for my hand. During the early months of 1918 there was a stirring of the dry bones of business, particularly a new interest in fur-buying. An old hand at the game was giving me a few sadly needed lessons in trading tactics and my own interest in its possibilities was growing. The position looked promising. Fur was becoming plentiful at Stewart. Ruby was in a position outside to dispose of skins for me to private buyers and Dawson DeWitt gave me another outside contact that would keep me posted on prices. I began to fancy myself as a fur trader and during the winter picked up quite a few furs from the prospectors coming to Stewart.

Then one evening during the first part of April a group of prospectors on their way to Dawson City arrived from upriver. One of them had a number of skins which I bought and he told me of several lots of fur along the river which he thought I could purchase at the same prices.

"Why don't you get a dog team and take a run upriver?" he suggested. "I think you can get those skins as easy as a wink. The weather is good. Be a sport and take a chance!"

I decided to take his advice and try it. There was no good team available so I had to content myself with a scratch team (a dog picked up here and there) and a driver that was at best only third-rate, but I assembled my forces and started. The trail was good as far as White River, but Harry Thorson, an old customer who was cutting wood at that point, reported it heavy in places beyond there and he insisted on giving me his snowshoes. I soon found that he was right as in places the trail was badly drifted.

With a poor team, worse driver, and heavy trail we made slow time and the afternoon was well under way when, about halfway between White River and Thistle Creek, there was a whimper from the dogs and they suddenly snapped into action. Looking for the cause I saw to the right marks in the snow where several animals had entered the trail. Stopping the team I went ahead to investigate.

On the beaten path I found the tracks of one lone caribou, evidently fleeing for its life, and those of a number of large timber wolves. The tracks were all very fresh and as I returned to the sled I wondered what would have happened if we had reached the spot fifteen minutes earlier. Caribou and wolves had followed the trail for about a mile, then the tracks led off to the left into some heavy timber. For the remainder of the distance to Thistle Creek, which the dogs made in record time, I rode with a cocked rifle across my knees. No further sign of the chase appeared. By that time the kill had probably been made and I was just as well pleased. I was looking for fur right enough, but not on the hoof.

To anyone who enjoys haggling and dickering over prices I strongly recommend fur-buying as a business! With many trappers it seems to be a foregone conclusion that you are out to "do" them and no matter what price you offer it is not enough. One such was included in the group that arrived at the roadhouse just after my own arrival. He would neither accept my price nor state his own. However, I was able to do business with the others in the party and they and I were both satisfied. I later learned that he was obliged to dispose of his catch in Dawson at a much lower average than I had offered him.

A chap named Edmunson chanced to be at the roadhouse with his dog team and he agreed to take me on the balance of my trip. So I sent the scratch team and driver back to Stewart. After picking up a number of skins here and there along the river we came, at Ballarat, to the cabin of an old fellow who had formerly spent considerable time around Stewart and was familiarly known as " Dad." He had a nice lot of skins which he proudly exhibited and he seemed friendly and agreeable enough until I asked, "Are the skins for sale, Dad?" Then for some unaccountable reason his manner changed instantly. It was almost as though I had wounded his dignity.

"They're fur sale," he drawled, "but you ain't got money enough to buy 'em."

"How do you know how much money I have," I laughed. "Let me make you an offer."

But he was firm. "No!" he persisted. "You ain't got money enough to buy my fur."

"In that case perhaps you'll make me a present of them." I bantered. "I need them in my business!"

A look of supreme disgust was the only answer to that sally.

We reached Britannia, end of the journey, late in the evening of the third day and were obliged to wait over as the next day was Sunday. I now had the opportunity of meeting for the first time one of the characters of the country about whom I had heard a great deal. John Egleson, known affectionately along the river as "Old John," had reached the ripe age of eighty-two years, but, nevertheless, his main object in life according to common report was to hoodwink Father Time. To this end one of his chief aids was a bottle of hair dye. Living so far from any beauty specialists it sometimes happened that his supply ran short and this was disastrous to his role. Or it might happen that at times he was too busy to apply the restorative and should visitors unexpectedly appear, particularly younger members of the fair sex, there was a great to-do until Richard was himself again. So I was advised to send word that I expected to call, but this was not necessary.

Bad news travels fast and when I arrived he was dyed, shaven, and shorn to the queen's taste. His brown, curly locks were more guiltless of silver than my own! But, joking aside, I found him a very fine old gentleman. He was a great reader and could discuss the current topics of the day with an ease that was refreshing. He was of a philosophical turn of mind and his views on the ethics of life were inspiring. I purchased a number of skins from him and after doing business with several other trappers in the vicinity we left for home.

It had snowed the previous night and as we started there was not a sign of the trail to be seen, but this bothered the lead dog not at all. Aided by some sense which I have never been able to understand he kept his course as easily as though it had lain beaten hard before him.

Edmunson had a message for Dad so we called at his cabin again. His skins were gone by now and his attitude on the fur question seemed to have undergone quite a change. His manner was almost conciliatory and he gave me several excellent opportunities for telling him what prices I was paying, but all his seed fell on stony ground. Later I discovered that shortly after I had left the cabin another buyer arrived and Dad had sold to him, only to learn that he had accepted several dollars per skin less than he might have had from me.

We had lunch at a woodcutter's cabin and about one o'clock reached the Indian village near Coffee Creek. While still some distance away I smelled the smoke from an outdoor fire and when we had finally succeeded in safely passing the cordon of snarling dogs that prowled in all directions we came in sight of the camp. As we drew near I realized that for some reason there was special rejoicing. There was great running hither and thither and a great clacking and jabbering to be heard from both old and young.

"You have skins?" I asked the first Indian I met.

"Uhm-uhm," was the answer, which I took to mean yes but might have meant anything.

"You sellum?" Again the gutteral sound. Then a squaw appeared and I put the same question to her. Considerable lingo passed between the two before she asked, "You want skins?" And I attempted to imitate their "Uhm-uhm!"

"You come me," and she led the way to what appeared the main cabin, council chamber, or what-have-you. Edmunson followed with the team, walking beside the dogs to protect them from the snapping curs, and as we passed along every Indian, squaw and papoose that we met fell in behind until we formed quite a procession. Edmunson's face as he trudged along was a study!

In the cabin we found a number of old Indians and squaws. One old squaw had heavy gold earings as large as quarters, and another ring about the size of a half-dollar in her nose. This hung well down over her lips and I have often wondered how she managed to eat with such a handicap. When our retinue had crowded in, the place was a little too well filled to suit me—my nostrils always have been rather sensitive—and I hurried to make the enquiry once more. "You have skins?" I asked, addressing all and sundry. At first I was met with blank looks, but I knew by their faces that they were stalling. So I dropped the subject of fur, asked one or two questions about the papooses, and started for the door.

Suddenly an old Indian stepped from the rear of the group with one lone weasel skin. As he held it up by the snout I almost laughed, it looked so funny. But he was as solemn as an owl. "How much?" he grunted and when I made an offer he eagerly thrust it into my hand. "You take him!" he declared. Immediately various skins began to appear as if by magic and for a short time business was rather brisk.

After leaving the cabin the trail led along the bank and when we had gone about a hundred yards we came to the fire and the cause of the rejoicing. Suspended from a tripod to roast in front of the fire was the carcase of an unborn moose calf, undrawn, head, hoofs, and hide, complete. It was being kept in a constant circular motion by the very simple expedient of whoever happened along giving the legs a kick.

"Where you get him? What you do him?" I asked a squaw.

"Injun killum cow moose, just not long time," pointing toward the hills. "We eatum. You stay, have some? Him hi-yu good!"

But I declined, with thanks, and we hurred on. My stomach stood the strain but in his struggles poor Edmunson almost threw up his immortal soul!

The result of this venture into a new field was that I returned with a very fine collection of skins which netted me a goodly profit.

If I, personally, saw a chance to prosper, however, the Yukon as a whole was enjoying no such fortune in that spring of 1918. We enjoyed no war prosperity. The main resource of the country is the mineral which it produces, chiefly gold, and due to the high cost of living, gold now held only half the purchasing power of pre-war days. All mining equipment was hard to obtain and some kinds impossible, for such material was badly needed for war purposes. Also the drain on the country in men, and in money for the various funds, was enormous. Large tracts of low-grade ground that had formerly yielded a small margin above operating expenses would no longer produce a living and were abandoned. The country in general was by now suffering severely. In contrast to this we heard glowing accounts of conditions outside. The boom was at its zenith, work was plentiful, wages high, and to judge by what we heard money was to be picked up in the streets.

Therefore, when navigation opened once again, a veritable exodus from the country began. Almost every boat that came from Dawson carried some old-timers on their way outside, all anxious to share in the general prosperity. The sight of so many familiar faces calling farewell from the decks of steamers filled me with dismay, until finally I refrained from going to wave to the departing travelers.

In other ways that summer was a very pleasant one. Physically, I was as well as I hoped ever to be. Business was such that I was making something more than expenses, without having to work as I had in former years. The attitude of "the boys" toward me was what they might have exhibited toward a younger sister and they seemed to vie with one another as to who should first tell me any pleasantry or joke, particularly on each other. I had every reason to think that I held the confidence and respect of the majority of those around me and I took great comfort in that thought. So the happy summer gradually slipped away.

During all these months the exodus from the country had continued and in the autumn I received a letter from Mrs. Pinska. They were going outside, too, and so was Miss Buckles. The latter was going for only the winter but the Pinskas would not return. She urged me to abandon the North and go outside, too, and live near them.

"Come to town as soon as you can and we'll talk over the plan," she concluded.

I felt as though my feet had been swept from under me. I had no idea what to think. It had never occurred to me they would go outside. They had appeared so happy, prosperous, and content! The result was that I went to Dawson earlier than usual and when the steamer refused to stop at Stewart I went downriver in a small boat. Getting to Dawson City about ten at night we went to a restaurant to eat before planning anything else.

In a few moments the door opened and in trooped the Pinskas, Dawson DeWitt, who had gone to town earlier than I, and Edmunson, my charioteer when fur-buying. They insisted on all crowding into one booth and what a merry party we made of it! That was the moment when I decided that with such friends as these life was worth living. The road back had been covered at last.

During all my stay Mrs. Pinska urged me to go outside. "Promise me that you will no longer bury your heart in that place at Stewart. Al intends to build a house when we've decided on a location and he says there must be one room that will be all yours."

In the end I went so far as to say, "I can't promise you that things will be just as you have planned, but I will promise to join you as soon as it can be managed." How—I had no idea.

The whole town seemed to be a fever of departure. Houses and possessions were being sacrificed for whatever they would bring and the question tossed from lip to lip was, "Are you going out this fall?" I began to wonder if there would be anyone left when the river closed.

On a Saturday afternoon, at the entrance to the dock, I met young Jack Maskel, a patron of the store and roadhouse at Stewart whose fine baritone voice had often entertained us. He held out his hand. "Just in time to say good-bye," he called.

"Are you going, too!" I cried in surprise.

"On the *Selkirk* and she's about to sail. I'm on my way to board her now."

"But . . . why?" I stammered.

"Going out to have my voice trained. I'll have a record made and send it to you as a souvenir of all the good times we've had at Stewart. 'Bye!"

We were to sail on the steamer *Whitehorse* and Mrs. Pinska insisted that Dawson, Edmunson, and I have supper with them. Miss Buckles was too busy to come. We demurred, but it was useless, although all were sailing on the same vessel.

"This is our last meal here and we want you with us, Smythie. We've had so many happy times together in the little house it seems only right that our last thoughts of it should be assoicated with you. Come and help us say good-bye to it."

So we went. In spite of the coming separation it was a merry meal. There was much laughing discussion regarding the house they were to build.

"Did Olive tell you there was to be a room especially for you?"

Mr. Pinska asked me. I nodded and he went on, "Well, now is the time to tell us the kind of room you want. Speak up, you little shrimp! What is it to be?"

With a lump in my throat at the raillery which I knew was all assumed, I answered:

"Better make it a round room. Then I'll not have to square the account of it!"

So the banter continued until the meal was over and we hurried away to allow Mrs. Pinska to make her final preparations for leaving. Then, at sailing time, we met again to share the journey until Stewart. The steamer was crowded and in the evening we formed a group in a corner of the saloon and talked until well into the night. The saloon slowly emptied but our group remained. Then the others said good night and Mr. and Mrs. Pinska, Dawson, and I alone were left. Midnight struck, then one, then two, and still we lingered.

When the hands of the clock were drawing near to three Mrs. Pinska yawned, then apologized, "Oh, I'm so sleepy, but I hate to leave. It seems a shame to waste the few hours before we must say good-bye by spending them in sleep, Smythie." But finally, she too said good night and went to her stateroom.

Stewart was reached about eight-thirty next morning and we went ashore amid much handshaking, waving handkerchiefs, and shouts of "See you in the spring," or "Be back with the ducks." Mrs. Pinska and Miss Buckles came only to the bow of the steamer on the lower deck and in her sweet way Miss Buckles said good-bye to me there. Mrs. Pinska said not a word, just a close embrace and as she laid her cheek to mine I felt her tremble. Then she gripped her hands tightly together and stood looking from brimming eyes . . . dumb. Both Mr. Pinska and Edmunson came into the store for a last word and each in turn kissed me and whispered, "Good-bye, little sister." My last glimpse showed the four of them standing together on the bow, in silhouette against the sparkling surface of the river, Edmunson and Al Pinska with caps in hand, waving both arms in farewell.

It was natural that my nerves should again be strained by all this rather sudden, certainly unexpected, separation from my dearest friends. To see them again at any early date, as I meant to do, would involve my turning away from my heart's home at Stewart. All this may serve for some as an explanation of the incident I am about to relate.

To me the matter goes deeper than that, beyond my understanding. I know only that it did happen.

Ever since that New Year Masquerade in Dawson City, when I had gone home sick with some unknown dread, I had felt times of great foreboding. I fought them off as nerves, tried to ignore them, but there was no denying their occurrence.

While the *Whitehorse* was still ploughing upriver with my friends on board, I went out about dusk one evening, leaving Dawson DeWitt absorbed in a magazine. It was a simple, routine errand: to lock the henhouse for the night. I was about halfway across the yard when I was seized with a sensation the like of which I had never before experienced and I sincerely hope I never shall again. There was nothing in sight except the ordinary everyday scene, neither was there any actual sound. But suddenly I stopped and stood as though frozen in my tracks, for the air about me seemed rent as with the knell of doom. I could not bring myself to continue my errand but instead I turned and, like a frightened deer, I fled in terror to the house.

Dawson looked up in amazement from his magazine when I burst in, sobbing and wringing my hands.

"What is the matter?" he cried.

"Oh, Dawson! It's . . . it's terrible!" I wailed.

Startled, he dropped the magazine. "What's terrible? Can't you tell me what's happening?"

I seemed not to have any control over the words that followed. They came tearing from my strangling throat without any volition of mine.

"O-o-h!" I moaned. "The air is alive with the shrieking of lost souls in agony!"

Now thoroughly alarmed he sprang to his feet and seized my writhing hands, while his eyes dilated and his face turned ashen. My mind must have given way completely, he thought.

"What do you mean?" he almost shouted, then quickly recovered himself. He gently forced me into a chair and chafed my hands and forehead as he repeated over and over, "Your nerves are certainly in a terrible condition!" When the shuddering and moaning had subdued he went to the kitchen and soon returned with his panacea for all ills, a cup of tea, and I did feel grateful for its soothing warmth.

The incident was never again referred to directly, but the next evening, when I was settled with my needlework, he opened the conversation.

"I want to talk to you about something that I think is for your good. Don't you think you had better reconsider your decision and go outside for the winter?"

"Oh, I can't!" I objected.

"I believe you can, if you make up your mind to it, and I really think you should. Your nerves are very much unstrung—and no wonder! You have gone through enough here to shatter the nerves of a person far more robust than you, but there is a limit to everything, so I really think you should go. You still have time to catch the last boat and join your friends on the coast. Think how delighted the Pinska's would be!"

But I only reiterated, "I can't!"

"Is it a question of funds?" he pressed. "Because if so, remember our compact. What I have is at your disposal and if you were in truth my mother or sister I would insist on this."

Again all I could say was, "I can't!" It was the whole truth. There were no reasons I could have given but my whole being rebelled at the mere suggestion.

At last Dawson gave up. "I'm sorry that you won't listen to reason. I think you're making a big mistake. But the decision is yours. I can do no more."

In the course of time the steamer *Whitehorse* reached the little town for which she was named and we wired our final farewells to "The Bunch" and signed it "The Residue." Her passengers and crew were joined by those of two preceding steamers and at noon one day Dawson announced, "The biggest load of passengers that has ever crossed the White Pass left Whitehorse this morning for Skagway and they plan to sail for Vancouver on the *Princess Sophia*. There was a big dance in Whitehorse last night and the sourdoughs did themselves proud. It was a gay affair."

"I wish I had been there," was my comment.

"Also me," he echoed, with a fine disregard for grammar.

I do not remember how many days elapsed after this nor the exact date, but the month was October and the day of the week Wednesday, when he informed me, "The *Princess Sophia* went on the rocks in Lynn Canal at two o'clock this morning in a blinding snowstorm."

"Good Heavens!" I cried.

"Don't be alarmed. There seems to be no cause for anxiety," he assured me. "The storm has abated, she's resting on an even keel, and one of her sister ships has been rushed from Vancouver to her assistance."

"There is cause for anxiety," I contradicted. "The trip from Vancouver will take more than three days and anyone who thinks that the lives of those people are safe on a ship stranded in Lynn Canal at this time of year when storms come up so suddenly has another think coming! That Inside Passage has swallowed more than one vessel with her cargo of souls!"

"You may be right," he agreed, "but worrying will do no good. So let's hope for the best."

On the Thursday I asked, "What about the *Sophia?*"

"Everything seems to be all right. People in launches and small boats cruising in her vicinity report hearing the passengers laughing and joking and someone playing the piano. So they all seem to be quite happy."

"Where is the relief ship?"

"I can't say definitely. Steaming along the coast somewhere, I suppose."

On Friday noon the question and answer were still the same, but that evening he was late for supper, came in very quietly, and avoided my eyes as he hung up his hat and coat.

"The *Sophia?*" I enquired, giving him a sharp lok.

There was a long pause. Then, "The *Sophia* is lost, with all on board."

It was little more than a saddened whisper, yet it struck my ears like thunder. "My God!" I screamed.

He took my hands gently in his. "I hate to have to tell you this, but that is the report. A storm came up this afternoon and she suddenly slid off the rocks into deep water. One of the lighthouse tenders picked up her S.O.S. and this message, "Just time to say good-bye. We're foundering." Although a comparatively small boat, the tender put out to her assistance in the teeth of the gale, but when she reached the place where the *Sophia* had been all that was to be seen was the top of her masts. The tender cruised around for some time, but failed to find even a bit of wreckage, so for the safety of his own vessel the captain made for shelter."

"The . . . passenger list," I managed to stammer.

"I can't tell you another thing just now. I'm going back to the office as soon as I've had a cup of tea and will get the list for you at the earliest possible moment. There is no chance to get a message through now, the wires are just humming with news of the tragedy. Hope for the best: the Bunch may have taken another boat."

I ate no supper, he very little, and as he laid his arm across my shoulders in sympathy before going out, he was trembling himself. Then for three hours I paced the floor. "The shrieking of lost souls in agony!"

When he returned he again avoided my eyes and with clenched hands and teeth I waited while he slowly drew from his pocket the familiar green slip.

"I've got a copy of that passenger list," he began, "and I don't see the names of Miss Buckles or the Bentons on it. Mr. Henry's is there . . . also E.S. Ironsides' . . . and his mother's . . . "

"For God's sake, Dawson, *tell me!*" I broke in and there was anguish in his voice as he little more than whispered the one word, "Yes!"

"The . . . Pinskas?"

He bowed his head slowly, then steadied me to a couch. As when Waldron went there were no tears—only that terrible iron band. I wished it would crush my brain into oblivion.

When the trembling had partially subsided he handed me the paper and near the top were the names of the happy pair that I had loved so well. Below I found that of Captain Locke of the *Princess Sophia* and his crew, from whom I had received such kindness when bringing Waldron home in 1912; of Captain Bloomquist, who had commanded the *Casca* on that same journey; of men from the crews of the river steamers plying past my home; of little Jack Maskell, going out to have his voice trained; of many, many more; of so many—so very many. Sick with horror I scanned the awful list. Whole families were lost and others cruelly broken. Among the more than three hundred and forty victims I found fifty-seven names that were known to me. Of our happy Christmas party of the year before Miss Buckles and I alone remained to grieve. The only living survivor of that terrible tragedy, which for utter fatality must be unbeaten in the history of the sea, was a small dog. About a week after the wreck he was found, famished and covered with crude oil, by members of the crew of a cannery operating in the vicinity, and was later identified as having belonged to one of the *Sophia's* passengers.

Recovery of the bodies was begun immediately. I think approximately one hundred and eighty were picked up along the coast. Of these it was reported that only one had been drowned and another had died before entering the water. All others had been suffocated by the crude oil which had escaped when the tanks were torn open as the vessel slid from the rocks. The bodies of Al and Olive Pinska were among the first to be found and I derived a small degree of comfort in the knowledge that they would be tenderly laid to rest.

Our loved Northland never recovered from the blow. I doubt if there was one person in all the country who had not been bereft in some way. In the eyes of many there remained always the look of one wounded unto death.

Pretty Crimpy!

Nothing that I had previously endured had so affected me. The suddenness of the blow, coupled with the knowledge that all those lives might have been saved, was devastating. There was little chance of consolation, for everyone, especially in Stewart, was sorrowing as well. So we shared our grief and the sad, weary days dragged by.

It was in this mood that the Armistice found us. Perhaps in the midst of our sorrow we were doubly thankful that the slaughter was at last over.

As the weeks passed I began to realize that life had once more been remade for me. The road back lay again before me, but this time there seemed no highway of return to the life that I had known. Instead, I found a new turning leading into spiritual ways as yet untraveled. This time I had not the ill health to contend with nor the burden of expense. Instead of the mental and physical lassitude, my sense of being alone, called out unexpected reserves of daring. Not for the first time I felt that my life mattered to no one but myself. Then I had rather morbidly grieved over my own loneliness. Now there was a sense of reckless freedom in the thought that none were left who really cared.

My life in the North with Waldron had been lived under protest at first and then under the compulsion of circumstances. Following his going I carried on because it was the thing to do and not from any desire to shoulder the burden. I did what must be done and nothing more. Gradually the severed links with the world about me had been renewed with added strength and I at last became assured that I had been weighed in the balance and not found wanting. The North had accepted me as its own. I had proved my mettle. Now that my friends were gone this knowledge still remained. It gave a new spirit of zest in my living. I was alone. If something did befall me, who was there at hand to mourn? There would be the Yukon salute to another sourdough gone home, nothing more. Had not Service once sung:

"And a bunch of bones on the boundless snows,
    The end of my trail . . . who knows? Who knows?"

Meanwhile, at the Christmas of 1918, we evened our scores against personal sorrows and our old enemies by doing the best good turn we could to the one who expected it least at our hands.

Over a year before, an older miner named Nordhof had rented my cabin only fifty feet or so from the store. He was past middle age and had suffered a partial paralytic stroke, making it impossible for him to continue mining. He had saved a little grubstake but not enough to last him outside and some of the boys around promised to help him occasionally if I would rent a cabin where he could "batch" and live on his savings. This was agreed and Mr. Nordhof had been a quiet and friendly neighbor ever since.

This Christmas someone suggested that we dress a tree as a surprise for him.

"He's a German," they reminded me, "and they all set great store by a tree at Christmas. It might cheer him up to have us remember him."

So the word was passed around among the boys, who were delighted with the idea and gifts of all kinds were donated. No group of school-children ever looked forward to a tree with more interest and excitement than those boys did to that one. I intended to serve dinner, to which Mr. Nordhof had been invited, about six o'clock and the plan was to dress the tree in the warehouse, entice him to the house before the dinner was served, whisk the tree into his cabin, and send him back there to find it.

On Christmas afternoon, Billie Middleton, my hired man, was detailed to lure the old man back and forth, so at the right moment he went to the cabin with a message from me. Mr. Nordhof came over quite unsuspectingly. When everything was ready Billie returned and informed the victim that he was wanted at his own cabin.

"But, I only came from my cabin a short time ago," he objected.

"I can't help that," Billie answered with a broad grin. "You're wanted at your cabin."

"But I tell you I've just come from there!" the other persisted, while the rest of us tried to keep sober countenances.

"I don't give a darn!" Billie laughed. "You're wanted at the cabin." Then, grumbling, the old man hobbled out.

After a while someone suggested, "Let's take a look." Like a group of naughty children we stole to the cabin window, but the next minute we regretted our curiosity. There were no lights in the cabin but the tree, looking very brave and pretty with its tissue, tinsel, and lighted candles, was nicely set up in the corner. In front of it stood the old man. His face wore a rapt look, his hands were clasped as if in prayer, and he swayed backward and forward while the tears coursed down his cheeks. One glance was enough. I fled back to the house, but the others were before me and it was a serious group that gathered around the fire. Some time later, when the old man tried to express his thanks to me, he seemed to be quite overcome.

"Don't say a word, Mr. Nordhof," I joked. "Once these boys get started one is as bad as the other."

As he groped his way to a seat I heard him murmur, with a tremulous sigh. "Yes—one is as bad as the other!"

When the evening was over and he said good night he shook hands with each one and told us earnestly, "It's more than thirty years since I left home and this has been the happiest Christmas I've known in all that time."

We were happy, too, and a year later the memory made us happier still.

In the following February I was told of a fine lot of furs on Barker Creek which I might purchase and determined to risk cold weather and make the trip. The keeper of the roadhouse at

Barker, Jim McLaughlin, would convoy me up and I could return with the mailman. At that time of year there was little traffic on the Stewart River and the trail was heavy. Even in the moderate temperature of twenty-five below zero the trip proved a hard one and I was more than pleased when Barker Creek was reached.

The sight of the place after so many years, with all that they had held, awoke many memories. How much had happened since that night, so long ago at Christmas, 1906, when Waldron and I had closed our new place at Stewart and gone to the house-warming party at Jim McLaughlin's new roadhouse. It had been my first experience of a Yukon party. When I went to the little room which I had then shared with Miss Geer (later Mrs. Pinska) I almost expected her voice to come to me from the silence. It was hard to take a matter-of-fact view of things and remember that the place was merely a roadhouse at which I was stopping while on a fur-buying trip.

I had never been up Barker Creek before but the trail would be good, with no rotten ice, and I determined to make the run alone. I did so without any difficulty, finding the locality one of unusual beauty and finding also a splendid lot of furs. Hearing of another lot on Scroggie Creek I made the five-mile trip to its mouth. Then I was caught for a week at the Scroggie roadhouse because the temperature had fallen to fifty below. Finally, it was only nineteen below one morning and I set out on the run up the creek, twenty miles each way. Unlike Barker there seemed little that was attractive about Scroggie, although I did get the furs and they were worthwhile. An added reason for not enjoying the trip was that all afternoon the glass was dropping again and I was far out on the trail. As the sun went down the decreasing speed of the dogs told me the temperature was still falling. When the moon rose the frost haze became noticeable and I knew it was at least forty-five degrees below zero. When I could hear my breath freezing as it came from my lips, I knew that a temperature of fifty below had been reached. Beyond that I had only the speed of the dogs to guide me. Slowly and more slowly they traveled until their pace became that of a person walking. Although I was unable to judge how far I had come I knew that I still had a good many miles to make and, with a view to keeping up my circulation I got out to walk behind the sled, being careful to wrap my fur coat about the foot-warmer so that it would be warm to put on again. The slow speed of the dogs made it easy for me to keep up without over-exerting myself and as they padded along the sound of their panting told me that they too were feeling the intense cold.

I was warmly clothed in two suits of woollen underwear, a man's flannel shirt, heavy cloth knickers, sweater, short skirt, and a parka. In addition to my own cashmere stockings I had on several pairs of men's woollen socks and moccasins with insoles. I also wore a man's fur cap and wool mittens covered with gauntlets of tanned moose-hide. I was not cold, neither did I have any distress in breathing, but when I had walked for some little distance I was suddenly seized with a violent trembling and a suffocating feeling of pressure around my heart. Instinctively I realized that all exertion must be abandoned so, stopping the dogs, I hurriedly donned the coat and wrapped myself in the robes. The trembling continued all the way to the roadhouse and the smoke from its chimney was a welcome sight to me!

A look at the thermometer showed that it registered fifty-nine below. "Pretty crimpy!" as the boys would say.

Early the next morning I heard a door open downstairs and an old fellow who lived near the roadhouse bawled, "Did Mrs. Smythe get in?"

"Yes," my host answered, "At half-past ten last night!"

"God bless my soul!" the other bellowed. "That woman will be picked up dead on the trail some day!"

For nearly another week I huddled by the fire at Scroggie, waiting for the weather to moderate. At last it came up to only twenty-five below and I decided to chance it. After such a double spell of cold it was almost certain to continue rising. So I set out early, trying to reach Stewart in the one day.

Barker was reached over an easy five miles. Jim McLaughlin offered to convoy me home again as he had coming up, but feeling sure that I should be in time to catch the mailman who lived a few miles farther on, I declined his offer and hurried on my way. Unfortunately I was about half an hour late in reaching the mailman's cabin and he was already en route to Stewart when I arrived. I was now between the devil and the deep sea. It would be necessary for me to do one of two things: either return to Barker Creek and enlist the service of Jim McLaughlin or make the trip over the treacherous ice of the Stewart alone. Neither alternative was particularly appealing. If I returned to Barker I should have to wait another day, with the possibility of the weather again turning cold. So, after debating the matter for awhile with myself, I resolved to take the risk and press on alone. There were two places where danger lurked and which were never considered safe even in midwinter. But I hoped to get past these before dark. Beyond them, I had no fear.

A few miles past the cabin I came to some very rough ice and got out to steady the sled. It was impossible for me to keep it upright and as it lurched and swayed, several times upsetting completely, I got the smell of something burning. Remembering that I had wrapped my coat around the foot-warmer again, I tore away the robe and pulled out the coat—with two large holes burned in it.

"Just my luck! There goes my three-hundred-dollar coat, the best rag I own!" I wailed, as I threw it in the snow and stamped out the fire.

Then I thought of my wallet in the pocket. I was willing to admit that it is better to be born lucky than pretty when I found that while the pocket, the portion of the coat surrounding it, and the end of the wallet, had all been burned away, bills amounting to more than two thousand dollars had remained untouched!

After having been tied up for several days the dogs were sluggish and made very poor time. Darkness had closed in and the moon was up before I reached Carlson Slough, the first danger-spot. My heart pounded like a hammer at every step along the trail because, in addition to the likelihood of encountering rotten ice or overflow, wolves were often seen in the locality. I had a rifle, which I placed close to hand, and I strained my eyes in an effort to scan the hillside in the light of the moon. But I am quite sure that had wolves—or even one wolf—appeared I should have been too terrified to even think about the rifle, much less use it. However, I saw neither wolves, rotten ice, open water, nor overflow, and I breathed a deep sigh of relief when I was well past the dreaded spot.

At Wildcat Slough there was considerable overflow which I at first mistook for open water but, aided by the moonlight and the sagacity of the dogs, I was able to pick my way around it without even getting wet.

I finally reached home safely about nine o'clock at night and of course pretended to think that I had done something quite smart.

But I secretly resolved that, furs or no furs, I had taken my last trip alone in midwinter.

It was an excellent resolution and, rather to my own surprise, I kept it. The effort to do so must have temporarily smothered my new zest for life, as I later said no to one of the most unexpected proposals I ever received.

When the rivers had opened, a dredge was required near Mayo on the upper Stewart. Excursion rates were declared on the steamer taking it up and I was a passenger, hoping to combine business with pleasure by picking up a few skins while there. One evening during the trip up the Stewart two men from Dawson City took chairs on deck beside me. One represented capital seeking investment and the other was a well-known sourdough. Both were successful men and of sound mind and memory, but when Mr. Pickering told me the purpose of the interview I began to doubt it.

"Would you," he wanted to know, "consider being nominated to represent the Stewart District in the next territorial election?"

When I was convinced of their sincerity I did consider being nominated. I was tempted to agree, but doubts of my ambitions really lying in that direction assailed me. In the end, I said "No," with thanks for the very real compliment.

But when I had gone to my stateroom that night I sat for a long time, thinking. Yes. My years in the Yukon had taken me a long way along the path of life! Not by any stretch of imagination could I picture those two men approaching that nervous, homesick girl astride old Dobbin on that sunny autumn morning in what now seemed a remote past, with the request that she stand as a representative of the people!

Pale Horse Rider

Christmas of 1919 promised to be quiet enough. Just what we should do had not been settled. We still recalled with pleasure our surprise tree the previous year for the old German miner, Mr. Nordhof.

The old gentleman was still living in the nearby cabin and about a week before Christmas he paid me an afternoon visit at the store. He often came across and while his hearing was poor and talking to him was often something of a strain, I realized how lonely his hours must be and always made him welcome. This day he appeared to be in unusually good spirits and assured me that he felt so much better.

"It's all in here," he said, laying his hand on his breast. "I don't know what caused it, but I'm like a different person. I feel so well!"

He stayed until Dawson DeWitt came in to supper but declined the invitation to remain and share the meal with us and, as the path to his cabin was rather icy, Dawson went with him to see that he reached his own door safely. When he returned I repeated Mr. Nordhof's words about feeling better.

"I'm afraid the old man is nearing the end of the trail," he remarked sadly. "This feeling better is probably the last flicker of the candle before it goes out."

That evening some of the boys were in for a game of cards and remained until about eleven o'clock. When they were leaving I asked them, as they passed the cabin, to see that all was well with our neighbor. They reported, "All okay," and things settled down for the night.

At three in the morning I went to my medicine cabinet for something to relieve a toothache. Through the window I saw Nordhof's cabin wrapped in darkness, a tiny wisp of smoke rising from the chimney.

Some time later, while the light in the buildings was still quite dim, I heard a door slam and then Dawson's quick footsteps as he ran through the store into the dining-room, then back into the store.

"Are you awake?" he called to me.

"A-almost," I mumbled sleepily.

"Did you sleep well?" was his next question.

"How silly! The idea of wakening me to ask if I slept well!" I snapped.

But his next words brought me to my feet. "I think you had better get up," he advised. "The cabin over there has been on fire and while I think all danger to these buildings has passed one can never be quite sure."

The cabin on fire . . . then it must be destroyed! I was half-dressed by the time he had finished speaking, for I knew well that once a spark caught one of our type of buildings they went up like tinder.

"Did the old man get out?" I cried frantically.

"I can't tell you, but it's useless for you to get upset about whatever has happened. If he got out, he's safe. If not, nothing can be done."

As he finished speaking I ran to the dining-room window, but all that remained of the cabin now was a heap of smouldering ruins. The fact that the main building remained untouched and that we escaped perishing in the fire—as we surely would have done had the building caught—has always seemed to me a miracle.

Death had passed us by so closely that had we been awake we should have felt his fiery breath. Had he taken our neighbor?

Frantically we searched all the buildings, in the hope that the old man had escaped and not wishing to disturb us had taken refuge wherever possible to wait until we rose. No trace of him could be found. I then prepared for a visit of inquiry to the other homes but Dawson accepted facts more readily.

"It might be as well," he agreed, "but I feel sure it will prove useless. Had he escaped he would not have gone to the neighbors. He would be here."

Of course he proved to be right, for I did not find Mr. Nordhof. During the forenoon a corps of volunteers shoveled snow into the ruins until all fire was extinguished, then searched carefully through it. The body was charred beyond recognition, but by its position and other evidence we all agreed that, five o'clock being his rising hour he had been astir early, had probably been seized with another paralytic stroke and fallen on his lamp, upsetting it.

Again we fashioned a coffin and again there was a new mound under the trees on the police reserve. The tragedy affected all of us deeply, but it left me particularly shaken. For the first time in my life I had the feeling that I had been deliberately suffered to live!

Two days after Christmas I left to visit some mining property on Barker Creek in which I was interested. Jim McLaughlin also had an interest in the venture and was traveling with me. I was gone about three days and on my return, I looked in vain for the familiar sight of Shand's buildings. All that I could see was smoking ashes. I looked again for my own buildings. They stood silent and untouched, looking unreal in the light of the hazy moon. Another miracle had been granted me.

As soon as we had reached the top of the bank Jim abandoned the team and started on the run in the direction of a cabin some distance away, in the window of which a light was shining. I was snugly wrapped in the robes and securely lashed into the sled. "Wait!" I called. "I'm going to get out of here!" But he paid no heed to me and I was obliged to extricate myself as best I could. Later, I chaffed him about his lack of gallantry and he drily remarked, "Well, I heard you say you was goin' to get out of there and I knew that if you said you'd do it, you'd do it!"

With the recent tragedy so fresh in my mind, as I followed Jim in the direction of the cabin I realized how one can live a lifetime in a few seconds. The question my mind kept repeating was, "How many—and who—perished this time?" Then from a distance I heard the cabin door open, a murmured question from Jim, and a voice inside answer, "They're all here, but some of them are pretty badly burned."

Thank God! This time the Pale Horse had merely galloped past.

The fire had started early in the morning while several of the guests and family were still in bed or at breakfast. Mrs. Shand, trapped upstairs, had a narrow escape. She had been obliged to make her way down the flaming staircase and her face, hands, and parts of her body were badly burned; while in their efforts to save her two others had been severely scorched. Also, several of the guests had got out only in the nick of time. The old couple lost everything the home contained, but true to the spirit of a big Northern family, friends rallied to their assistance and it was not long until they were again doing business.

For me, however, the end was not yet. Within a few weeks more I was to look into the very eyes of the Pale Horse's Rider and know that he is a coward.

During the preceding summer it had been necessary to have a man's help and I had hired a fellow whom I shall call Brown and who came well recommended as a worker. His work did prove satisfactory, but the job was scarcely finished when he insisted on paying me the very doubtful compliment of laying his affections at my feet. At first I regarded the matter merely as a regretable incident and tried to handle it as delicately as possible. I have always been an exponent of the theory that it is easier for all concerned to have one's hair barbered than pulled out by the roots. I think Dawson had an inkling of the situation for, without giving a reason, he quietly advised me to get rid of the fellow. A woman also spoke a word of warning to me, so when Brown reopened the subject later I took a much firmer stand. He then become rather disagreeable and the upshot of it was that he was told to remain away from the place. Shortly after this he left the locality, presumably to trap for the winter, and I considered the matter closed.

One winter night, when making my rounds with a lantern to see that all was well, I found that the fire in the warm storage needed replenishing, so I filled the stove and sat down to wait until all danger from gas was past before closing the draughts. Just as I had finished doing so a while later and was picking up the lantern to return to the house, the door opened and Brown appeared. Some intuition warned me that his visit boded evil, but I tried to conceal any sign of fear.

"I'll be through here in a very short time," I explained and busied myself with some unnecessary attention to the fire. "If you want anything from the store you can wait for me there."

"I don't want anything from the store and I can say what I came to say here," he growled.

"As you wish," I answered, careful to put the stove between us. My heart seemed about to choke me and my knees almost refused to bear my weight, but I tried hard to appear at ease. If Dawson would only return from the office and come to look for me! But the door remained closed and I thought I should faint when he came close to me, slipped his hand in his pocket, and barked, "Is it all over between you and me?"

I believe my voice was steady, as I answered, "I don't know what you mean."

"You do know what I mean. Is it all over between us?"

The lout's impudence began to anger me and, frightened though I was, I shot back, "There never was anything between us! I hired you to do certain work, for which you were paid. When you presumed, I was kindly and patient. But understand this: I want no more of your impudence! Do I make myself clear?"

He took a step nearer and I held the lantern ready to hurl at him. I watched that hand in the pocket. Did he have a gun?

He thrust his face still nearer and hissed, "If I can't have you, then—by God!—no one else will!'"

I waited to hear the gun bark. Nothing was happening to me . . .was it bluff?

Could I bluff, too? But how? The Mounties! Yes. . .like whist . . .when in doubt, lead trumps!

Though sick with terror I forced myself to meet his evil face squarely.

"You have me at a disadvantage," I sneered. "I am alone here. No one is within call. But don't think that I'm afraid of you! You may even be coward enough to kill me, but you would merely be taking a life that has seen its best days. So, before it's too late, I want to remind you that we have an organization in this country which deals with criminals as they deserve. My record is clear and I have friends in the Force. If harm comes to me the country will be combed for the guilty one and he will pay the price! So, if the idea of swinging at the end of a noose appeals to you, go ahead! Do your worst!"

But while I pretended defiance I was turning as cold as ice.

His face twitched. Slowly his hand came from his pocket. "Damn you!" he snarled.

The next moment the door slammed behind him.

Too terrified to move, I remained where I was until Dawson returned from the office and came in search of me. But I spoke no word to him, ever, of what had occurred.

Lonely Heart

The shocks which these few weeks brought to me were probably among the first causes that ultimately resulted in loosening me in a measure from the grip of the Yukon and of Stewart. Experiences like them bring home to any person, even if subconsciously, the true tenuity of life. The message was clear that one's temporal possessions or surroundings can be swept away in a flash and there is instinctively a self-defensive withdrawal of any absorbing interest in them.

Some six months after these events I received a letter from Miss Buckles, now once more in Dawson, announcing her coming marriage to William Rinehardt. She told me I must be present.

I knew she was making a wise choice but in some strange vague way I almost envied the man. I realized the effect her marriage would have on our relations and the more I thought about it the more my attention was drawn to my own case. Among my friends there were those who, having my welfare at heart, regretted that I had remained alone so long. Some even remonstrated with me. May I be pardoned if I say that it had not been necessary? There were men of my own age who could have given me the comforts of a home and who appeared willing to risk life with me as a helpmate. But when it came to a final decision Waldron's face always rose before me and the yes became a no. Then, too, there was Dawson. I could not tolerate the thought of anything which would interfere with our splendid friendship.

Yes, I knew that with the Pinskas gone and Miss Buckles married, life for me in the North would be much more lonely. Still, when the time of her marriage came I donned my brightest smile and if there was a lump in my throat as the words which changed her name were spoken no one suspected it. The ceremony was performed in the manse and later about twenty of us sat down to a wedding supper at the home of friends of the bride and groom. It was a happy gathering and we rose only when the closing hours of the old day had given place to the opening ones of the new.

For some reason I lacked the usual urge to hurry on this visit to Dawson City and also felt the desire to do a number of things which I had long intended to do, sometime. My general feeling was what I might have felt when visiting a place to which I had little hope of returning.

Back at Stewart there was still no need for hurry. Again we looked forward to a lonesome and nerve-trying winter and it proved to be just as lonesome and nerve-trying as we anticipated. Life at Stewart had changed completely. Gone were the jolly good times of former years. Business was practically at a standstill, at least temporarily. There was little or no travel and we occupied ourselves as best we could. I was again on the horns of a dilemma: in allowing myself to become so attached to the place which I hoped would be a home I had gradually alienated myself from all other interests. Could I continue to live on in this state of practical isolation?

Then in the midst of this perplexity it seemed as though fate took a hand. My father was now well past the allotted span of life and his rugged constitution showed signs of breaking down. He had never been reconciled to my persistence in remaining in the North after Waldron had gone and as his strength failed he repeatedly expressed a longing to see me. So when I received another pleading letter shortly after the river closed, I took long and serious counsel with myself. My final decision was to reduce the stock to a minimum and to close the place and go to him as soon as it could be done. I still could not tolerate the thought of selling. Even to close and leave it for a while caused a pang such as none have ever guessed.

I made no mention of this conclusion to Dawson DeWitt until I knew that my mind was unalterably made up. He had known of my father's repeated requests, but in spite of this the information came as a surprise. He made no comment at the time, but a few evenings later reopened the subject. Did I have any idea as to when I might be going? Because it would be necessary for him to go outside sooner or later for surgical treatment. The operation was not likely to prove serious, merely the removal of a fatty tumor, but he had been advised to go to the Mayo Institute. Could we not go outside at the same time? And would I not go to Rochester with him? Man-like, he quailed at the thought of encountering hospitals, doctors, and nurses alone. When the treatment was over I could continue on my way to my old home, he would convalesce with relatives, and perhaps when all this was over we might even return to Stewart at the same time.

This was extremely different to the program I had in mind, but I finally agreed and with a homesick heart I set about making preparations for carrying out the plan. I think if the business of leaving could have been accomplished quickly it would have hurt less. I repeatedly told myself that I was closing only for a time but deep within me some strong intuition told me it would be forever and as each article of merchandise was disposed of it seemed to be another farewell.

So time went and Christmas was again with us. We had no guests so Dawson and I and an old prospector named Card who was cutting wood for me sat down to a fowl together. The day ended just as quietly.

On the following evening a group of the boys, including Shorty Doner and our old friend Wilkins, dropped in for a game of cards. Wilkins had not visited us for some time and he was as pleased to be back as a school-boy home on vacation. Shorty Doner was everybody's darling, so to speak. Well past middle age, he was undersized and from his wrinkled gnome-like face a pair of piercing eyes popped at you through perfectly round lids. He knew everyone for miles around, as well as their affairs, both public and personal. But what he knew he kept to himself; consequently he was a prime favorite with all. His greatest delight was in a game of solo, a card game in which you bid according to the hand you hold and in which the ten-spot always ranks highest. A run of good luck would send him home in high spirits. The opposite was also true and he was often made the victim of the boys' love of a practical joke. They would stack the cards so that Shorty would draw an apparently unbeatable hand, only to find that his next neighbor held the one card necessary to take the trick. At such times his remarks were punctuated with phrases which he never learned in Sunday School, but his resentment was always directed against the cards or his luck. I doubt if he ever suspected he was being hoaxed.

On this evening he was as pleased to see me as though I were a dearly-loved and long-lost relative. From my seat in the dining-room I could hear their merry banter and Wilkins's laugh told me each time Shorty lost a ten-spot. Wilkins had always enjoyed a game with Dawson and when it was over he rose to make his usual request, "Well, Missus, the game's over and now will ye jest play 'Me Wild Irish Rose' before I go? Ye know it's me favorite song and that's certainly a lovely record ye've got!"

So I played it for him twice and then he picked up his hat.

"Thank ye kindly, Missus. Me visit to Stewart is never properly finished without hearin' 'Me Wild Irish Rose.' Good-night, Dawson. I'll be back soon and, by cracky, I'll beat ye on a heart solo!"

Then he closed the door behind him and went whistling up the trail.

We had scarcely greeted the New Year when the mercury began to drop. It fell rapidly and in a few hours had reached the terrible level of sixty-five below zero, where it remained for several days. While the biting cold searched for the tiniest crack through which it might penetrate, we all huddled around our cosy fires nor dreamed of the tragedy being enacted at our very door. On January sixth the weather started to moderate and by the next morning it had reached the comfortable temperature of only twenty-five below. Dawson and I were seated at breakfast when the door opened to admit Shorty and one glance told me that he was the bearer of bad news. His round bright eyes held a look of horror, his kind little face twitched, and he was gasping for breath. He lost no time in giving us his news.

"Dawson," he began, without even taking time to extend a

greeting, "there's a dead man lyin' in the trail up there!"

"A dead man in the trail! Where?" cried Dawson, springing from his chair.

"In the trail on the river just around that little bend above Shand's. I started out this mornin' to go over my trapline an' was goin' along with my head down an' my cap pulled close. First thing I knowed I was right up to him. It give me quite a scare. I thought I better let you know so's you could tell the police."

"Do you know who it is?"

"No. I didn't examine him nor nuthin'. I know it's against the law to interfere with a body any."

"All right, Shorty, I'll be with you in a minute," Dawson assured him and went for his coat and cap.

"Who can the poor creature be?" I wondered, as Dawson returned dressed for the outdoors.

"Without a doubt it's someone we know. You needn't keep breakfast for me. I'll not be back until the police have been notified and I've received their instructions."

Then he and Shorty left together. My own breakfast remained untouched. To realize that a fellow-being had perished almost within sight of our door was terrible. I knew everyone within miles in all directions and over and over again my mind checked them off. Which one was it?

When Dawson returned a couple of hours later, he looked very grave and I could see that he was deeply moved. So I waited in silence. His own voice was unsteady when he spoke.

"That dead man . . . lying in the trail up there, is . . . poor Frank Wilkins."

"Frank Wilkins! Are you sure?"

"There is no doubt about it. The police asked me to go with Shorty to identify the body and have asked that it be brought here till the Coroner comes to hold an inquest. Have I your permission?"

"Certainly," I agreed.

So once again we had the sad offices to perform, but this time over one of the best of companions. When all was ready poor Wilkins, with his happy laugh forever stilled, entered the door which he had closed behind him with gay raillery but a few short days before. I think nearly every resident of the village attended the little service, held in our sitting room. When it was ended one of the men stooped to close the coffin but Card, the old hunter and prospector, stepped from the group. Grizzled and stooped, it was not hard to see that his footsteps too were nearing the Long Trail. He raised his hand and his voice quavered as he turned to me.

"We all knew Frank," he began, "We knew his kind Irish heart and his love of Irish music. If he could speak to us I'm sure he'd ask, as he did so often, to hear his favorite—'My Wild Irish Rose.' Will you not play the record for him, Mrs. Smythe, once more?"

My throat tightened and I hesitated, but at a murmur of approval from the group I went to the machine and in a moment the sweet strains of the beautiful Irish melody filled the room— Wilkins's funeral hymn. As I looked at him, lying so peacefully, I wondered if he heard and understood.

So ended the life of another sourdough and so I mourned the stilling of one more voice that had made Stewart merry in the days that I had known. I steadily pursued my course of reducing my stock and in April, 1921, I went to Dawson City to find sale for some surplus. I went by dog team but returned by stage over a trail fast breaking up. We were obliged to change from wheels to runners and back again several times during the day's run to Blackhills. From there I was returning on my own. I would not risk crossing the summit of the mountains with Casey, but had wired to have him taken to Sixty Pup and would cross to there on foot.

There was still considerable snow on the summit and in order to get across while the frost held I was up before the dawn. I started on my twelve-mile mush to Sixty Pup just as the first golden rays appeared in the east. My trail led through some of the best of this mysteriously fascinating country into which I now knew my very heartstrings had become entwined. The route followed the stage-line for a short distance, then swung to the right and led up Dome Creek toward the summit. About halfway up the creek, as I emerged from a small thicket, I came suddenly upon a small band of caribou. They showed not the slightest fear and I stood watching them for some time. As they roamed about in the light of early morning, stopping now and then to clear away the snow with the broad flat horn or shovel with which nature has provided them in order to get at the moss on which they feed, they made a fine picture of contentment. Even when I clapped my hands and shouted they merely raised their graceful antlered heads and looked at me, then continued with their feeding.

The sun was quite warm by the time I reached the summit and I sat on a fallen tree to rest after the steep climb and to feast my eyes on the familiar scene before me. Then I rose, tucked my parka into the knapsack which I carried and began the descent to Sixty Pup. I had not traveled many miles when the little cabin— my first Yukon home—could be seen nestling among the small hardwood trees on the hillside and the sight of it took me back to the night of my first arrival, atop old Dobbin, at its door.

I reached it as the hands of my watch pointed to eight o'clock and found Casey tied to a tree at the rear, contentedly munching his breakfast. The man who owned the cabin now was not at home, but I took the musher's privilege of making tea and ate the lunch which I had with me.

That lunch was not simply a meal to me. It was a sacrament. I caught myself listening for the owner's return, but the step *I* listened for sounded now only in my heart.

"Hi, there! Albert says if you don't hurry you'll get no breakfast!"

Hot mush . . . buckwheat cakes . . . maple syrup . . . coffee. How miserable I was!

"All you need to do is swear loud and long!"

My first dogs . . . Think of coming down the Stewart alone through wolf country after dark over rotten ice!

You nut, you had more sense fifteen years ago, I do believe!

"When the flames froze he snipped them off and sold them for strawberries. That did it."

"I should think it would!"

What a little fool I must have been! But Waldron loved me . . .

The creek of the windlass . . . since long before dawn?

No! Only a door swinging! You've had your past and savored its sweetness. Let it rest . . . let it rest . . .

The lunch over, I dared not linger. Besides, what would it bring me? So I harnessed Casey and in the bright spring sunshine said good-bye to the humble little cabin on Sixty Pup—the happiest home my life has ever known.

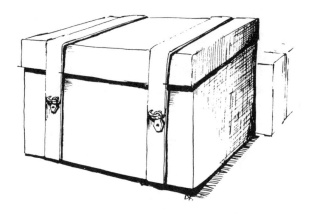

Away from Stewart

T he last summer was a busy and a lonesome one. The inevitable was drawing slowly nearer. Gradually all stock and equipment was being sold, except Casey and some pets. For these I found homes where they were to be held till called for.

During September I paid my last visit to Dawson City. It was not a happy one, although I said no good-byes. So, alone I ascended the gangplank and stood to watch the dear old town recede from view. And my heart was heavy, heavy.

Then came October second, 1921. Sixteen years before the day, on October second, 1905, I had stepped ashore at Stewart as a bride. Now I was waiting for the *Whitehorse*, southbound from Dawson, to go Outside.

Then I had trotted disconsolately behind Waldron on our way to Smith's Grocery, dreading the strange country in which I had landed. Now I paced nervously back and forth in Smythe's Store and Hotel, sick with the heartache of leaving it. For this land which had filled me with aversion was now everything to me. I had come a bride, full of bright hopes and dreams. I was leaving it a widow, with my hopes and dreams shattered and gone.

It seemed as though my whole life had been lived there. Oh, the memories—glorious and agonizing! Waldron . . . the laughter and the pain. Friendships . . . Aish . . . Olive and Al Pinska . . . Dawson DeWitt, now sailing with me. The fellowship of so many sturdy souls.

"Ma guidness, Mrs. Smythe! There isna a man on the river but thinks he has tae look out for ye!"

At ten p.m. the searchlight of the steamer appeared, still several miles away. With trembling limbs and a bursting heart I saw my trunks and suitcases carried out. I followed—closed the door behind me.

"Oh, if I should perish my ghost will come back to dwell in you, cabin, once more. How sad, still, and lonely—how empty you look . . . !"

A man from Barker Creek drew me aside.

"I don't want you to think me impertinent, Mrs. Smythe. But I know you've had a hard fight and carried a terrible load. If ever you run short of funds and want to come back, let me know. I've a few dollars—they're yours for the asking. Don't forget!"

Unable to speak, I pressed his hand and bowed my head. This was the spirit I was leaving.

Our baggage was carried on board. The few good-byes were spoken. Dawson took my arm, for the gangplank was treacherous with heavy frost.

My dog was close at my heels. They took him back by force.

The steamer backed into the stream—away from Stewart.

Ah, yes, I was planning to return. But deep in my soul I knew that it would never be.

My life in the Yukon lay behind me.